MW00989962

The Life That Prays

REFLECTIONS ON PRAYER AS STRATEGY

Minette Drumwright

Woman's Missionary Union
Birmingham, Alabama

Woman's Missionary Union
P. O. Box 830010
Birmingham, AL 35283-0010

For more information, visit our Web site at www.wmu.com or call 1-800-968-7301.

©2001 by Woman's Missionary Union
All rights reserved. First printing 2001
Printed in the United States of America
Woman's Missionary Union® and WMU® are registered trademarks.

Dewey Decimal Classification: 248.32
Subject Headings: PRAYER
                  MISSIONS
                  CHRISTIAN LIFE

Scripture quotations identified NIV are from the Holy Bible, New International Version. Copyright ©1973, 1978, 1984 International Bible Society. Used by permission of Zondervan Bible Publishers.
    Scripture quotations marked NKJV are taken from the New King James Version. Copyright ©1982 by Thomas Nelson, Inc. Used by permission. All rights reserved.
    Scripture quotations marked KJV are from the King James Version of the Bible.
    Verses marked TLB are taken from *The Living Bible,* copyright 1971 by Tyndale House Publishers, Wheaton, IL. Used by permission.
    Scripture quotations identified CEV are from *Contemporary English Version.* Copyright ©American Bible Society 1991. Used by permission.
    Scripture quotations from *The Message.* Copyright ©1993, 1994, 1995. Used by permission of NavPress Publishing Group.

Diagram on page 69 adapted from Harold Lindsell, *When You Pray* (Wheaton: IL: Tyndale House Publishers, 1969), 45.

Design by Janell E. Young

ISBN: 1-56309-489-4
W014116•0101•5M1

To my cheering section—my grandchildren: Lauren, Bradley, and Emily; my daughters and their husbands, Meme and H. W. Perry, and Debra and Max Underwood; my sister and brother-in-law, Dodie and Liston Beazley. You have loved me extravagantly, prayed for me earnestly, and given me sheer joy in who you are and what you are doing with your beautiful lives.

I also dedicate this book to the memory of one who is among that "great cloud of witnesses"—my husband, Huber Drumwright Jr. If there is a heavenly cheering section, he is in it, giving enthusiastic affirmation to those listed above, to his former students and colleagues, and to all whom he touched—as the impact of his life, love, and laughter lingers on and on.

Contents

Standing on My Tiptoes in a Box Seat

I have never felt I had it in my bones to write. Of course, I have written, but only when I have agreed (without enthusiasm) to accept an assignment on a specified topic. Across the years of doing much more teaching and speaking than writing, gracious people have urged me to write out the things about which I have been teaching and speaking. Living a full to overflowing schedule most days, I have never created the time and space to give serious attention to my promises to give it some thought.

Until now. Today, I am sitting at my computer because Robert Garrett, professor of missions at Southwestern Baptist Theological Seminary and former missionary to Argentina, patiently and gently guided me into a firm commitment to fulfill this task. Indeed, I became convinced that it was the Father Who directed him to prompt me into writing about the development and implementation of prayer as strategy in Southern Baptist overseas missions. Let me quickly say that even though that portion is largely a Baptist story, I believe earnest pray-ers from other Christian perspectives will find the content applicable to their experiences.

My understanding that prayer as strategy does not have its beginning point in missions. It begins, if it begins at all, in one's own life. Indeed, the concept's basic motivation must come from a personal passion for God and His glory, which brings with it, as a natural result, a passion that all people will come to know and worship the Savior. In other words, without this central core in one's heart, there is no authentic progression toward the further reaches of prayer. Thus, incorporating prayer as strategy begins at home and affects all that God leads one to be and to do, creating a life that prays. Hence, the development of one's personal prayer strategy brings prayer to the place of a deep, pervasive, intentional commitment that stays in place consistently and reaches out in concentric circles to the ends of the earth.

As the concept naturally moves our praying outward, prayer first includes our families and those close to us. How crucial is strategic prayer in the life of a family! A family prayer strategy is another step in being responsive to the Father's desires for His people. Then the church! What a challenge the church has in being true to Jesus' intentions: "My house shall be called a house of prayer." Every church needs to have a *prayer strategy*—whether the congregation calls it by that term or not—in order to become an authentic house of prayer. It is a matter of obedience. We encourage the incorporation of this same principle of an intentional prayer strategy in every agency, institution, association, convention, and organization that has as its mission bringing glory to God and joy to the world.

Therefore, prayer as strategy has an impact on all aspects of the life and relationships of the Christ follower. Strategic prayer is not the saying of certain words and phrases at appropriate times and places. It is the living out of a life that prays—a life that stays connected, sensitive, and responsive to the Father and His desires at all times and places.

I did not use the term *prayer as strategy* until circumstances confronted us with prayer's strategic nature in our work at the Foreign Mission Board (now International Mission Board) as we sought to relate to unreached peoples. Prayer rose up before us as the only strategy we could employ at that point. Our traditional missionary strategies simply were not allowed in the restrictive lands in which the unreached peoples resided.

The dawning of prayer as strategy was a stunning moment that took me on a reflective journey of retracing my own deep beliefs and prayer experiences. I saw clearly in my rearview mirror (that's often where I have my clearest vision!) that prayer had been God's strategy all along. Indeed, the Scriptures reveal that the concept of prayer as strategy goes back to the early days of God's dealing with His people. It has reverberated through the ages and reached its highest visibility in our extremity of having no other strategy to employ. Climactically, chapters 7 through 10 document the progression of this path.

I acknowledge with deep gratitude to the Lord that I have had extraordinary opportunities for meaningful prayer experiences with Him in my own home, across our land, and around the world. During my years of serving as director of the Office of International Prayer Strategy for the International Mission Board, I had a box seat (although I stood on my tiptoes most of the time) to watch God at work in magnificent ways. I cannot imagine a more meaningful way to have invested these latter years of my life—a life that had been traumatized by the sudden loss of my dynamic, impactive husband/best friend in the prime of his life and ministry. God took my broken heart, and in a more encompassing way than ever before, He placed the world in it. He gave my colleagues and me the unparalleled privilege of being partners with Him through prayer and in linking many individuals and churches in serious prayer involvements He has used to make a difference for His kingdom. I treasure this matchless privilege.

In preparation for this writing project, I went into the far corners of my attic. I am a "keeper." I have retained files, papers, memos, calendars, notes, messages, presentations, favorite Scripture passages, quotations, articles, letters—just because they mean something to me. I got them out of their boxes and covered my home with the spread-out keepsakes. I read and reflected and read some more, my cup filled to overflowing. When at last I began writing, I often found my own tears distorting my view of the screen, with chill bumps covering my body.

I have been much more personal than I dreamed I would be. I sat down to "just write," and that which appeared on my screen turned out to be chunks of my life. I went back to work to change my approach, but then somehow it seemed to be hollow any other way.

My intention is that this book will be for all Christ followers of all denominations, wherever they find themselves in their journey with the Father. Although my life and work have taken place largely in the context of the Baptist arena, I have been blessed with opportunities to interact with earnest pray-ers from across the denominational spectrum. Wonderfully, authentic prayer has no boundaries or labels. Therefore, my quiet hope is that this book will be considered applicable to all intercessors; that all who have a heart for prayer will find information, challenge, and usable material.

Now I pray our Lord will use this humble writing effort to create within its readers new or renewed longings to know more intimately the God of prayer. My deep desire is that Christ followers will seriously embrace prayer as a priority strategy in their own personal lives and ministries; in the lives of their families, their churches, their work, and relationships; and in participating with the Father, through prayer, in accomplishing His heart's desire of making Christ known and worshiped by all the peoples of all the nations. In His loving, full-of-grace, just, sovereign, gentle way, may He deal with you and with me at those places within us that need His touch, His teaching, His correction, His re-formation that will make us more like Him— for Jesus' sake, for His kingdom's sake, and for the sake of those who do not yet know Him.

MINETTE DRUMWRIGHT

Acknowledgements

I acknowledge with gratitude those who have had a special ministry to me in the unfolding of this manuscript.

First, Robert Garrett, professor of missions at Southwestern Baptist Theological Seminary, is responsible for leading me to a commitment to fulfill this project. He insisted that we needed as a resource for missions classes a written account of the beginning stages of the development of prayer as strategy in the work of the International Mission Board and shared his conviction that I was the logical one to undertake the task. I am glad Bob was persistent.

Next, I must acknowledge my daughters. With much hesitation, I placed a partial and very rough draft of the manuscript in the hands of my older daughter, Meme, an accomplished and published writer. Her affirmation (although I realize her usual objectivity is highly questionable in relation to her mom's work!) gave me courage to proceed. Debra, my younger daughter, soon read a draft and made excellent suggestions, almost all of which I incorporated.

A breakthrough in the project came from the expertise of Leland Webb, retired editor of *the COMMISSION* magazine. His respected skills, knowledge, and constant encouragement made all the difference. I am deeply indebted to Leland.

Other readers of the complete manuscript, each with helpful suggestions, were my close friends and experienced writers, Al Fasol and Millie Bishop. Karen Bullock, Leon McBeth, Catherine Walker, and William O'Brien read certain chapters to check the accuracy of those areas related to their expertise. International Mission Board staff members were responsive to my every contact and expressed need in the development of the project. My deep gratitude to each.

It has been sheer joy to work with my editor, Jan Turrentine. From the point that she came into the picture, she made everything seem easy. Jan was already my good friend; but through this experience, our bond has deepened. I am most grateful for her superb contribution in bringing this manuscript to publication. Kathryne Solomon, my copy editor, brought her many years of dedicated experience to bear on my work, and I thank the Lord for her careful attention and essential role. Another key participant in this project is graphic designer Janell Young, creator of the beautiful cover and book design. I must also acknowledge my close, "forever" friend, June Whitlow. This manuscript went first into her hands on its way to being accepted for publication by WMU.

Very importantly, many friends have prayed me through and kept in touch as to progress and developments. In addition to others named in these acknowledgements, cherished prayer partners who have been especially attentive are Dot Forester, Karen Keister, Donna Dee Floyd, Sandra Nash, Cindy Gaskins, Kim Templeton, Sybil Carroll, and Ethel Lynn Patterson. My indebtedness to them and to other intercessors is great.

There are a host of treasured friends in my church (most of them the age of my children and younger) who could be listed in my cheering section (and I could be listed in theirs). They have a special place in this chapter of my life and have demonstrated the sweetest level of caring and understanding in the midst of the comings and goings of my hectic schedule. They are truly kingdom people, a consistent inspiration—Summerfields Baptist Church.

I am blessed by these and other current relationships, and in a lingering way by the influence of many meaningful persons from my other life—my past. Almost daily I have the joy of picking up on various bonds formed through the years and around the world. A significant influence throughout my adult years has been, and continues to be, the inspiration and love of many missionary friends—too numerous to name names. Even so, I want them to be reminded of their special place in my heart. These acknowledgements would not be complete without sharing that at the beginning of this endeavor, the Father gave me His quiet, certain assurance that He would take every step with me. I acknowledge—and cherish—His constant companionship and steady guidance. I want to express to Him in this venue that which I have said many times—in the midst of ecstasy, in the depths of sorrow, and many places in between: Of all people, I am most blessed. My most constant prayer is that my life will bring, wonder of wonders, glory to Him.

1

Indelible Impressions

"Because of the Lord's great love we are not consumed, for his compassions never fail. They are new every morning; great is your faithfulness" (Lam. 3:22–23 NIV).

"In His divine condescension God has willed that the working of His Spirit shall follow the prayers of His people."—Andrew Murray[1]

The night was moonless and starless. I was traveling alone on an all-night train toward Kishinev, the capital of Moldova, located in the former Soviet Union. I had boarded this train in Bucharest, Romania, not exactly the center of the universe—unless you live there! My travel agency —a large one at that—had never booked anyone to Moldova. They were learning on me. The little nation had not been open to Westerners very long, and our missions agency had no missionaries there. In fact, our field administrator for that part of the world had strongly objected, and so had my family, to my traveling alone. A major concern involved the gypsies. I dislike stereotypes, but I was told the gypsies had a reputation for riding the trains and robbing fellow passengers. In fact, two of our volunteer nurses serving in Romania had been robbed at knifepoint as they traveled by train. They were so traumatized by the experience that they returned to the United States before completing their term. "I would not have that happen to you for anything," my administrator/ friend said with a worried look. Thus, I agreed to have a traveling companion accompany me on the train trip from Bucharest to Kishinev.

Concurrently with my travel to Moldova, the little nation was much in the world news because of the desperate scarcity of food and basic essentials. The people were suffering. Our government only recently had sent several planeloads of food to help the needy population.

As the train sped into the darkness, I reflected on the factors that had led to my unusual destination. The previous year, 1990, I had attended the Baptist World Alliance (BWA) in Seoul, Korea, and the Women's Department meeting that preceded it. For the first time in BWA history, Baptists from the newly crumbled former Soviet Union had been allowed to leave home and attend such a meeting. Five women from the former USSR were in the delegation; one of them was their interpreter.

The presence of the five women at the Women's Department events created excitement. To my delight, this group of five attended the conference on prayer I led and lingered afterward to visit with me. I asked for the privilege of taking them to lunch, and we had a warm time of sharing together. During the rest of the conference we found ourselves gravitating toward one another again and again. We kept the interpreter busy!

On the last night of the Women's Department meetings, they invited me to their hotel room. We had an old-fashioned prayer meeting, and then Olga Mocan, from Moldova, talked to me about the possibility of my coming to her country to teach about prayer. To be honest, I had already learned that I needed them to teach me about prayer instead of the other way around!

My heart warmed to the invitation. I told her I would need as much lead time as possible because of schedule and budget constraints; but if I combined her invitation with another planned trip abroad, it would be possible to include Moldova in my long-range planning. Soon after I returned to my home and office in Richmond, Virginia, I received an official invitation, seal and all, from the Baptist Union of Moldova, to come and teach prayer in a series of churches—in just two months! Something had gotten lost in the translation of "lead time" and "long-range planning." Working out plans took much longer, of course, but eventually I went. To say Moldova was off the beaten path would be an understatement. At that time, it was so remote that I had to produce a map to show my family and friends where I was going. Just in case you are fuzzy about the location, Moldova is northeast of Romania in the far southwestern part of the former Soviet Union.

As is my custom before leaving on an assignment, I wrote the wonderful people who make up my personal prayer support base. I did not choose them; God did. He called them to pray for me daily, consistently. This blessing dovetails with a simple, yet powerful principle of prayer: *Every spiritual work brings with it an inherent need to be covered with prayer—one's own prayers and the intercessions of others.* While every work should be done "as to the Lord," some tasks are more directly related to kingdom purposes than others and therefore more vulnerable to the evil one's attention and more needful of God's released power. When an activity has a vital connection to kingdom work, I covet intensely the specific prayer attention of my team of intercessors. I want them to be specifically aware of my needs and potential stress points when I am traveling overseas on a spiritual assignment. Schedules, communications, and relationships can easily go awry. Spiritual warfare is always a potential factor. Fatigue and any number of other complexities can cause various problems to surface.

I sent my prayer partners my day-by-day itinerary, including specific needs and requests, and I included an especially stressful concern, "Pray that I will make connections on my flights." From Richmond, I would change flights in Boston, then change from Heathrow Airport in London to an airport newly converted from military to civilian use and located many miles away. The third flight in the sequence, from London to Bucharest, *had* to be on time. Otherwise, I would miss the overnight train, my fourth connection, and not make it to Moldova in time to fulfill my first day's teaching assignments in Kishinev.

I included in my requests my health and energy, and placed much importance on my spiritual readiness. Then I gave some details unique to the itinerary. Without mentioning the gypsy matter, because I expected someone to accompany me, I concluded generally, "Please pray for safety on the train trip to Kishinev."

I did not know what to expect in Moldova except that I had been told (1) I must not wear makeup at any time, and (2) I must have a scarf on my head at all times in public. I had three huge suitcases with me, filled by my Sunday School class and other friends with pantyhose (which created grateful excitement), aspirin (which the women were most excited about); cough syrups; antihistamines; other drugstore medicine; and, of course, a shower of candies, cookies, and other goodies.

I made the connections smoothly, with much praise to the Lord at each change. A Romanian "sister" met me at the airport in Bucharest to accompany me to the proper train. But there I discovered that the arranged plan for a traveling companion had evaporated. I would be traveling alone on the overnight train, which also meant coming back alone. I did not feel particularly unsettled. I had reserved a private compartment. Surely it would have a lock, I reasoned. I anticipated no problem.

Settled in my train compartment, I was mentally reviewing the events leading to this point when the first of many officials threw open my sliding door. There was no lock. He began speaking in either Romanian or Russian, of which I did not understand a word. I spoke to him in English, of which he did not understand a word. I guessed that he wanted to see my documents, and I got them out. He took my visa and the exit card I had been issued upon arrival at the airport in Bucharest and placed them in his folder. When the exit card had been handed to me at the airport, I had been told emphatically, "Do not surrender this to anyone. You will have to have it to get out of the country." Of course, that impressed me. I knew I would want out.

"Sir, please, I was told not to surrender these," I said to the official, pointing to his folder with my exit card and visa inside. I indicated that I preferred them in my possession. Raising his voice in a futile attempt to help me understand him, he yelled (I have no idea what!).

At that noisy moment, a handsome young man appeared in my open compartment door, to say calmly in broken, but beautiful English, "May I be of help?" The atmosphere changed immediately. I explained my concern. The stranger conferred with the official and then explained to me that I must surrender the exit card because I was exiting the country; I would be given another one on my return trip to Bucharest that would get me out of the country. That made sense. A more complicated matter was that I would have to get another visa in Kishinev. How in the world was I to do that? I did not know how to get a visa in my own country, for my travel agent always takes care of that!

I expressed strong gratitude to the young man who had come to my rescue. In a moment, both he and the official were gone.

Soon another gruff official slid open my door with a bang. I had heard him coming down the corridor, throwing open doors of compartments and slamming them shut as he went on to the next. Just as he finished his first unintelligible (to me) sentence, the charming young gentleman appeared again in my doorway, and once more he translated for me.

All through the night this scene repeated itself as the young man appeared in my doorway at exactly the right time. I soon picked up that he was traveling with two other men in the compartment next to mine. In one of his late night appearances he had changed to a warm-up suit. By this time I had grown a little more adept at dealing with these brusque officials who streamed in and out, but my friend was always there in the doorway seconds after my door flew open. Mostly, by now, he said nothing, just making sure he was not needed, then disappeared when the official closed my door.

I don't say this glibly: The deeper we got into the night, the more I saw this young man as my angel, hovering, protecting, caring. I developed the most secure feeling I have ever had in traveling. In between those "official" visits, I actually fell asleep. I am not a champion sleeper in good conditions. For me to be able to sleep in these unusual circumstances was a small miracle.

On one such appearance after sunrise, my friend had changed clothes for the day, and I had freshened up. I invited him in and expressed my tremendous gratitude, which had heightened all through the night. I said, "You have lost a night's sleep getting up and down to look after me, and I am very indebted to you." He smiled with a certain radiance and told me that it was important to him that I have a good experience in traveling in his country, and this was something he could do to contribute to that. "I did not want you to worry," he said.

I told him he had given me a most incredible gift of care, and I would like to share with him the most wonderful thing in my life. I took that opportunity to plant seeds of the gospel, which he received with some interest and wonder. Although he had a nominal Catholic background, the concept of a personal relationship with Jesus was new to him. I had with me some copies of *The Message of Hope,* a small booklet of selected Scriptures from the New Testament with the plan of salvation clearly stated. Giving him a copy, I urged him to find a believer who would share with him fully, and I told him I would be praying that God would provide such a person. At that point we were arriving in Kishinev. My "angel" helped me get my multiple heavy suitcases off the train, which placed me further in his debt. We had a fond farewell. We had truly bonded.

One adventure ended, and another began. What I found in Moldova was first an entourage of believers welcoming me. Soon I learned that Olga, my hostess, was widely known because of a television documentary about a prison ministry in which she was involved. A most remarkable woman, she had arranged two streamlined, well-planned prayer seminars a day, each in a different Baptist church. This took us like a whirlwind all over the small country. I was amazed to find so many Baptist churches—185, they told me! I did not find all of them, but we were scheduled in two each day. Every church was full and overflowing; I did not speak to an empty seat the entire time. An equal number of women and men attended. It was easy to tell, for men sat on one side of the center aisle and women on the other! In First Baptist Church, Kishinev, on Sunday morning people stood in every possible spot as I spoke, around 2,000 in all. That evening, I spoke in the worship service of the First Baptist Church of Beltsie, again to a standing-room-only crowd of about 1,500.

Although Sunday was an exceptional format, our typical seminar had Olga beginning each session. A lovely woman, quiet in manner and conversation, she dynamically expounded the Scriptures. At each seminar a woman from prison whom Olga had led to the Savior gave a moving testimony. Increasingly, I was impressed to see how the Lord was using Olga.

In getting to know Olga in Seoul, I had no idea of her leadership gifts and effectiveness, although I certainly had been aware of her deep devotion to the Lord. I was very interested in knowing her background, so I inquired.

Olga had received training from a woman named Lidia Caldararu, a 1935 graduate of the Baptist Womens' Training School in Bucharest, Romania. Missionaries had established the school in the 1920s, sponsored by Woman's Missionary Union and the Foreign Mission Board (now International Mission Board). Baptist women of the South had raised the money to establish and support the training school.

After Lidia graduated from the training school in Bucharest, she moved to Moldova to work as a home missionary with women in the churches. Olga said Lidia walked from village to village and from town to town, organizing women's groups and Sunday Schools in the churches; visiting prisons; teaching women to pray, witness, give, and minister to the needs of the people around them.

In 1941, the Communists arrested Lidia, beat her, and sentenced her to 25 years in prison because of her faith and teaching. Released after 15 years, she returned to her work among the women in Moldova. Her health had broken, but Lidia continued to work faithfully as long as she could, organizing and motivating women to prayer and good works.

One day she called Olga in and said, "Olga, *you* must lead the women of Moldova to do the work of Christ. I will teach you how." Olga said she received Lidia's careful teaching, preparation, and training as if from the Lord.

As Olga told me this story, keeping interpreter Raisa Doga very busy, I better understood Olga's passion and effectiveness. Radiantly, she showed me a portrait of Lidia displayed in the foyer of First Baptist Church of Kishinev. Lidia was her mentor, her inspiration.

Lidia's investment has borne fruit for years and continues today, not only in Moldova but also across the entire former Soviet Union. In recent years Olga has served as the president of the Euro-Asiatic Federation of the Unions of Evangelical Christians-Baptists, giving leadership to women across that vast part of the world. God has taken the gifts and efforts of one generation and stretched them to the next generation to make a difference in lives and even in a nation.

My time came to a conclusion in Moldova. I had never been with such devoted, responsive people. Every family had stories of loved ones who had been persecuted relentlessly by the Communists, with many having lost their lives because of their faith in Christ. Their economy was in shambles, yet they were a radiant, grateful people who were joyful in all circumstances. Aglow from my experiences with the inspiring believers in Moldova and with my new visa in hand (secured for me by a woman doctor, a believer, after much hassle with local officials), I boarded the train to Romania to catch my flight out of Bucharest. My cup was full. I did not know another adventure lay just ahead.

My train had come from Moscow; Kishinev seemed to be a major stop on the way from Moscow to Bucharest. I boarded in midafternoon, scheduled for arrival in Bucharest the next morning. My first surprise was that my private compartment had in it two persons—an older Russian-looking woman (a *babushka*) and a 20-something young man, apparently her son. My Moldovan hosts, expecting to tuck me into a private compartment, led me to find the conductor. We showed him my ticket for a *private* compartment. He shrugged and said all three of us had tickets for the same private compartment. Finally, we shrugged and headed for "our" private compartment.

Having completed the exchange of lingering and fond farewells with the large contingency of my new dear friends, I greeted my compartment mates with my best

Texas smile. I deposited my one remaining suitcase (I had left the others with Olga) beneath my seat. *I will be spending the night with these people, so I am going to make friends with them, beginning right now,* I thought. I sat down directly across from the young man. The grandmotherly woman huddled in the corner, very solemn.

I had a great idea. I pulled out pictures of my grandchildren to show them. I said their names, slowly and clearly. The woman would not look at the pictures, but her son did. When I said, "Lauren," and held up one finger to show her age, the young man's face brightened. In Russian he told me he had a 1-year-old daughter, Tanya, as he held up one finger. I understood, and cooed approvingly. Then I introduced him to Bradley and Emily, held up the appropriate number of fingers, and finally put my pictures away.

I then reached into my carry-on bag and brought out candy to give my cohabitants. I offered it first to the babushka, but she declined without looking at me. Next I offered it to the young man. He smiled, took the candy, held it high, and said, "Tanya." Then he put in it in his small bag. I smiled and nodded approvingly for him to save it for Tanya. Immediately I reached back into my bag and pulled out more candy. "For you," I said, chuckling and pointing my finger directly at his nose. He shook his head as he took it, also chuckling, and said again, "Tanya," putting it away. I brought out more candy. This time he laughed heartily, nodded a thanks, and put it in his pocket. By this time there was a faint smile on the face of the woman. Again, I offered her candy, and she reluctantly accepted it in slow motion, her eyes never meeting mine.

The compartment had warmed considerably. *Thank You, Lord, for placing me in this nice family situation. I believe we are going to make it through the night together just fine,* I thought.

Soon an official appeared at the door to check our documents. I could not have believed it if it had not happened to me, but a man came to the door, looked over the shoulder of the official, and said directly to me, "No problem."

Plain as day, here was another angel. This time he was located on the other side of our compartment, traveling with his wife and two young daughters. He could speak only two English words: "No problem." What I heard him say in plain, unspoken English was that he would be there in my doorway to make sure I had no problem during the long trip ahead.

After awhile, we seemed to come to the border between Moldova and Romania. Since no one spoke English, I did not know for certain. Wherever we were, the train stopped and a group of officials got on board and began to go from door to door. Two of them came to our compartment and gruffly ordered me, with added hand motions to make sure I understood, to open my suitcase. I quickly complied. Before I got very far, they motioned and loudly told me not to open it further and to put it back under the seat. I obeyed.

Then they told my new friends to open their bags. The young man reluctantly, in slow motion, unzipped his. One of the officials pushed into our crowded compartment, threw open the flap of the case, and pushed aside a thin layer of clothes. I caught my breath as I saw hundreds of small, resealable plastic bags with some kind of substance in each. Both officials started yelling, quickly closed and zipped the suitcase, and threw it into the corridor.

They went through the same noisy procedure with the woman's bag, found the same type of contents inside, and tossed that suitcase into the corridor also. All this time, the babushka whimpered. The officials left, taking the young man with them. My angel, whom I had seen out of the corner of my eye, watched from a short distance, then came to the doorway to say to me, "Problem!" and linger outside my door. The train did not move. I could see a small station from our window.

The woman began pacing our tiny compartment, wringing her hands, not crying or sobbing, but whimpering. Filled with sadness for her, I said aloud many times, "I am so sorry." She continued to pace and check the view outside the window. I wondered if she expected to see her son removed. Finally, she made motions to me that she was leaving and asked, in sign language, if I would look after her heavy shoulder bag. I assured her I would. After some time she returned, picked it up, gave me a faint wave of her hand, and for the first time looked into my eyes. Hers were the saddest eyes I have ever seen, haunting me to this day. She left.

My angel came to the door. Again he said, "Problem." I asked, with added motions, "Do you know what was in those suitcases?" He seemed to know what I was asking. He answered at some length, although not one word sounded like any English word I knew.

Just then I glanced out the window and saw the officials carrying the two bags, accompanied by the babushka and Tanya's dad moving toward the little border station. Almost immediately the train began to move and we were once again on our way.

An official delivered my new exit card.

Time and again I think of that mother and son and Tanya. I will never know what the whole story was, but I will always pray for them, every time they come to mind.

On another level, I have smiled many times as I recall being convinced that I was in a cozy, safe family situation, when in reality I may have had a front row seat in observing a drug-smuggling operation.

I now had a private compartment after all. Throughout the night my angel appeared at my door only seconds after an official threw it open. Again, I was able to get some sleep between the visits.

The next morning, I went to their compartment next door and expressed my gratitude to my angel, his wife, and two young daughters, giving them the remainder of my candy. I knew they could not understand any of my words. Yet my heart told me they understood the essence of what I was communicating. It was a sweet moment. I thanked the Lord for another angel.

After returning to Richmond, I called my friend, Sandra Nash, in Clinton, Mississippi. Some years ago the Lord had led Sandra to give regular, intentional time to intercession for me. On many specific occasions God has prompted her to pray for me when I have not been able to get word to her that I was in special need of intercession. Somehow she just knows *when.*

In giving her a report of my extraordinary trip, I began describing this experience. When I had finished, Sandra told me it had been difficult not to interrupt. From the moment she had read my letter requesting prayer for safety prior to my departure, she had been especially impressed and somewhat bothered, she explained. During the time frame when she knew I was on the overnight train, she felt so much anxiety for me that she expressed it to her husband, Ben. He said, "Let's just pray right now for an angel to watch over Minette." They specifically prayed for an angel to be on that certain train somewhere in Romania making its way through the night in an out-of-this-world part of the globe. Sandra told me that Ben also prayed, "And, Lord, she is going to need that same angel, or another one, on the way back!"

Together we rejoiced over this special demonstration of God's grace, love, provision, and faithfulness, and we thanked Him as we prayed together on the phone. I hung up my receiver and fell on my knees and worshiped Him.

I got up humming: "We are standing on holy ground . . ."

Another experience with a lingering, indelible impact on my life occurred in a restricted-access country on a prayer journey with 20 prayerwalkers, including 7 who had served as missionaries. They were an outstanding group of intercessors.

Our prayer journey took us to a strongly Muslim nation, the identity of which I must not reveal. In the orientation preceding our journey, we learned that probably only a few hundred Christians lived in this country's population of 27 million. Of course, no one knows the accurate number of believers. Their identity is revealed in guarded tones.

The government claims to afford religious freedom. In actuality, that means foreigners residing in the country are free to choose their religion—but not the citizens of the nation. A familiar saying there is, "To be a *(citizen of this country)* is to be Muslim." In recent years, many highly publicized incidents of persecution of Christians in this land have surfaced. The irony is that Christianity flourished in this country centuries ago, but gradually was stamped out by the Arabization of the region.

In the midst of this restrictive culture, I had opportunity to meet one of the rare believers—a woman who spoke English fluently. It was not advisable for her to meet with our large group. Just having contact with Christians places a believer in a position to be questioned and mistreated or perhaps face even more serious consequences.

Only the two of us were there that day, face-to-face. It was obvious she was not comfortable. I explained, "I am here with a group of believers who love the Lord and love all His family. We have come to pray for the people of this land, that they will be allowed to hear the gospel and be free to accept Christ and worship God as they choose. Also, we have come to pray God's blessing and comfort and protection upon the believers here. Will you help us know how we can best pray for you and the others?"

She was guarded in what she said. First, she cautioned me that she would be in grave danger if any of the information she gave me ever got traced to her name. Therefore, she said, it was extremely important that I *not* know her name. I assured her I was highly sensitized to her circumstances and the risks involved. Even with that assurance, she cautioned me again during our discussion that I must not know her name. I assured her I had no need to know it.

Articulately, she then described prayer needs. She said, "We believers live in constant danger of arrest and persecution. We are scrutinized, and officials pick us up and question us for no reason. Police brutalize us, ordering us to give names of other Christians. Sometimes, a fellow believer finally will break down and give a believer's name, and that destroys our trust of one another. Our lack of trust is so sad, for it means we are further isolated. We feel very alone. Often, we are cut off from one another. Satan takes advantage of our fear and lack of trust by telling us no one knows about us and no one cares about us. Satan is constantly telling me that. I love Jesus so much. He stays close to me and I want to be true to Him. He means so much to me, but still I have a tendency to get depressed. Pray especially for this problem, for all believers here struggle with matters of trust, isolation, and depression."

She told of those she knows personally who receive Christ as Savior but then face such opposition and persecution from their own families and former friends that they "cool off" (her words) and turn away from their Christian faith. I recalled reading that in some areas as many as 90 percent of Muslim converts to Christianity return to their old ways because of isolation and discouragement.

I said, "Please remember that Satan is a liar. There are Christians who are aware of the persecution of fellow believers in these difficult, restricted places. We don't know names and faces; but as best we can, we do pray for those of you in these painful circumstances. We care intensely! This busload of people is here because we are aware and we care. We came wanting to get word to you and other believers that you are our family in the Lord. We want you to tell other sisters and brothers about our commitment to pray for you and for them. Tell them we represent others in America who care about you. Tell them our hearts break with their hearts, and we pray for the day when all of you will know the joy of freedom to love and worship God openly and to rejoice with other believers."

There was a pause, and I felt overwhelmed by a combination of emotions, including anger at the repressive government and at Satan's attempts to deceive, destroy, discourage, and depress. But I also felt a keen sense of God's love, grace, and power to sustain a child of His in terrible circumstances.

Then she said, "Another big need is that many believers rarely have anyone to teach them the Bible. That makes us prone to misinterpret and distort the real meaning of Scripture. We have not been trained in the Scriptures, and we easily get into false doctrines. Please ask people to pray that the Holy Spirit will be our teacher and that we will be able to understand rightly God's word to us." I assured her I would make that request known.

I cherished every moment with her, but I knew we had to be cautious. I knew officials were outside the building, and we must not be seen together, for her sake. All they could do to me was to ask me to leave the country. I hated to think what they could do to her.

I asked if I could pray for her. She replied, "Please do." I put my arms around her and she clutched me tightly. As I held her close, I was so aware that she was a vivid representative of thousands of believers worldwide who pay such a high price because of their faith. I remember wishing I could hold them all in my arms. I thanked the Lord for her and her Christian husband, for their strength and steadfastness.

I pledged directly to the Lord that I would tell others in America about this sister and her prayer requests. I asked the Lord to give her and the other believers a new courage, a lifting up of their spirits. I prayed for God's peace that passes all understanding to saturate her being. I prayed that I would be a good steward of this blessed experience and insight.

After a few moments, I wept an "Amen." She continued to cling to me tightly. Neither of us moved or broke the silence. I felt her tears on my cheek and wondered if she could feel mine on hers.

Then she spoke into my ear, "My name is . . ." and she told me her name. I felt a melting within, for I realized she was entrusting to me her most precious and fragile gift—her name. As we reluctantly parted, I spoke her name quietly and added, "I just hope, that when we get to heaven, my hut is next to your mansion." For the first time, she smiled. I treasure that moment also.

Later that day, I learned that several years earlier, my new friend had been picked up by the police and questioned. Because she refused to give names of other believers, they tortured her and humiliated her sexually. My understanding of her fears went to an even deeper level. I felt awe that I had been in the presence of one who lives faithfully in the midst of constant danger simply because she is a follower of Christ.

Will you pray for this woman? Not only now, but continually. Give her a biblical name: Phoebe. Lift to the Lord the thousands of believers in similar circumstances.

Here in our land and in our churches, we have the opportunity of warm, sweet Christian fellowship in every direction we turn. I am grateful and I celebrate this precious privilege. Yet that is not possible in many places in this world.

Missions researcher David Barrett estimates 165,000 people are martyred every year because of their faith in

Jesus. The Sudan, Egypt, Iran, Iraq, India, Pakistan, Vietnam, and China are only a few of the countries where Christians suffer persecution. This is the price they pay for their devotion to our Lord.

Will you open yourself in sensitivity to this dimension of kingdom praying—for those who are in pain because of their faithfulness and courage? Our prayers can release God's comfort and blessing upon them. We can be a part of a prayer support base that is missing in their stark circumstances.

This level of praying requires depth of faith on our part, for we do not have the spiritual pleasure of seeing or knowing God's answers to our prayers. Our faith is called forth as we entrust our prayers to Him, and then as we trust His answers.

Please pray daily for Phoebe, her husband, and the thousands of others in similar circumstances. I promised her I would ask you.

Full name: _____

Questions for Reflection
Do you have family and friends who pray for you specifically?

When you take on a spiritual challenge, are you aware of a special need for prayer?

Do you communicate specific needs to those who pray for you?

Has God impressed you to be a part of another Christ follower's prayer base?

Do you need to grow in your sensitivity to those who are persecuted because of their faith?

Will you pray regularly for the Phoebes of the world in terms of the prayer requests articulated by the believer in this chapter's concluding story?

[1]Andrew Murray, *Prayer: A 31 Day Plan to Enrich Your Prayer Life* (Uhrichsville, OH: Barbour and Co., n.d.), 10.

2

One Pilgrim's Progress

"For who is he who will devote himself to be close to me?" declares the Lord" (Jer. 30:21 NIV).

"Nothing is ever wasted in the kingdom of God. Not one tear, not all our pain, not the unanswered questions or the seemingly unanswered prayers. . . . Nothing will be wasted if we give our lives to God. And if we are willing to be patient until the grace of God is made manifest, whether it takes nine years, or ninety, it will be worth the wait.
—Rebecca Manley Pippert[1]

I am a pilgrim, and this is a story of my progress. I come to you as a fellow struggler, a learner, a disciple of our Lord Jesus Christ. I come just as I am to share with you simply from my own heart and life and experiences with God, His Word, and His people.

My journey began in San Antonio, Texas, where my dad served as pastor of the same small church for 25 years (all my growing-up years). It was a typical Southern Baptist church of that era: evangelistic, missions-minded, revivalistic (at least two revivals a year, at least two weeks in length), no movies, no dancing ("Would you want to be at the movies or on a dance floor if Jesus returns?"), no cards ("the devil's tools"), no slang words, or any of the things of the world. We were so typical we even had a church split!

Our lives revolved around church activities. Mother made sure we had all the missions organizations functioning full speed ahead. Mrs. Washam was my Junior Girls' Auxiliary (now Girls in Action) leader. She patiently put up with us wiggly, giggly GAs, who were more interested in refreshments than in her plans for us to learn about the Chinese and the Africans who did not know Jesus. She no doubt despaired that she was getting through to us at all, but she was. It took about 20 years for me to tell her so, but the Lord used her to plant seeds in my heart that later took root and grew into a caring concern for the world.

On Sunday afternoons, I went with Mother and Daddy to the little Mexican mission our church sponsored on Dora Street. We literally rounded up Hispanic children and their parents for the service where Mother played the piano, we sang, and Daddy told a Bible story. He always explained how to be saved and made an appeal for each and all to ask Jesus to come into their hearts. Over the years, many did. Those missions experiences helped sensitize me to God's desire that all people come to know and love Jesus.

Daddy was a conscientious pastor, and both Mother and Daddy worked long and hard in serving God and the congregation. They had high expectations of themselves as servants of the Lord. As a child, I was slightly embarrassed by their intense dedication, but in time I grew to be very proud of them and to appreciate their sheer fineness.

They also held high expectations for us. Mother, especially, sought to instill high ideals in us and in everyone else in her sphere of influence. My sister, Dodie, was 6 years older than I. I looked up to her, and wanted to be just like her. I still do! Glen was 4 years younger than I. As the middle child, I . . . Well, I suppose everyone knows the reputation middle children have for mischief. I managed to live up (or down) to that reputation.

My recollection of my childhood is that, in the midst of Mother's ideals, I was nearly always in trouble. We had at least 1,000 rules at my house, and I was usually challenging one or another of them. Some of those rules, I just flat broke. Many of them I did not altogether break but seriously bent. At our house, that meant punishment with a peach tree switch. We had a beautiful peach tree in our backyard; at least, it started out that way. My parents actually killed that tree—on me! I even got a switching one day when I said, "Oh, look, our switch tree has a peach on it!"

I am very grateful for my heritage. I don't remember not knowing about the love of God in Jesus. It was a natural part of the atmosphere in my home and church. One Sunday evening when I was 9 as I walked to church with my dad, we got into a conversation about Jesus. Daddy led me to understand that Jesus' love was for me personally, and that He died for my sins so that I could live in heaven with Him forever. In a simple way, I asked Jesus to forgive my sins and come live in my heart.

I understood very little of what I was asking. To borrow someone else's words, "All I understood of myself, I gave to all I understood of Jesus." It was very childlike, but it was real. I meant it. I treasure that beginning point in my spiritual life.

My home and my church represent those who took patient—and at times impatient—interest in me, taught me, affirmed me, cared about me, rebuked me, disciplined me, nurtured me. I had many opportunities to learn the things of the Lord. My home and my church were imperfect, as they are for all of us, but I acknowledge gratefully the many attempts there to show me the way. But I must also acknowledge that deep down there was not much taking place in my soul.

An exception occurred when, as a young teenager, I attended Intermediate Girls' Auxiliary camp at Alto Frio in the beautiful Texas hill country. During the invitation at the concluding service, I walked down the aisle under the old tabernacle and rededicated my life. To me, that meant I was willing to know God's plan for my life. It was a spiritual marker. Later I learned that, as significant as that decision was, the most important reality is to know God, and to know His heart. Somehow I missed that understanding. Later that became my passion.

I recently went back to Alto Frio for the first time since that teenaged experience. Although everything else has changed into a lovely conference center, that old tabernacle is still the same. Alone, I made my way to the tabernacle and to the middle aisle. Here I was, 55 years later, walking down that same aisle. I offered myself to my Savior all over again, as I do every day. However, now that offering takes place deep in my soul, and it is total. It means that I want to abide in Him intimately, and I want Him to abide in me fully. I found it difficult to put into words the depth of my expression of rededication. I stood there with tears and chill bumps and thanked God for hearing my wordless prayers.

When my dad retired from the pastorate at age 65, his life became remarkable in new ways. He began to work as a chaplain in the county hospital, which had no chaplaincy program or spiritual ministry at the time. Daddy already had years of pastoral experience, of course, but he began taking chaplaincy training at every opportunity. Soon he was enlisting and training volunteers to minister alongside him at the hospital. He developed a sustained, active volunteer program. Over the years, a staff of chaplains came into being to direct the ever-enlarging program.

Mother lived to be 83. We honor her memory and often quote her. After she had been deceased for 5 years, Daddy remarried—at the age of 91½. I enjoy telling where Daddy met his bride—in the Singles Department of Trinity Baptist Church! When he was 98, Daddy cut back on his weekly schedule at the hospital—from five days to four days! His health broke for the first time when he was 100½. He lived to be two months short of 102. He had become an institution at the hospital and, to a certain extent, in the city. My own observation is that he became the pet of the staff—they honored him in many ways and with many awards. Daddy was dearly and sweetly loved, by them and by us.

I went off to college not intending to marry a preacher; in fact, intending not to marry a preacher. But I met one who was irresistible, and I married him—Huber Drumwright. We moved as bride and groom to a little farming village, Huber's student pastorate. Soon he was pastoring a new church in a booming part of north Dallas. At the same time, he began teaching as an instructor at Southwestern Baptist Theological Seminary, which meant commuting from Dallas to Fort Worth. He was also working—haphazardly, at that point—on his doctorate. We lived a hectic, harried, hurried life, juggling responsibilities, activities, and events in both cities, trying to stretch the hours to cover the matters that clamored for our hassled attention.

There were times when, as Huber kissed me good-bye to leave for Fort Worth, he would say, "Honey, I have not had time to write the pastor's column for the church bulletin, and it is due today. Would you please write it for me?" I was barely 21 years old when I wrote my first pastor's column!

The time came when, after 6 years of teaching at Southwestern Seminary, Huber was eligible for a sabbatical leave. He chose that we would go to Princeton Theological Seminary in New Jersey for special study in his field of New Testament and Greek.

I signed up for two courses—one was on prayer and worship. I had spent my life in the middle of prayer and worship. Thus, I did not expect to encounter anything new. Yet the Lord used that class and its godly professor to cause me to make some disturbing discoveries about myself. I found I was shallow in my soul and therefore shallow in my understanding of the real meaning of prayer and worship. This meant I was shallow in my relationship with God in Christ. And I was lacking in the power, the spiritual energy God makes available through His Holy Spirit, for the living of my daily life.

Shallow and *lacking.* Those two terribly descriptive words loomed before me. The old cliché came to my mind and convicted me: I was "a mile wide and one inch deep." That was hard to take. I was a pastor's daughter, a pastor's wife, a seminary professor's wife, and I was seeing myself as God saw me in my soul. I was beyond humbled. I felt broken before Him. I tasted contriteness.

Deep within, I heard the still, small, loving, gentle, firm voice of Jesus saying, "Learn from Me. Open your life to Me and to what I want to teach you and do within you." I felt a stirring throughout my being. I knew I wanted Him to be my Teacher. I wanted to know Him intimately. I wanted to love Him with all my heart and live my life in the way that would please Him.

He began to teach me. I am still learning.

There is much I could write about those classes at Princeton, but the professor's lecture on one specific day is a particularly important marker for me. That morning, he directed our attention to Hebrews 9. We read the words referring back to Exodus about the Tabernacle erected according to the instructions given to Moses.

"You recall the outer room called the Holy Place?" asked the professor. I did, of course. He continued, "The priests went there to perform their duties. Then there was the Most Holy Place, where dwelt the presence of God, the most sacred spot on earth for the Jews.

"Only once a year—the day of atonement—the high priest, and he only, entered the Most Holy Place with the blood of an unblemished animal, which He offered to atone for his own sins and the sins of the people (Heb. 9:7).

Obviously, there was no access to the direct presence of God by the people. The people were far removed from Him. There was even that veil that further separated the people." I followed the professor closely, familiar with what he was describing.

He continued, "But when Jesus came, of course, things radically changed. Because His life was sinless, perfect, as required by the Old Covenant, He fulfilled the requirement of an unblemished sacrifice to atone for the sins of believers for all time. He met every condition of the Old Covenant."

The professor, after going over the familiar facts, read Matthew 5:17–18. Then he reminded us: "When Jesus became the sacrifice for our sins on the Cross, a remarkable happening took place over at the Temple. The veil separating the presence of God from the people was torn in two— from top to bottom!" (Matt. 27:51–53). I knew that too.

What really happened in that Princeton classroom that day? Why has that day stood out as a spiritual marker in my life all these years?

As the professor pointedly questioned us, I realized that I had been living my life, figuratively speaking, in the outer court. At the age of nine, when I accepted Christ, I literally began living under the New Covenant. Yet in a sense I was still living under the old one. It dawned on me that morning in class that God was longing for me to live close to Him while I was going about my busy way, doing good, fine things (for Him!), not even realizing that I was missing out on something of ultimate significance. I was *not* receiving what Jesus had provided. I had *not* gone into the Most Holy Place, that inner part, as He intended. As I sat there with these thoughts burning my heart, the professor gently said, "Look, it is not too late. You can experience (and he seemed to be looking right at me) the personal, loving, consistent presence of the God of the universe within, right now and moment by moment."

God was getting through to me. The Most Holy Place was in me, for through Christ, that's where God lives. Christ in me! That rang a most familiar bell. That's exactly what I had prayed as a 9-year-old—that Jesus would come into my heart—and He did. However, I had not learned or experienced all that transaction meant. I still haven't!

That morning, the Father convinced me that He was yearning for me to move beyond the place where the veil had been and to live constantly in His presence, day by day. I felt an intense new longing to be close to Him with nothing, not even a thin veil, between my soul and my Savior.

Are you living your life in the outer court in your relationship with God? In your experience with Him, is that veil, figuratively speaking, still intact, creating an invisible barrier that looms up time and again? Hebrews 10:19 assures us we *can* enter and live in the Most Holy Place near to the very heart of God. If you have not made your way into the Most Holy Place, or if you have been there and moved away, listen! Wonder of wonders, our Lord is asking you to come close to Him and allow Him to be close to you (Jer. 30:21).

In the meantime, God was using another set of circumstances to deal further with my heart. We had rolled into Princeton on Friday evening before Labor Day. My energetic, dynamic husband commented, "I may dry up and blow away while we are here because I will not be preaching a single time during these months!"

Moments after our arrival we received an emergency telephone message. Hurriedly returning the call, we were relieved to learn what the emergency was. A group of Southern Baptists whose jobs had taken them to the East had begun to meet on Sunday mornings in the YMCA building on 23rd Street in Manhattan. They needed someone to preach Sunday morning—in just 36 hours! Was

Huber available? Was he ever! The Billy Graham crusade had been taking place in Madison Square Garden that summer. The group had been able to find visiting preachers to preach for them every Sunday morning during the crusade, until that final Sunday. With the concluding crusade service in Times Square that evening, Labor Day Sunday, they were searching for a preacher, and Huber was able to meet this need. I was not sure who was more grateful, Huber or the church members!

The little congregation, Manhattan Baptist Chapel, had already begun taking steps to call a pastor and constitute as a church. Just as we completed our leave at Princeton, Paul James arrived to begin his leadership of the congregation. Later, he became the executive director of the Baptist Convention of New York/North Jersey, and served with distinction in that key responsibility.

In our beginning days with the congregation, with Huber now available as interim pastor, the little group wanted evening services on Sunday nights and Wednesday nights. Church members in the northern New Jersey cities of Chatham and Morristown agreed to host those services in their homes. Huber did not dry up and blow away! We were having a delightful time.

Soon the women wanted to organize a WMS (now Women on Mission). For their charter meeting, they asked me to teach the spiritual life development book, *A Practical Primer on Prayer*. As I prepared for the study, I realized God was using the little book to reinforce the personal probing He was pursuing with me in my seminary class. Out of my study and preparation I made some commitments to God and to some disciplines of prayer that remain a part of my life today, especially in the area of praying for missions.

The Lord used that combination of events to teach me that prayer must become an integral part of my daily inner life: real prayer—not just routine, prayer-type words, but

authentic words and thoughts that come from staying
closely connected to Christ day and night. Jesus' words in
John 15 became deeply meaningful to me. "I am the vine;
you are the branches. If a man remains in me and I in him,
he will bear much fruit; apart from me you can do nothing" (John 15:5 NIV). His words throughout John 15 continue to grow more important in my understanding of how
He wants me to relate to Him and others. He says to me
daily, "Stay closely connected to Me. Only as you do so will
you receive the resources that flow from the Vine into the
life of the branches. Only as you do so will you bear fruit—
your role in the kingdom. Apart from Me, you will accomplish nothing." This is the secret of life in Him, the secret
of fruitfulness: to be a good branch, constantly connected,
not just at certain times and places, but receiving the flow
of His life resources consistently, every day, in every circumstance. That became and remains one of my goals.

We returned to Fort Worth. Outwardly, I looked the
same. Inwardly, my soul was being transformed. Jesus had
become my daily teacher.

As time unfolded, God led me into a variety of experiences, some related to prayer and the inward journey with
Him. At the same time He led me into ministries related
to my outward journey with Him, avenues of service
through my church, and even some outside that framework. I worked with unwed mothers and taught a Bible
class of economically disadvantaged women for 12 years
(and they taught me a lot!). I led a women's Bible study
group in the federal prison in Fort Worth. I worked with
internationals and related to other ministry opportunities
provided through our church's outstanding WMU and its
extensive outreaches. Involvement in Texas WMU provided many challenging life-changing experiences. I felt a
new joy, a new energy, a quiet, deep fulfillment in my soul
beyond anything I had experienced before.

My family seemed to sense this. In our family time each morning, in addition to praying for missionaries, we prayed for one another in specific, intentional ways. One morning our younger daughter, Debra, then about 7, prayed first for her sister, Meme: "Dear God: Meme is so worried about that test she has been studying for. Please help her to do her best on it. Help her remember what she studied. . . . And God, bless Daddy as he works in his office at the seminary today, and help him as he teaches the students in class how to teach the Bible and how to preach about Jesus. . . . And dear God, please bless Moms as she . . ." She paused and I could almost hear the little wheels turning in her mind. I remember thinking, "This is going to be one of those moments of truth. I'm about to see how my child perceives my day and all the things I do." She repeated herself. "Bless Moms," and paused again, then prayed, "as she plays around all day!"

They burst into laughter! I admit my sense of humor was slow to respond. "I've got to impress upon this kid that my days are full of worthwhile things. I am not out there just having fun all day," I thought.

Then the light dawned: "Oh, yes, I am! She's right. I am having so much joy—real joy, God-given joy—and she is catching accurately the essence of what I am feeling about my day-by-day journey with the Lord."

I would not have worded it exactly the way she did, but in her childlike discernment, she had tuned in to the joy I was experiencing in my soul.

As I sought to be intentional in living out my new commitments to God and to His Word, I developed a deep conviction that (1) God had called me to a ministry of prayer, and (2) He had given me a heart for prayer. I soon learned He calls every Christ follower to a ministry of prayer, and He gives a heart for prayer to every one of His children who will receive it.

Another spiritual marker contributing significantly to my life and pilgrim growth was a Yokefellows group to which I submitted myself for a 2-year period. This prayer therapy group followed a format that probed deeply into my inner soul and demanded strict honesty and accountability. In becoming members of the group, we made a commitment to spend 30 minutes with the Lord every day concerning the specific discoveries we were encountering—discoveries involving our relationship with Him and with others. We prayed intensely together each week. The group sessions were sometimes painful, sometimes exhilarating, always stirring to my soul. The Holy Spirit did transforming work.

In 1980, God had a big surprise for us. Huber was dean of the School of Theology at Southwestern Baptist Theological Seminary, and I had not dreamed of our being anywhere but Southwestern forever (in this world). The Lord and Arkansas Baptists called Huber to become the executive secretary-treasurer of the Arkansas Baptist State Convention. After a long period of soul-searching and a recommitment of our desire to know and do God's will, we moved to Little Rock.

One of the shocks of my life was to find, when we arrived to plant our lives in Arkansas, that I had an instant feeling we were home. After a lifetime in Texas, how could this be? Indeed, often we commented to one another that this was the most joyful period of our lives together. Our daughters were happily situated at Baylor University, and Huber and I spent much of our time "running around Arkansas together" (Huber's description). We felt a renewal of our souls in the Lord and His kingdom work and a renewal of our hearts with one another.

This beautiful period was short-lived. On Sunday, November 1, 1981, Huber preached with his usual vitality morning and evening at First Baptist Church, El Dorado, Arkansas. We had returned to our home in Little Rock, when late that night, with no previous warning, a massive heart attack took his life.

Our lives had been intricately intertwined for nearly 31 years. To put it mildly, I was traumatized and devastated. I struggled with how to do my life without his life and love and laughter.

For many years, I had given myself to the principle of gratitude in the midst of every circumstance. However, I found it very difficult to apply this principle to a shattered heart. Gradually, in the midst of the loving ministry of my family and friends, I slowly came to a recommitment of myself to a stance of gratitude for the years Huber and I had, rather than focusing on the years we would not have. I came to the reaffirmation of the truth that even in life's most difficult loss, this is a requirement for abundant life in Christ. I continue to encounter Huber's friends and former students in this country and around the world who tell me Huber Drumwright stories of his impact on their lives and ministries. I love those stories. To this day, they minister to my heart. I have more than a few Huber Drumwright stories to tell of my own! I am again overwhelmed with gratitude for our lives together.

In due time, William O'Brien, a longtime friend and one who ministered meaningfully to me in my grief, asked if I was ready to think about what I was going to do with the rest of my life. He was at the time executive vice-president of the Foreign Mission Board (now International Mission Board). Soon thereafter, I was invited to join the Foreign Mission Board staff as his assistant. As I sought to know God's mind, I received other challenging opportunities for missions and ministry. Gradually, He began to give me a strong sense of rightness about investing myself in what I was being asked to do at the Foreign Mission Board. I moved to Richmond, Virginia, away from my family and roots, still in brokenness. That move became another spiritual marker in my life. Of course, I would never have chosen this life apart from my husband, but God was faithful to minister to my brokenness and bring good even out of dashed dreams and the wrenching rearrangement of my life in midstream. He is true to His promises.

My work with the Board represented to me a paradox—both a disconnection with my past and a continuity with it. I sometimes, even now, refer to my life with my husband, family, friends, and simple ministries through those earlier years as my "other life." At the same time, life on this side of the stream has taken on extraordinary meaning to me because it has represented, among other significant matters, continuity with my life on the other side of the stream. That continuity has remained very important to me. God, in His creativity, took the commitments and disciplines this struggling pilgrim made many years previously, and in my latter years of brokenness incorporated them into another arena of His world; and in a small way that was significant to me, He included me in His plan for the nations.

I went to Richmond thinking I would be there several years, then return to my Texas roots. However, I became so caught up in the work God had given me to do that when I did return, I had been away 14 years.

At the time of this writing, I live in a carefully chosen location in Fort Worth 20 minutes from two of my grandchildren, 3½ hours from the third. My older daughter, Meme, teaches business ethics at the University of Texas at Austin, where she and her husband, H. W., are both on the faculty. They have Lauren Minette, born in 1991. Debra, my younger daughter, is a stay-at-home mom, although she doesn't stay at home! Her husband, Max, a CPA, commutes to Dallas in his work. They have Bradley Huber, born in 1986, and Emily, born in 1988. I take seriously my role as grandparent and delight in the opportunity to have impact on the lives of my grandchildren. We are best buddies!

I belong to a small congregation of young families near where I live. Unlike any I had chosen before, the church is contemporary, seeker-friendly, come as you are, mostly new Christians. I had assumed the Lord would lead me to a traditional church. That is what I would have chosen. However, it was another of God's surprises when I discerned clearly His leading me to invest my current energies in this congregation. Once again, I am learning. Many of the young adults come from dysfunctional family backgrounds and are determined to avoid repeating the same patterns in their own families. I believe God has entrusted to me a special gift in placing me among these young families. My favorite time of the week is the women's Bible study I teach in my home, for there God comes, and in the midst of our studying, sharing, tears, and laughter, He reveals Himself to us as He teaches us and grows us.

I have been down a variety of roads in my journey during these years. I have had many wonderful experiences in prayer, here and around the world. For a decade, I worked in the area of prayer, mobilizing people to pray, especially for missions. Even though I have been deeply involved in prayer, personally and in my work, I still periodically need to stop and reevaluate the authenticity and freshness of my current prayer experiences and prayer disciplines. I need to assess the place prayer has in my own life right now. Even with my commitment to the power of prayer, which goes back many years, prayer has a way of floating out to the periphery of my life. Again and again I need—deliberately and intentionally—to bring prayer back to the center of my life. More accurately, I need to bring the God of prayer back into the center of all that I am and do. Frankly, I periodically need a revival of prayer; I need to rediscover again the familiar aspects of prayer and to seek new depths in prayer.

Daily I hear our Lord's question as found in Jeremiah: "Who are the ones who will devote themselves to be close to Me?" My answer is "Lord, I will." I am still unwrapping all that His question and my answer mean.

Today He is asking *you*, "Who are the ones who will devote themselves to be close to Me?" What is *your* answer?

Questions for Reflection

What does prayer really mean to you?

How often do your thoughts turn toward the Lord in simple, heartfelt prayer?

Is prayer vital—at the center of all you do—or is it simply tacked onto your life at convenient points?

Are there days when you make your way without, in your heart, connecting with God?

When you pray, do you talk with God naturally, spontaneously, from the bottom of your being, or do you just go through the routine of saying more or less the same words you said the last time you prayed?

Do your spontaneous prayers usually begin with "Help me" and/or "Give me"?

Do your prayers reveal a subtle attempt to use God rather than offering yourself to Him for His use of you?

What do your prayers reveal about your relationship with God in Christ?

36

Do you need a revival of prayer, a rediscovery of prayer, that stirs the core of your being, transforming your perspective and attitudes, your capacity to love, your relationship to God and others, your very life?

[1]Rebecca Manley Pippert, *Love Has Its Reasons* (San Francisco: Harper and Row, 1989), 194.

3

Prayer's Foundational Truths

"'I have come that they may have life, and have it to the full'" (John 10:10 NIV).

"You will seek me and find me when you seek me with all your heart" (Jer. 29:13 NIV).

"We are not here to prove God answers prayer; we are here to be living monuments of God's grace."—Oswald Chambers[1]

Most of us instinctively think of prayer as a resource and support in our lives, in the lives of others, and even in a broader worldwide perspective. And it is. All earnest pray-ers give testimony to that fact. Yet at another level, prayer is strategy, a primary strategy in the Christian life.

A strategy is a means or plan that contributes to the accomplishment of some end or goal. Early Christians called their disciplines and commitments to spiritual growth a "rule of life." Every monastic order had its rules of life—an intentional plan for accomplishing their spiritual goals. The Latin word for "rule" is *regula,* meaning something done regularly and intentionally. Today's word is *strategy*— an intentional plan involving regular actions for accomplishing one or more goals. Thus, once we define the God-given goals of our lives, our family, our church, or any ministry or institution or cause, then prayer can become a strategy for accomplishing these goals.

Before we can formulate a prayer strategy, some familiar truths from God's Word need to become a part of the spiritual fabric of our being. Periodically we need to rediscover these truths, reaffirm them as vital, and realign our lives in relation to them. Scriptures are filled with these truths. This is an attempt to acknowledge some that are on the front burner of the Christ-following life in terms of daily need and application.

The Goal of Prayer

This goal actually is the goal of all aspects of the Christian life and is stated best in the classic statement from the Westminster Shorter Catechism: "The chief end of man [and woman—my addition] is to glorify God and enjoy Him forever." Is your heart's desire to bring glory and pleasure to God? Paul wrote, "Whatever you do, do it all to the glory of God" (1 Cor. 10:31 NIV). That includes prayer.

Jesus said, "Whatever you ask in My name, that I will do, that the Father may be glorified in the Son" (John 14:13 NKJV).

John Piper comments on this verse: "In other words, the ultimate purpose of prayer is that the Father be glorified. The other side of the purpose comes out in John 16:24. Jesus says, 'Till now you have asked nothing in my name; ask, and you will receive that your joy may be full.' The purpose of prayer is that our joy may be full. The unity of these two goals—the glory of God and the joy of His people—is preserved in the act of prayer."[2]

The psalmist agrees. He wrote, "Delight yourself in the Lord" (Psalm 37:4 NIV). Paul said, "Revel in him" (Phil. 4:4 *The Message*). Do you actually enjoy God in your praying? A meaningful part of the goal of prayer, and of all the Christian life, is to enjoy Him forever—as we are bringing

glory to Him, and being obedient to His greatest com-
mandments (Matt. 22:38) and His Great Commission
(Matt. 28:19–20).

The Premise of Prayer

The premise of prayer (from the Drumwright Catechism)
is this: All the good, fine things we do for God are largely
futile (1) unless they come from the mind of God, (2) unless they are offered to God and others in the Spirit of
Christ, and (3) unless they are carried out in the power,
energy, and stamina of the Holy Spirit, and not by our energy. This means the most important thing about prayer is
not prayer. The most important thing about prayer is God
and His glory, and our current, close, costly relationship
with Him. This, in turn, means that God does not just answer our prayers. He answers our *lives*. Thus, the significance of the life that prays.

The Major Purposes of Prayer

Prayer has two major purposes. The first is to know God
in Christ intimately, to know His heart, His Word, His
character, His ways, His will, His voice; to love Him increasingly; and to become more and more like Him. The
second major purpose is to participate with Him in what
He is doing in this world through prayer, to become His
prayer partner.

Consider the first purpose: knowing God, simply and
profoundly. Paul wrote "everything else is worthless com-
pared to the priceless gain of knowing Christ Jesus, my
Lord" (Phil. 3:8 TLB). Is knowing Christ your passion? Is
your relationship with Him more important than anything
else? Somehow in all our worthwhile activities, the priority
of *knowing Him* has a way of quietly fading in the rush of
going and doing. Corrie Ten Boom said, "Beware the bar-
renness of a busy life."

Knowing God more deeply and becoming more like Him involves daily solitude with Him, daily worship of Him. It means inviting Him daily into the midst of our lives, rather than keeping Him on the fringe. It requires listening, not just hearing; not only reading His Word, but absorbing it and living it in a way that makes a difference in our attitudes, perspectives, habits, and relationships. It involves staying intimately connected to Christ, abiding in Him, and drawing resources from Him for the living of every day. Is that a picture of you and Him? Without that close connection, the words we call prayer are not really prayer, but only routine, spiritually correct prayer-type words. Our intimate walk with Him must be vital today in order for our words to be authentic prayer today.

Although the foundational truths of this chapter apply to both purposes of prayer, we are focusing now on the first purpose. Chapter 7 gives in-depth attention to the second purpose, understanding kingdom praying, partnering with God in what He wants done in this world. These two purposes interrelate and intertwine. Even though we discuss them separately and distinctly, they are each intrinsically important to one's relationship with God in Christ.

Rediscovering Familiar Truths About Prayer
In making prayer the priority strategy in our lives, we need periodically to rediscover familiar truths about prayer.

1. We must develop, and live our lives in harmony with, an accurate understanding of the real meaning of prayer.
One of the constantly amazing matters in all of life is that, through Christ, we have direct access to Almighty God, the maker and sustainer of the universe—and of us! God has chosen to relate to us as a personal, present, loving, forgiving, just, sovereign, trustworthy Father. Jesus taught us to address God as Abba, an Aramaic word from Jesus'

heart language,[3] the sweet, tender word with which a little child addressed an earthly parent.[4] Jesus' use of the word was extraordinary and revealing, for this view of God was new to people at that time. God is initiating intimate, loving fellowship with us. He longs for us to respond to Him. At the same time, prayer is a gauge of our relationship with Him. Our prayer habits, attitudes, and content reveal the state of the relationship. This revelation serves as a reality check, perhaps a sobering one.

Prayer has been referred to as either the greatest thing we can know and do or the most cruel hoax possible, as "the primary fact, or the worst delusion."[5]

Prayer is difficult to describe with mere words. In defining a concept, it is sometimes helpful to state both what it is, and what it is not. Prayer is not a supernatural credit card. It is not a magic wand to wave away misfortune or a rabbit's foot to keep us from disaster. Biblical prayer is not a letter to a celestial Santa Claus. It is not a campaign to persuade God to do something He would otherwise leave undone. Biblical prayer is not begging or bargaining with God. It is not merely a routine, spiritual exercise. Real prayer is not a blank check on which God's signature appears, guaranteeing anything on which we set our selfish hearts. Authentic biblical prayer is not a way to get God to give us what *we* want.

Then what is prayer? Prayer is, of course, communication with God, simply, honestly, from our hearts, talking to Him like we talk to our best friend—because He is! Prayer is inviting God into the very midst of our lives. Prayer is offering ourselves to God all over again each day.

Archbishop Temple wrote, "The essential act of prayer is not the bending of God's will to ours, but bending our will to His. The proper outline of a Christian's prayer is not 'Please do for me what I want,' but 'Please do in me, with me, and through me what You want.'"[6] O. Hallesby wrote, "Prayer is something deeper than words. It is present in the soul before it has been formulated in words. And it abides in the soul after the last words of prayer have passed over our lips. Prayer is an attitude of our hearts, an attitude of mind."[7] Hallesby goes on to say that the attitude of the heart, which God recognizes as prayer, is a combination of helplessness and faith.

Other writers have offered further insights. Richard Foster states, "Prayer is the central avenue God uses to transform us.[8] John Piper said, "Prayer is God's appointed means of bringing grace to the world and glory to himself."[9] Watchman Nee wrote that prayer is "none other than an act of the believer working together with God."[10] E. Stanley Jones described prayer as the will to cooperate with God in all of one's life. Samuel Zwemer wrote, "True prayer is God the Holy Spirit talking to God the Father in the name of God the Son, and the believer's heart is the throne room."[11]

This dimension of prayer changes our perspective and causes us to begin to think God's thoughts after Him. We begin to pray what the Holy Spirit wants us to pray. Slowly, imperceptibly, we begin to have the mind of Christ.

Authentic, biblical prayer is a means God uses to give us what He wants us to have and grow us into becoming what He wants us to be.

2. God's answers come in various forms.

Probably the most asked question about prayer has to do with answers. As I was growing up, I learned that God has three answers to our prayers: yes, no, and wait. As I have become a bit more experienced in my own relationship with Him, I have discerned other answers. One is, "I will give you something better."

Often we hear stories and testimonies of answered prayer. One of my favorites: A missionary family was preparing to leave their assignment in Africa for stateside assignment in about two months. They found that they had barely enough powdered milk to meet the needs of their 5-year-old daughter and their 5-month-old baby. No more would be available. Then a single missionary arrived at their home, became ill, and could take only milk. About the same time an African baby was brought to them whose Christian mother could not take care of him and whose father they were seeking to win to Christ. The baby, of course, needed milk. The meager supply could not begin to provide for four people for two months.

They prayed intensely. That evening at prayer, the wife's eyes fell upon a verse of Scripture that she was seeing for the first time: "And thou shalt have goats' milk enough for thy food, for the food of thy household, and for the maintenance of thy maidens" (Prov. 27:27 KJV). This looked for all the world like a promise from God, but they had never heard of any goats in the area!

The next day at the village store, a man whose reputation was less than godly asked if the missionaries could use some goat's milk. He had just returned from a long trip, bringing back a truckload of goats. He would have milk going to waste every day. Could they use some? Well, could they ever! And we hear the words of the Lord: "Before they call, I will answer; and while they are yet speaking, I will hear" (Isa. 65:24).[12]

I love such stories and praise the Lord for them. In my own journey, however, I rarely have such dramatic experiences. The deepest answers to my prayers have been less measurable; not less real, but less tangible. My own passionate belief is that God's greatest answer is the gift of Himself. Thomas à Kempis's prayer strikes a responsive chord in me: "It is too small and unsatisfactory, whatever thou bestowest on me, apart from Thyself." Noted twentieth-century scholar W. T. Conner wrote, "What man seeks, or should seek, in prayer is not, first of all, some thing that God may give, but God Himself."[13] Oswald Chambers observed, "Spiritual lust makes me demand an answer from God,

instead of seeking God Who gives the answer. . . . The
meaning of prayer is that we get hold of God, not the answer."[14] When our heavenly Father is the desire of our
hearts (Isa. 26:8), then *He* is our greatest answer.

In our petitions and intercessions, questions regarding
God's answers and seeming lack of answers will always be
with us. Can God be talked into answering our prayers?
Why does God need me to tell Him something He already
knows? Why should I ask Him to do that which He already wants to do? Were the answers really answers or were
they coincidences? If I had not prayed, would the same
things have happened? Does God *really* intervene?

How our prayers affect God's sovereignty remains a
mystery. Yet even in the midst of the ever-present questions, we simply know that God answers prayer.

Consider these thoughts:
If the request is wrong, God says, "No."
If the timing is wrong, God says, "Slow."
If you are wrong, God says, "Grow."
But if the request is right,
The timing is right,
And you are right,
God says, "Go."[15]

Adoniram Judson observed, "I never prayed sincerely and
earnestly for anything, but that the answer came at some
time—no matter how far distant the day—somehow, in
some shape, probably the last I should have devised, it came."

The more important question is not Does God hear and
answer us when pray? but Do we hear and answer God
when He speaks to us?

3. We must learn to listen to God.
Most of us are much better at talking to God than at listening to Him. An Indian proverb says, "Listen, or thy tongue
will make thee deaf." How true this is in our communication

with God. How possible it is for us to do all the talking and be deaf to what He has to say to us.

My goal is to spend as much time listening to Him as I do talking to Him. Yet I am prone to express to Him all I have on my mind and in my heart; and when I stop talking to Him, I tend to consider the time complete. I neglect to wait, to be still and quiet.

Too often I say in essence, "Listen, Lord, for your servant speaks," instead of "Speak, Lord, for your servant is listening."

4. Our hearts must become private chapels.

Jesus said we "should always pray and not give up" (Luke 18:1 NIV). Is it possible to be obedient to this clear instruction of Jesus?

Thomas Kelly wrote, "There is a way of ordering our mental life on more than one level at once. On one level we may be thinking, discussing, seeing, calculating, meeting all the demand of external affairs. But deep within, behind the scenes, at a profounder level, we may also be in prayer and adoration, song and worship and a gentle receptiveness to divine breathings."[16]

Praying without ceasing is turning our hearts and minds to the Lord all through the day and night. It is abiding in Him. It is what I call lifestyle praying. It is the practice of the presence of God.

Brother Lawrence wrote a classic book by that title. He was assigned to work in the kitchen at the monastery, and called himself the "lord of the pots and pans." He wrote, "To think that you must abandon conversation with Him in order to deal with the world is erroneous. . . . The time of business does not with me differ from the time of prayer; and in the noise and clatter of my kitchen, while several persons are at the same time calling for different things, I possess God in as great tranquillity as if I were upon my knees in the chapel."[17]

He insisted that we make a private chapel of our hearts where we can retire from time to time to commune with God. Just as the kitchen can be our private chapel, so too can an office or shop or car. All through the day we too can turn our thoughts to the Father.

I have developed reminders that nudge me to say, "This is one of those times to lift my thoughts to the Lord." As I wait in line or at a red light, I can thank God, intercede for someone, pray for the person in line with me, or pray for the clerk soon to handle my groceries. Replacing the receiver of a phone is an alert to pray for the person with whom I have just conversed. Many years ago, I began the practice of praying for the people affected whenever I hear the sound of a siren. So often, that eerie sound means trauma, heartbreak, and sudden rearrangement of lives. Always, there is urgent need for intercession.

For 18 years now, my praying in that regard has come from a deeper level of my soul. When my husband suffered a massive, fatal heart attack, he and I were the ones in the ambulance with the siren screaming in the night. We were the ones in need of unseen, unknown people praying for us. This kind of lifestyle praying means being in touch with the Father throughout the day and the night. How this kind of praying and this kind of life has sustained me through deep and troubled waters! As best I can understand, this is how we abide in Him. This is how we pray without ceasing. This is how we can walk and not faint. This is how we can know Him more and more intimately. This is how we can become more like Him.

Making our hearts private chapels is the response of the life that prays and of the Christ follower who has a heart for prayer.

5. *Prayer brings Satan's opposition.*

Even though Satan will ultimately be defeated, he is busy at work today, seeking to undermine and destroy the people of God and the work of God. Yet no one is a firmer believer in prayer's power than he, not because he practices it but because he suffers from it!

Satan must feel smug when we fail to pray, for we become vulnerable to his invasion of our attitudes and behavior when we neglect to be in consistent communion with God in Christ Jesus. Peter warned, "Be self-controlled and alert. Your enemy the devil prowls around like a roaring lion looking for someone to devour. Resist him, standing firm in the faith" (1 Peter 5:8 NIV). Satan opposes prayer because prayer destroys him. We need to rediscover the ultimate value of prayer in voiding the power of evil around us.

6. Prayerlessness is sin.

"As for me, far be it from me that I should sin against the Lord by failing to pray" Samuel declared (1 Sam. 12:23 NIV). I suggest two generalizations: (1) Christian believers believe that we believe in prayer. (2) I have a fear that we do not pray very much. We especially neglect to pray for God's heart desire—the salvation of a lost world. Someone suggested that in too many of our churches, we spend more time praying to keep sick saints out of heaven than we do praying lost people into heaven.

This does not mean we should lessen our prayers for the sick. It means we need to align our hearts with the Savior's heart and balance our praying for personal burdens with an equal prayer concern for those who do not know Christ.

James Leo Garrett Jr., noted Baptist theologian and friend of my husband from their earliest days of childhood, affirmed that while "prayer is imperative for the Christian, . . . prayerlessness is the taproot of the Christian's sins and failures."[18]

One of our greatest prayer concerns needs to be that God's people will pray, for prayerlessness is sin. We may call it neglect or spiritual dryness, but God considers it sin.

48

7. Prayer has conditions.

God has given us guidelines for prayer that, when we
follow them, enable Him to respond to our prayers without compromising His character or our well-being. The
conditions are:

a) Abide in Christ. "If you abide in me, and my words
abide in you, you shall ask what you will, and it shall be
done unto you" (John 15:7 KJV). Abiding means intimate,
constant fellowship with our Lord. Abiding in Him and
absorbing into our beings His words and Spirit provide the
resources we need for obedient living as well as for effective
praying.

b) Be cleansed from known sin. Do you confess and repent daily? We tend to use spiritual cosmetology on our
problems of ego, competitiveness, jealousy, criticism, envy,
irritability, negativism. The psalmist warned, "If I regard
iniquity in my heart, the Lord will not hear me" (Psalm
66:18 KJV). Often we take lightly our need for repentance
and continual cleansing. We shrug off the grief our sins
bring to God. Sins, even subtle ones, rob us of closeness
with the Father. We must be quick to confess and repent.
This means agreeing with God about the seriousness of our
sin. When we confess humbly and contritely, God is instant in forgiveness and cleansing (1 John 1:9).

c) Pray in Jesus' name (John 16:23). Knowing what we
do about His character, mind, and name, we are to pray
those prayers He will endorse and approve. To pray in His
name means we are praying the prayers Jesus would pray if
He were here among us in the flesh.

d) Pray according to God's will. We are not to pray,
"Thy will be changed," but "Thy will be done" (Matt
6:10). Prayer is the means whereby our desires can be redi-
rected and aligned with the will of God.

e) Pray in faith, believing. "If you believe, you will receive whatever you ask for in prayer" (Matt 21:22 NIV). What a bold promise! And what a big *if.* When we come to God with an abiding, cleansed life, approaching Him in Jesus' name, seeking His will, then we can have the assurance that God will do what He says. He is utterly trustworthy. Our praying must evidence our effortless confidence in Him and our recognition of His power. Our faith must not be in prayer, but in God. As a child, I was taught an acrostic for simple FAITH: Forsaking All, I Trust Him.

f) Pray in humility. This means acknowledging our helplessness, brokenness, and total need for God. "If my people . . . will humble themselves" (2 Chron. 7:14 NIV). Humility is the first requirement in that important statement of our Lord. "God opposes the proud but gives grace to the humble" (James 4:6 NIV). In the light of the significance God places on authentic humility, how rare is it in our daily relationship with Him and others?

Stating the conditions of prayer in yet another way, Scripture is clear about the hindrances to prayer:

• Unconfessed sin—Isaiah 59:2; Psalm 66:18; 139:23–24
• Pride—James 4:6*b*
• Disorder in marriage relationship—1 Peter 3:7
• Busyness—Luke 10:41–42
• Wrong motives—James 4:3
• Unforgiving spirit—Colossians 3:13
• Disobedience—1 John 3:22
• Hypocrisy—Matthew 6:5; 1 Peter 2:1
• Lack of compassion—Proverbs 21:13
• Critical attitude, negativism—Matthew 7:1–5

8. Jesus is our example in prayer.

Jesus' life is the model of what our lives should be. With our imperfect natures, of course we cannot mirror His life perfectly. Still, the goal remains to be like Him.

How did He pray? Jesus prayed often in secret and in public, for His friends and for His enemies, for Himself and for others. He prayed when He faced decisions and in times of crises. Prayer was central and crucial in His life. He knew He needed to be in touch with the Father at all times. If He needed it, how much more do we?

Jesus instructed His disciples to pray, and He taught them how to pray. It is interesting that He did not teach them how to preach. He taught them how to pray. Jesus is our example in prayer.

My desire is to pray for a person or situation or nation as I discern Jesus would pray if He were beside me in the flesh as my prayer partner. The reality is that He *is* with me as my unseen prayer partner, praying through His Holy Spirit *within* me and *alongside* me even as I pray *to* Him and to the Father.

9. Our greatest need is God's power.

This is the most basic truth, and we must acknowledge it daily. Our greatest deficiency is power—not training or prayer materials or seminars or retreats—or books on prayer! Our greatest need is power—power for worship and witness, ministry and mission; power for living joyfully and abundantly day by day; power to stay closely and constantly connected to God.

How do we access God's power, His spiritual energy and stamina? The early verses of Acts reveal the disciples' lack of clarity and understanding. In Acts 1:6 (NIV) they asked, "Lord, are you at this time going to restore the kingdom to Israel?" They still did not get it. They were tentative and uncertain about their own futures and the future of the floundering movement they were leading. Oh, they

knew and loved and wanted to serve the resurrected Lord.
Yet it was only after they rediscovered prayer in a prayer
meeting that lasted for days, "as they all joined together
constantly in prayer, along with the women and Mary the
mother of Jesus, and with his brothers" (Acts 1:14 NIV)—
only then did God's transforming power come. Prayer, not
preaching, brought Pentecost. Prayer brought the Holy
Spirit, Who brought the power that transformed, clarified,
and energized the disciples.

Only after Pentecost did their lives overflow with courage, clarity, fruitfulness, and joy. Only then did they become the powerful people who turned the world upside
down for Jesus.

How can we be recipients of that power? How can our
lives overflow with the joy, courage, thanksgiving, and
fruitfulness that characterized those first-century disciples
after Pentecost?

The answer is the same for us as it was for them. We
need to rediscover prayer. Prayer leads to the Holy Spirit's
filling, which leads to effective living (and dying) and to a
portion of all the Christlike qualities. God can do within
us and among us and through us what He did in their
midst. But we must meet the conditions of prayer and
open ourselves to the Holy Spirit's filling. We must have a
rediscovery of prayer in our lives. Do we dare?

These affirmations come from the Word of God and
form the foundation of intimacy with Christ and partnership with the God of prayer. In deeply believing these essentials, absorbing them and living them day by day, the
Holy Spirit brings transformation to our lives and churches.

As a young man, Beethoven made a long journey to a
distant cathedral where a great organ had been installed.
Though he had already attained fame as a musician, he was
still unknown to most people on sight. Travel was difficult,
and he made most of the journey in an open carriage and
on foot. He arrived at the cathedral looking like a vaga-

bond. Presenting himself at the side door, he was met by an old monk.

"I have come to see the great organ," the great musician said. "I have traveled many miles so that I might look at it." The monk slowly appraised the unkempt, seedy-looking young man, but then led him down a long dark corridor where he could get a view of the instrument. Coming closer, Beethoven asked, "Sir, could I be permitted to run my fingers across the keyboard?"

"Oh, not so, my friend," said the monk. "Please do not ask such a favor. This organ is reserved only for the touch of the masters."

Beethoven was persistent, and the monk saw the deep earnestness in the young man's face. Relenting, he whispered, "Just for a moment."

Beethoven eagerly seated himself. With artistry and skill, he swept the keyboard with his fingers, and the lovely music rose and reverberated through the arches of the cathedral. "Who are you?" asked the amazed monk. "I am Beethoven," the young man replied. The monk peeled the skullcap off his head. With tears in his voice, he prayed, "O God, forgive me for almost missing letting the master use this humble instrument."

Tragedy is not always something that happens. More often, it is something wonderful that could happen, but does not.

The greatest tragedy is not what we are. We are good, fine folks who believe in prayer and have a genuine desire to serve the Lord. The tragedy is not what we are, but what we do not become because we do not really pray. The tragedy is not what we do, but what we do not do in giving ourselves, individually and corporately, to united, persistent, authentic, extraordinary prayer.

Lord, teach us to pray.

Questions for Reflection
How do your prayers reveal your understanding of the real meaning of prayer?

What is your level of expectation of God's answers to your prayers?

Are you becoming more and more selective of what you ask of God?

What is the ratio of your listening to God and your talking to Him?

Do you think of the Father all through the day and talk to Him spontaneously, intimately?

Within the framework of your lifestyle, what are some reminders that can serve as prayer alerts?

On a scale of 1 to 10, with 10 the highest, what is your awareness level of Satan's opposition to prayer? Are you confident that your praying voids his power?

Do you consider prayerlessness sin?

What is your greatest need in your spiritual life?

[1]Oswald Chambers, *My Utmost for His Highest* (New York: Dodd, Mead and Company, 1935), 219.
[2]John Piper, *Let the Nations Be Glad* (Grand Rapids: Baker Books, 1993), 56.
[3]Aramaic is a dialect of Hebrew and was the language spoken by the Jews in the first century.
[4]Huber L. Drumwright, *Prayer Rediscovered* (Nashville: Broadman Press, 1978), 17.
[5]George A Buttrick, *Prayer* (New York/Nashville: Abingdon-Cokesbury Press, 1942), 15.
[6]William Temple, *Reading in St. John's Gospel* (London: Macmillan and Co., 1940).

54

[7]O. Hallesby, *Prayer* (Minneapolis: Augsburg Publishing House, 1931), 16.

[8]Richard Foster, *Celebration of Discipline* (San Francisco: Harper and Row, 1978), 30.

[9]Piper, *Let the Nations Be Glad*, 220.

[10]Watchman Nee, *Let Us Pray* (New York: Christian Fellowship, 1977), 3.

[11]Samuel Zwemer, *Into All the World* (Grand Rapids: Zondervan, 1943), 160.

[12]From story told by J. G. McCauley, *A Devotional Commentary in the Acts of the Apostles* (Grand Rapids: William B. Eerdmans, 1953), 133.

[13]W. T. Conner, *A System of Christian Doctrine* (Nashville: Sunday School Board, 1924), 488.

[14]Chambers, *My Utmost for His Highest*, 82.

[15]Anonymous, quoted by Bill Hybels in *Too Busy Not to Pray* (Downers Grove, IL: InterVarsity Press, 1998).

[16]Thomas Kelly, *A Testament of Devotion* (New York: Harper Brothers, 1941).

[17]Brother Lawrence [Gene Edwards], *Practicing His Presence* (Goleta, CA: Christian Books, 1973), 103.

[18]James Leo Garrett Jr., "Prayer," *Encyclopedia of Southern Baptists* (Nashville: Broadman Press, 1958), 2:1103.

4

A Prayer Strategy for the Christ Follower

"'For the eyes of the Lord range throughout the earth to strengthen those whose hearts are fully committed to him'" (2 Chron. 16:9 NIV).

"The greatest people of the earth today are the people who pray—not those who talk about prayer, nor those who say they believe in prayer, not those who can explain about prayer, but those who take time to pray."—S. D. Gordon[1]

Recently many people have begun to use the term *Christ follower* rather than the word *Christian*. I prefer the newer phrase. Although *Christian* began in New Testament days (Acts 11:26) with the descriptive meaning of "little Christs," the word no longer has that connotation. Today *Christian* can stand for many different levels of devotion to our Lord, or even a nominal, inherited relationship. To say a person is a Christian does not necessarily indicate he or she is a disciple of Christ.

What is your impression when someone identifies himself or herself or is described as a Christ follower? Surely the phrase sounds a serious note of discipleship.

Jesus Embodied the Life That Prays

A Christ follower can be defined as one who lives connected to God in every area of life, including prayer. With the goal of Christlikeness clearly in mind, the Christ follower studies what Jesus taught and seeks to absorb and incorporate even the nuances of His words and example into the fiber of the soul and life. Jesus embodied the life that prays. Thus, the Christ follower is especially observant of how Jesus incorporated prayer into His life. What was Jesus' prayer strategy?

From the study of His life, we know that Jesus kept closely in touch with the Father consistently. We know He also withdrew often to spend periods of time in solitude and communion with His Father. Then He would reengage with the persons to whom God led Him. So should we be intentional Christ followers.

This chapter is devoted to discerning, developing, and living out a personalized prayer strategy. To whatever extent our personal commitments, disciplines, and convictions are active and authentic, they are reflected in our personal prayer strategy, or lack of one. Many Christ followers have a prayer strategy without using that term. The words we use are not the important issue. The important matter is to have a plan that will assist us in accomplishing our (and His!) intentions and purposes in making prayer central and vital in our lives. Our plan is our prayer strategy. Of equal importance is faithfulness to the plan.

Jesus said, "When you pray, go into a room alone and close the door. Pray to your Father in private" (Matt. 6:6 CEV).

Since solitude time with the Father was of utmost priority to Jesus during His time on earth, consider first this facet of the life that prays. For today's Christ follower, what is an effective plan for daily communion with Him and for keeping the time fresh and vital? How can our solitude with Him be consistently meaningful? No one disputes that time alone with God is essential. Yet many who believe in it simply do not do it.

What is the ideal time for solitude with God? I have always read and heard that the saints traditionally had their special time with the Lord very early in the morning. Indeed, the psalmist (Psalm 5:3; 88:13) seems to emphasize early morning as the preferred time. Evidently, Jesus did also (Mark 1:35). I quickly agree the ideal is to give to the Lord the first of our day. I affirm the concept.

I am about to make a confession. I am not a morning person. The most difficult thing I do all day long is to begin the day. Morning people believe down deep that night people can and should just become morning people. They just do not understand! Ordinarily, I do awaken early, but my body resists arising. After a slow start, I am blessed with good energy that lasts through the day and half the night. I even get a second wind about 8:00 P.M. In these years of living alone, I often find myself beginning a new project while my neighbors are turning off their lights, sensibly going to bed. Sometimes I get a day's work done at night. The next morning I still awaken on the rather early side and ease tentatively into the waking world. My muscles do not want to move. My brain does not want to function.

Granted, I have spent most of my life functioning in the early morning, but it has always felt against the grain. Through the years of family life, of course, every day began early. My morning person husband (morning people nearly always marry night people) would bring a cup of coffee to me in bed, which helped considerably in my coming to. Even now, after 18 years without him, I am still adjusting to not having that lovely, loving ritual with him in the early morning.

Years ago, when I became serious about daily, set-apart time with God, I decided I needed to be biblical and saintly. That meant getting up and spending the early-morning-before-anybody-else-got-up portion of the day with Him. So I did. I got up (even ahead of Huber) and met with the Lord early, wanting to be transformed at the point of my weakness. However, my groggy mind was . . . groggy. It did not wake up sharply like I believed it should and would, considering that I was in His presence. For a period of time I mentally gritted my teeth, toughed it out, kept it up, and hoped for that transformation of my sluggish self into a bright-eyed morning person.

One morning as I was badgering my sleepy body and fuzzy mind out of bed for my time alone with the Lord, I recalled my Mother's teaching that I must always give the best of whatever I have to Jesus. The lesson comes from one of my favorite childhood stories: Jesus and Mary and the expensive perfume (John 12:3). As I reflected on this passage, my sleepy heart heard again the words of the old song "Give of Your Best to the Master." It occurred to me that I was not giving Him my prime time. In fact, the time I was giving Him was at bottom level of my alertness and energy. What I needed to be giving Him was a chunk of time when I was at my best. "Lord," I asked, "is this Your idea, or only mine?" I know my expertise as a rationalizer, and I wanted to be careful not to be guilty of that sneaky trait.

My next thought (perhaps it was from Him) was, "Why not try it differently?" So I did. The next day my quiet time took place in the afternoon. It was wonderful! I reveled in Him. I suspect He enjoyed me more. I felt His affirmation. Later, when our daughters started to school, I gravitated to the kitchen table with my Bible and prayer folder immediately after everyone was off and gone in the mornings. This timing lasted for years. Now my time with Him is usually in the evening. Somehow I feel the Father understands. I hope so. He made me!

Back then, as I was finding my way into a somewhat delayed, but regular time of meeting with God, a form of early morning communion did begin to take place. Not the crisp, eyes-wide-open, more organized time with Him, which happened later in the day, but a sweet, groggy time of beginning the day with Him. I think of it as my own version of the saints' early time with Him. I continue to follow this general pattern. I treasure these tender moments.

They match my state of being, and He is faithful to receive me into the holy of holies "just as I am."

Here is how those early moments usually unfold. As soon as I first start coming to consciousness, before I have moved a muscle, my heart says to Him the easiest Scripture I know, except for "Jesus wept." I slowly paraphrase Psalm 118:24: "Lord, this is another day You have made. I am glad I can be in the middle of it. I want You to know I will rejoice and be glad in it—all through this day and into the night."

Then I bring to mind other Scriptures, personalizing them as I talk them to Him, not quite so slowly now. Lamentation 3:22–23 is one: "Lord, because of Your great love, I am not consumed. Your compassions and provisions and watch-care never fail. They are new every single day. I thank You and praise You. I am awed by the greatness of Your consistent, everlasting faithfulness."

Next, I restate to Him one of my life goals, from *The Living Bible* paraphrase of Paul's words to the Ephesians: "Lord, today I will lovingly follow the truth at all times, speaking truly, dealing truly, living truly, and so become more and more, I pray, in every way like Christ. This is my vow once again to you concerning this day" (Eph. 4:15).

Then I offer myself all over again to the Lord. I ask Him to fill me to overflowing with His Holy Spirit. I pray His fruit will be evident in my attitudes, perspective, words, behavior, and relationships. I tell Him of my awareness of my total need of Him. I ask Him to cleanse my heart and make me pure. I state my desire to keep my life clean and express my frustration that I fail so often and thus grieve Him. I attempt to describe my love for Him, and ask His guidance of my every step, word, thought, attitude, and action for this day.

As I become clearer in my head and heart, other matters of concern begin to come to my attention, and I pray for these. In this current season of my life, most mornings I

am able to linger in this prayerful state for quite a while
before I even move a muscle—my favorite way to begin
the day.

I have followed this sequence, generally, for years. Even
though it may sound routine, it reflects my soul and continues to be intensely meaningful to me. The day takes on
a certain complexion that does not happen when, for some
reason, I have to hit the floor running without this spiritual luxury. Usually, I can find a spot for it later, but it is
not quite the same.

Those who awaken suddenly at their brightest (as my
husband did) and who want to put their feet on the floor
immediately will meet with the Lord in a different frame
of mind and degree of energy. At this point, I suggest you
may want to find a book written by a morning person!
And read it early each morning!

Seriously, when we experience solitude time with our
Lord is not the major matter. That it is done consistently is
of great importance. And even for those of us who do not
conform to the more saintly time, remember that we too
can begin the day with our precious Savior in a way that
reflects our love for Him and desire to be in His presence
at all times.

There is no one right way to experience quiet time as
long as we come regularly to God with open, contrite, listening hearts and share with Him honestly and authentically. Concurrently, we recognize that anything we do on a
daily basis is vulnerable to becoming routine and to having
varying levels of meaning. I am always open to ways to enhance and vitalize my consistent meetings with God.

Don't expect every time of solitude to be a spiritual
high. As with human relationships, there will be differing
degrees of closeness with the Lord from day to day. It is
important not to be frustrated when you do not always feel
like being consistent and obedient. Just be it and do it! We
should keep our appointments with Him because of the

shared relationship and commitment. We should show up because our bottom-line desire is to please, honor, and glorify Him. Remember: He longs for this time with us. He initiates it. He is waiting. As we set apart time for prayer, we discover so many people and situations for whom and for which to pray. Many of us have made commitments to pray for numerous people and situations, here and around the world. Every day through my computer's email I receive at least 30 new specific prayer requests, sometimes more. That adds up to 1,000 or more each month! Can I include all these prayer requests in a way that is real and earnest? How can we do justice to all the needs clamoring for our prayer attention?

Those who have many prayer involvements obviously need to determine ways to organize our time. Again, a personal prayer strategy can be helpful. You do not have to have a so-called strategy to pray, but the simple truth is that a plan, a strategy, assists us in using our time effectively toward accomplishing our goals and intentions. A strategy assists us in being a life that prays.

Recall the major purposes of prayer: (1) to know God in Christ intimately, to love Him increasingly, and to become more like Him; and (2) to participate with Him in what He is doing in the world. A disciplined plan helps cover those matters the Holy Spirit has in mind for us to pray and makes the solitude time with the Lord effective and fruitful. For most of us, any plan we adopt needs to be very simple and easy to carry out. Few people will adhere to a complex prayertime over the long haul.

Even a simple plan should be flexible. Some days, put aside the plan altogether and pray whatever the Holy Spirit brings to your heart and mind. There are days when I sense He says to me, "Put your prayer folder down, My child. Don't even get out your list. Just be with Me." I believe He gets special joy from that time. He wants that closeness with us that has no other agenda. I relish it also.

62

Most of the time, however, it is imperative to give some order to the time of solitude. Here is something of my own simple plan, my own personal prayer strategy.

A Personal Prayer Strategy
For daily use, I have never found a better suggestion than the ACTS acrostic. Most days, I work through my own version of the ACTS of prayer: adoration, confession, thanksgiving, and supplication. Under supplication come the asking prayers: petition and intercession. Interwoven throughout each of these forms, I add the prayer of surrender, of yielding my will to God's. I also add a time of listening, either interspersed among the other forms, or else at the conclusion of talking to Him. Thus, the adjusted acrostic looks like this: ACTS(SL).

Adoration
Confession
Thanksgiving
Supplication
  Petition
  Intercession
Surrender
Listening

Every prayer we breathe takes one of these forms. Yet no one form comprises the totality of prayer. To be complete, the Christ follower includes each of these, not in the same order and not necessarily in the same prayertime, but often. A periodic checkup can keep the forms in some degree of reasonable inclusion and balance.

My own strategy is to usually include each form at least briefly most days, though I vary the time frame as to which form I give the major portion of my focus. Please don't make a bunch of rules. Flexibility and the free-flow of communion are important.

Periodically, read over one or more of the following paragraphs as a part of your quiet time. Share them with your prayer group, your Sunday School class, deacon board, choir. Even though familiar, they continue to be effective in retreat settings. They lead us to God.

Adoration
The highest form of prayer is adoration. Adoration is sheer worship and praise of God. It is acknowledging God as God. Adoration does not ask anything for ourselves or others. It seeks only to be in the presence of God. Jesus taught His disciples (and us) that adoration is our first duty to God as we turn our hearts to the Father: "Hallowed be thy name" (Luke 11:2 KJV). We are to hallow, to worship, to adore this One Who is both near and far.

Adoration places all else we pray in proper relationship and perspective. This form of prayer is foundational to all other kinds of prayer, for it brings us into immediate and direct contact with our Lord, Master, Creator.

Adoration happens when we acknowledge God's nature and character. It is praising Him for Who He is, while thanksgiving is praising Him for what He does. It is because of Who He is—love, grace, mercy, power, sovereignty, and so much more—that we respond with adoration, worship, and awe. Then, as we respond, we discover that adoration has done something important for our souls.

Focus even now on God's nature and character, on Who He is to you. What have you experienced personally with Him that brings forth adoration and worship from your soul? You may want to quote a Scripture verse or sing your praise to Him. "O come, let us worship and bow down: let us kneel before the Lord our maker" (Psalm 95:6 KJV). Sing, "Father, I adore You" or "Come, let us Adore Him."

Adoration:

- lifts our hearts in reverence, awe, love, and gratitude before God's worthiness and holiness;
- expresses the worship and praise of our hearts, minds, lips;
- acknowledges God's attributes and His character;
- is the highest form of prayer;
- is our first duty to God, and our highest privilege;
- brings glory to Him.

(Psalm 63:3; John 4:23–24; Psalm 95:6; Isa. 6:3; Heb. 13:15)

Confession

The psalmist made a sobering statement in Psalm 66:18 (KJV). He said, "If I regard iniquity in my heart, the Lord will not hear me." We know from God's Word and from our experience that unconfessed sin is a barrier to our intimacy with God. Sin is a hindrance to His answering our prayers. We tend to misunderstand the seriousness of our sin. Jesus died on the Cross because of our sins. How prone we are to forget the astounding cost involved in God's forgiveness. Do we know what it is to mourn because of our sin problem?

"He was pierced for our transgressions, he was crushed for our iniquities; the punishment that brought us peace was upon him, and by his wounds we are healed. . . . The Lord has laid on him the iniquity of us all" (Isa. 53:5–6 NIV).

I fear we take confession too lightly and glibly. Confession means literally "to speak the same words," to agree with God about our sin. It means we say, in essence, "Lord, I know You grieve about my sin. I grieve also. I am deeply sorrowful. With Your forgiveness and help, I am not going to repeat my sin. Give me Your guidance as I seek to make restitution for the wrong I have done." This, from the heart, is true repentance.

Four brief statements about confession:

1. God is holy. The closer we get to Him and His holiness, the more aware we become of our sinfulness—and the more grieved we become.

2. We must name our sins. We must be specific. God knows anyway. We must be scrupulously honest with Him.

3. Confession is not an end in itself. It is a means to a greater end. Just as surgery is not an end in itself but a means to health and wholeness, so confession is a means to spiritual health and wholeness. Confession leads to a changed attitude about our sin, to a changed relationship with the Lord, to changed actions in our lives. It leads to making things right with those we have harmed.

4. When we truly confess, the Father's forgiveness is instant. The apostle assures us, "If we confess our sins, he is faithful and just and will forgive us our sins" (1 John 1:9 NIV). We know from the prophet Micah that God will "hurl all our iniquities into the depths of the sea" (Mic. 7:19 NIV).

Right now, imagine Jesus and you are sitting together. As you confess, pray something to this effect: "Lord, You are Lord, and I have been disobedient. I am truly sorry to grieve You. I take Your grief very seriously, and I grieve also. Please forgive me. I want You to know I am turning around and going in the opposite direction from my sin. Whatever I need to do to make amends for my sin, reveal that to me, and I will do it. For Your glory and in Your holy name, I will."

Confession:
- involves our sinfulness and unworthiness in the presence of God's holiness and purity;
- means to agree with God about our sin and its seriousness;
- expresses repentance for the specific sins in our lives;
- is preceded by God's desire and promise to forgive in response to our repentance;

•clears the channel for God's hearing and answering prayer;
•must be accompanied by appropriate acts of amends (restitution) and changed behavior;
•deals with the insidious danger of secret sins.

(Mic. 7:19; Isa. 43:25; 1 John 1:8–9; Psalm 139:23–24)

Thanksgiving
Paul said to the Thessalonians (and to us) in his first letter (5:18 NIV): "Give thanks in all circumstances, for this is God's will for you in Christ Jesus." We are to "forget not all his benefits" (Psalm 103:2, also NIV).
Yet, too often we take His benefits for granted.
Recently I was in the home of my dear longtime friends, Wilbur and Gladys Lewis, who served some years ago as medical missionaries to Paraguay. Highly regarded as a surgeon and outstanding Christian layman, Wilbur was one of the founders of the Baptist Medical-Dental Fellowship. He has led many missions trips around the world and enlisted hundreds of doctors to use their vacations for overseas missions ministries.
Five years ago, he had an accident injuring his neck—the same injury suffered by actor Christopher Reeve. Paralyzed from the neck down, Wilbur is dependent on a ventilator for every breath he breathes. He can do nothing on his own, not even scratch his nose. This once-vital, dynamic, impactive man has to be fed every bite he eats for the rest of his life, unless God chooses to do a miracle.
Yet, even in his circumstances, he looks for something for which to give thanks. He expresses gratitude to the Lord for every possible blessing, even the tiniest one. I visit the Lewises at every opportunity. Wilbur has taught me at a deeper level than ever before "to forget not all his benefits." Gladys, a brilliant professor and gifted writer, models eternal love and valiance as she responds to the constant,

overwhelming demands of caring for her husband. Neither does Gladys forget "all his benefits."

Jesus expects the expression of thanks. In Luke 17:17 (NIV), when one of the ten lepers came back and threw himself at Jesus' feet and thanked Him for the healing, Jesus said, "Were not all ten cleansed? Where are the other nine?" When we fail to say thank you, I believe Jesus says, "Have you forgotten, My child? Every good thing you have is from Me."

How long has it been since you thanked God for being able to breathe on your own, for being able to lift food to your mouth, for having the ability to lift your arms and put them around someone you love?

Our thanksgiving should be specific. We are specific in our requests, as we should be, but often we are not specific in expressing our gratitude. We tend to say, "Thank You for all our many blessings. Amen." We are to name our blessings, one by one, and to thank Him.

Right now, with your eyes open or closed, with your head bowed or not, thank the Lord for something specific in your life. Thank Him for another blessing that comes to your mind, and another.

Thanksgiving is praising the Lord for what He has done. Let us "enter into his gates with thanksgiving, and into his courts with praise" (Psalm 100:4 KJV).

Thanksgiving:
- is offered to God, for He is the source of every good gift;
- was taught and practiced by Jesus;
- is a consistent biblical principle;
- is an antidote to our vulnerability to self-pity;
- produces spiritual and physical energy;
- contributes to a positive spiritual perspective;
- is a matter of obedience.

68

(Psalm 136:1; 1 Thess. 5:18; 2 Cor. 9:15; Col. 3:17; Psalm 9:1; James 1:17; John 11:14; Psalm 86:12)

Supplication

Supplication refers to those prayers in which we ask God for something—for ourselves or for someone else. Asking prayers are petition and intercession. Jesus dealt with this form of prayer more than any other.

Supplication:
•includes asking prayers: petitions and intercessions;
•is the form of prayer most dealt with by Jesus in His teaching on prayer.

(1 Tim. 2:1–2; Luke 11:9; 18:1; John 14:14; James 5:16*b*; Matt. 21:22; 1 John 5:14)

Petition

Perhaps we are most familiar with petition. Petition is asking God for things for ourselves. Someone said that about 90 percent of the average person's prayers begin with "Give me" or "Help me."

Petition is quite legitimate. God wants us to bring our personal burdens, needs, hurts, and desires to Him. He is concerned about every aspect of our lives. Always remember that He wants to be intimately involved with us. We are needy, and we are to come to Him just as we are. But we must be careful that our petitions are not selfish, that is, not for our own comfort. If so, we would be praying for our glory, not His—and praying amiss. We must continually gauge our prayers by the goal of all prayer: that God be glorified.

Therefore, we need to be careful not to make petition the primary part of our praying. This diagram makes this point graphically. An unbalanced amount of petition throws our praying out of kilter and reveals self-centeredness.

FORMS OF PRAYER

The closer we get to our Lord, the more careful we are about what we ask Him. As I grew and matured, I tended to ask my parents for those things I sensed they wanted me to have. That is a part of close, intimate, maturing relationship. As we get closer to God, we ask Him more and more for what He wants us to have and to be.

What are some of those things? We get clues from God's Word and from His Holy Spirit within us. He wants us to have a firm grasp of His truth as revealed in His Word and through His people. He wants us to have His character and integrity within us. He wants us to have the fruit of His Spirit within and applied throughout our everyday experiences. He wants us to be filled daily with His Spirit and to experience the sweetness and challenge(!) of His constant presence. He wants us to have physical, mental, emotional, and spiritual health, and energy to serve Him and bring glory to Him. He wants us to have the willingness and ability to witness boldly and to bear fruit. He wants us to be holy, thankful, and humble. He wants us to have abundant life. He wants us to care passionately about others and the salvation of all peoples. And I believe He wants us to petition Him for these blessings and gifts from Him. Why? There is something about humble, earnest asking in accordance to His will that places us in a stance to receive what He already desires to give us.

One principle of prayer supersedes our own discernment of what God wants us to have: When we ask the Holy Spirit to pray through us, He brings to our minds the very things the Father wants us to ask.

Petition:
- is asking for ourselves—our own requests and needs;
- means that our requests should relate to God's purposes;
- acknowledges God's concern about every aspect of our lives;
- teaches us that the closer we get to Him, the more careful we are about what we ask Him to do for us;
- leads us to ask for health, wisdom, inspiration, strength, courage, character, integrity, knowledge, and understanding of God's truth, God's adequacy, God's presence, and God's companionship.

(Psalm 25:4–5; Phil. 4:6; Matt. 7:7; 1 Peter 5:6–7; Matt. 7:11; Phil. 4:19)

Intercession
Intercession is simply asking God on behalf of others. A very special form of prayer, intercession has been called love on its knees. There are certain aspects of intercession that God, in His Word, encourages us to embrace.

Embrace the priority of intercession. Only two-ninths of the asking prayers in the Bible are petitioning in nature. Seven-ninths are intercessory prayers. Although both are important, this ratio indicates God's priority. The role of Jesus as intercessor is a wonderful study. He is at the right hand of God interceding for us (Rom. 8:34; Heb. 7:25).

The Holy Spirit also intercedes for us (Rom. 8:26–27). Paul began every letter except Galatians and 2 Corinthians by giving assurance that He was interceding for the people to whom He was writing. Intercession is a biblical priority.

Embrace the powerful nature of intercession. Time and space cannot limit intercession. We can pray for someone on the other side of the world as effectively as we can pray for our next-door neighbor. I often think of that as I email my dear friend in Hong Kong and missionaries in remote places of the world. I click my mouse, and my message is there. Even faster is the reach of our prayers.

Embrace the purpose of intercession. We intercede for others to pray that God's will be done in that person's life, or in that situation, or in that people group or nation. Not what I want, but what God wants for them. The purpose of intercession is to secure the grace of God for the individual or group for whom we intercede so that fellowship with God and usefulness to His kingdom will be established and maintained.

Ethel Lynn Patterson is one of the most devoted, consistent missions intercessors I know. A longtime resident of Corpus Christi, Texas, my 93-year-old friend spends her mornings praying through her lengthy prayer list. She breaks down in weeping again and again as she lifts to God's throne the myriad of needs that come from around the world to her heart. That is love on its knees. Ethel Lynn represents to me in human form a passion for God, a love for people, and a desire to have Christ known among all the peoples of the earth. She is praying for me now, even as I am writing.

Intercession:
- is asking God on behalf of another;
- is releasing God's power into lives, situations, nations;

•is a dynamic partnership between God's power and
our prayers;
•is the most crucial work we can do;
•is love on its knees;
•is walking in the Spirit and abiding in Him.

(1 Tim. 2:1–2; John 17:11; Eph. 1:18–19; Rom. 10:1)

Surrender
The prayer of surrender weaves itself into and throughout
each of the other forms. Surrender involves submission to
the will of God. It needs to be inherent in every request we
pray.

The passions of Jesus' life are revealed in the first words
of the Lord's Prayer. In response to the disciples' desire for
Jesus to teach them to pray, He said, "After this manner
pray ye: Our Father, which art in heaven, Hallowed be
Thy name. Thy Kingdom come. Thy will be done." We
see clearly that Jesus' passions were the Father's name, His
kingdom, and His will. Jesus wanted God's name to be
known, honored, and glorified through all the earth. He
wanted His plans fulfilled according to the Father's desire.
Not only did He want these matters, He became intensely
involved in bringing them about.

This should be our passion as well. The prayer of surrender desires God's plan to be fulfilled—but desires it to
the point of willingness to be involved in accomplishing it.

Surrender means we have in our hearts a genuine, personal love for our Savior and for people. Love creates a
spirit of yieldedness and humility, which produces contriteness and acknowledgement of our dependence on
God. Surrender involves deep awareness of our brokenness,
our weakness, and our helplessness. It requires receiving
His resources into the midst of our weakness. Finally, it requires an understanding of our ineffectiveness and futility
without the daily filling of His Spirit.

As a college student, I heard Vance Havner declare in a chapel message, "God intends for us to take care of the humbling of ourselves. If we do not take the initiative, then He allows the circumstances of our lives to do the job of humbling us." Frankly, I would rather do the job myself!

The prayer of surrender is not easy, for a fact of life is that we are deeply and chronically self-centered. Yet, when this form of prayer is sincerely prayed daily over many years, God transforms self-centeredness, to the degree that we allow Him to do so. Surrender is giving, all over again and again every day, our lives to the lordship of Christ. It is praying, "Lord, without you, I can do nothing. I simply want what you want, whatever it is. I yield myself to you in every aspect of my life."

Surrender, when authentic, combines with *every* element of prayer. Whatever other form of prayer you pray, include surrender to the Lordship of Christ and to the Father's will. They are the same!

Thomas Merton wrote, "The deepest prayer at its nub is a perpetual surrender to God."[2]

Have you yet today expressed an up-to-date prayer of surrender to our Lord?

Surrender:
- requires an attitude of humility and a passion for God's will to be done;
- acknowledges the sovereignty of God.

(Matt. 6:10; 1 John 5:14; James 4:15; Psalm 40:8)

Listening
Listening to God may be the most ignored form of prayer. Yet communion is not communion unless there is a mutual, reciprocal, alternating, free-flow with each tuned in to the other—authentic communication.

A major part of listening is the reading and absorbing of God's Word. To put it another way, the Scriptures are the Father's clearest way of speaking to us. We are quick to see the necessity of listening in our human relationships. How much more essential it is to be on the listening end in our communication with God. I acknowledge this is a difficult challenge, for it usually requires silence and waiting in His still, quiet presence.

God constantly communicates with us. We just fail to be still, to listen. Most of us are acclimated to focusing our praying on persons, situations, needs, and crises. These concerns are appropriate and even necessary in our balanced approach to prayer. However, we need to develop the ability to truly listen to our Lord through His Word, through His quiet whispers to our hearts, through the impressions He wants us to have from His mind to our souls.

We may not be very comfortable with silence, for there is so much noise in our lives! Many of us have little experience with stillness. We need silence more than we may realize, in order to discern His still, small voice.

I especially respond to a period of corporate silence as a part of a worship service. Many regular worshipers may go through an entire service without having an authentic experience of worship of our living, reigning Lord. A period of silence tends to bring us face-to-face with God for the purpose of turning our full attention to Him. How we respond to such an encounter is up to us.

"'Speak, for your servant is listening'" (1 Sam. 3:9 NIV).

Listening:
- •is most effective in quietness;
- •can take place in the midst of noise;
- •often gets left out as an intentional discipline;
- •reveals a sensitive, attuned, close relationship.

(Heb. 4:12; Deut. 30:20; Prov. 1:5; John 10:27; James 1:19; John 8:47; Psalm 119:11,103,105)

Remember that each of these forms of prayer is important and should receive adequate time. When we authentically include these forms in our time with the Lord, our prayer life tends to be sane and balanced.

And remember that all prayer is spiritual warfare. Any prayer that gains ground for God's kingdom simultaneously loses ground for the enemy. Spiritual warfare is not one certain type of praying—it is all authentic prayer.

Components of My Prayer Strategy

•Daily Solitude with the Father
Daily quiet time is the cornerstone of my personal prayer strategy. It seems elementary; yet our busyness can easily allow us to neglect this regular time alone with God. Frankly, it never gets easy in the life of an involved person. Periodically I must renew my commitment to spend this set-apart time every day with Him. I feel irresistibly drawn back to the altar as I remember again how He longs to have this time with me even more than I have the capacity to want it with Him. It is essential in my everyday living.

I regularly pray through the ACTS(SL) acrostic and experience the intentional time of opening myself for divine replenishment of my fading resources, of renewing the core of my soul, of loving the Lord with all my heart in worship of Him.

I also spend time in the *Scriptures,* either a particular study I am preparing to teach and need to absorb, or a study interest I am pursuing on my own. I seek to do some heavy-duty listening at this point, as I read, reread, study, reflect. This is God speaking to me—more important than I know how to stress. I seek during this time not only to read from His Word, but also to absorb it day by day, to allow Him to be my teacher.

Books have been very important to me. Some are spiritual markers in my walk with God. I enjoy reading from a current author who challenges my growth, but I also am blessed by the spiritual classics. Nearly every day I do some reading in my quiet time.

Of course, each day I pray for *my family* and their specific needs. I lift each to the Lord and ask for His hovering over them and His Spirit dwelling within them. I pray each will be aware of Him this day and come to love Him more. I always pray that their thoughts will turn frequently toward Him, even without knowing how or why.

For many years, I have had a commitment to pray each day for *missionaries* on the prayer calendar. This allows me to pray on behalf of many I know personally, but also many I do not know. It stretches my heart to prayerfully care about them and their needs.

I use a folder with pockets to hold the names of *people and their requests* for which I will pray. Periodically, as the life of the prayer request comes to an end, I discard that reminder. Most days I pray through these special commitments.

Although I give special focus to *my people group* on Fridays, I turn my heart toward them and all unreached peoples briefly every day and toward all the lost. I know I need to be sensitized daily to them and their eternal lostness.

As the Holy Spirit leads, I pray concerning *my own needs and concerns.* I lift them to my loving, merciful, full-of-grace Father. This is when I bring to Him my burdens in a systematic way. And throughout the day as these come to mind, I place them before Him again and again.

Generally, this is how I pray every day. In addition, there are certain large areas of prayer I bring to the Lord on certain days of the week. These needs are not relegated to that particular day, but usually, I place a unique focus on them one day a week. The following schedule is informal and flexible and has some ebb and flow. At times, I change completely. However, it gives me a guide for covering my concerns in a rather systematic way. Notice that the concerns move outward in an ever-enlarging pattern of concentric circles.

Saturday is a family day, generally the most leisurely day of the week. Therefore, I give my unique focus on this day to praying for my family and close friends. This is probably the most natural, spontaneous praying I do because of the built-in capacity to care about them intensely. I am so aware of their burdens and concerns (for their concerns have a way of becoming mine also), and I place them before the Lord in detail.

Sunday, of course, is a special day of worship, although I insist the other days are worship days as well. My prayer focus is on my church, my pastor, my fellow believers, my Sunday School class, those with whom I am involved in spiritual ministries. Realistically, things are not always ideal; relationships can become strained. How much more important does prayer become at times like these? If you have a point of discomfort or difficulty with someone in your congregation, do the spiritually radical thing: pray, really pray for him or her. Eventually, as the Lord leads, pray with them, humbly and openly.

I also pray on this day for other churches and other believers, that they will be effective in bringing people into the kingdom. I pray for fellow believers around the world—for their growth as disciples, for their boldness in witness, for their development as leaders. I include those who live in restricted countries where persecution is a reality. I pray in a general way that Jesus' name will be lifted in clear, winsome ways all over the world as people gather for worship. I pray this day will contribute to the hastening of that day when "every knee will bow and every tongue confess that Jesus Christ is Lord."

This is also my time to focus on prayer for revival and spiritual awakening. I long to see a sweeping move of God's Spirit in my church, across our land, and around the world, beginning in me.

On **Mondays** I pray especially for my neighbors. My intercessions move up one side of my street and down the other side, home by home. Many times during the week, I spontaneously pray for them as I visit with them or wave to them in passing; but on Mondays, there is an intentional focus on them. As I discern the Holy Spirit's guidance, I tell a neighbor that I am praying for her or him. I have lived in this location for three years, and now I often have a neighbor come to me with a prayer request, even some who are turned off, they say, by churches. Realistically, neighborhoods often include "irregular," or difficult persons. A deeper step in prayer involves the commitment to pray regularly for such people. That intercession truly becomes love on its knees.

On **Tuesdays**, I am committed to be especially attuned to pray for those whose paths I cross randomly—at the grocery store, the post office, the service station, the mall, the restaurant, wherever my schedule takes me. We must become responsible for praying in this way if we are to be obedient to Christ's intentions for us as His followers. More and more, this lifestyle praying should permeate every day.

You have probably heard the thought, "We are the only Bible some people read." Are they reading a distorted version of the gospel as they read your life, or an accurate portrayal of Jesus' love, grace, mercy, and forgiveness?

A still deeper step in prayer is to move in my focus beyond my own environs. **Wednesdays**, I pray for those people, situations, and places in our own nation needing intercession. God calls me to stretch and pray beyond that which my eyes can see or my experiences include. This is not easy. In fact, it is work—crucial work that requires an intentional commitment, strong discipline, and a caring, determined heart. Yet I find the Holy Spirit will provide these necessities as I do my part in loving, caring response. I pray for our government leaders, that they will be people of character and have sensitivity to righteousness. I pray their decisions will be for the good of the people. I pray that those of our leaders who do not know Jesus will come to know and worship Him.

The most challenging days are still to come. On **Thursdays,** I focus on people of other nations. This includes the leaders of other nations and the missionaries and fellow believers involved in God's kingdom work in those lands. On this day I ask the Lord of the harvest to call forth more laborers. Actually, I believe He is calling more than are responding. I pray each one He is calling will hear and heed His call. I also pray on this day for mission strategists and decision makers who have the responsibility of discerning God's plans related to world evangelization. I pray for many by name, and ask God to give them wisdom for implementing His plans for having His name known and worshiped by all peoples of all nations.

The farthest out in my prayer journey is the outer circle of the limited access nations and people groups, the unreached. In many of these locations, it is very difficult to get strategies approved by government officials. Yet my prayers—and yours—can go directly there. Although I pray for unreached peoples on other days of the week, on **Fridays,** they are my focus. Perhaps we stretch the farthest in our intercessions to reach with our hearts to those lost people who have not yet been introduced to Jesus. We may have come to the deepest level of prayer, in God's eyes. The lost are so lost! Think of how God's heart must ache. Two thousand years, and we still have not gotten the word of His Son to the hearing and understanding of all the world. Yet we live in an age that makes it possible. We can help take, send, and embody the gospel to *all* peoples. It *can* happen!

What is the place of prayer in causing this to happen? Important, priority, essential, ultimate. And if we fail to pray? Impossible to achieve.

•*Listening*

Always, interspersed throughout my focused time with the Lord, I pause to listen. I seek to respond to His impressions upon my heart.

Toward the end of my solitude time, I ask the Lord to bring to my mind what He wants me to pray that has not occurred to me. I wait and let my mind wander. Many times it wanders to someone or some situation that I recognize should have come to me without prompting. How awesome to hear from the God of the universe.

• *Retreating*

Periodically I include a morning's personal retreat or an entire evening of set-apart time with the Father. Once I went to the Pocono Mountains alone and spent most of a week in fellowship with Him, one of my best times ever with Him. That is not easy to arrange, of course, but it can be a memorable and most meaningful tryst. And we can arrange the briefer periods of several hours of just being with Jesus. It is not easy, but it is possible!

• *Praying with Others*

Another area of my prayer strategy has to do with joining with others in spending time in prayer. This begins with my family, then moves to other fellow believers. Praying comfortably and naturally with other believers is a simple but profound way to bear one another's burdens. When we speak to another about a concern, ours or someone else's, why not together lift the matter to the Lord on the spot? We don't have to fold our hands, bow our heads, and close our eyes. We can simply say, "Lord, we place this in Your hands and ask for You to minister in this situation. If there is something You want us to do in relation to it, give us light and understanding of what our role needs to be." We should intentionally ask God to grow us to the place that we will pray *with* other believers as freely as we discuss *any* matter of mutual importance and/or interest to us.

• *Arrow Prayers*
Another part of my personal prayer strategy is to turn my thoughts to the Lord all through the day and night about what is in my thoughts and on my heart. This deals again with the intimacy of relationship God wants with us, that abiding quality of staying connected with Him at all times and in all places.

Years ago I read of Frank Laubach's reference to the chinks of time we all have—those little pauses in our day that give us opportunity to turn our thoughts Godward and breathe a brief prayer. That struck a resonating chord in me. I began to make it part of my life: a brief "Thanks, God!" or "I love You, Father"; lifting someone in intercession. Arrow prayers mean "glancing at the Lord," and doing so frequently.

• *Prayer Alerts*
Arrow prayers and prayer alerts are closely akin. Both are a part of lifestyle praying, incorporating prayer into the very fabric of my days. Lifestyle praying requires a relaxed alertness in recognizing those moments when we can breathe a heart prayer. No matter how busy and involved, we all have those moments. Throughout the day there are snatches of time to breathe an honest, in-the-midst-of-the-day expression or intercession to Him.

I developed a series of prayer alerts, reminders that nudge me to say, "Hey, this is one of those times to lift my thoughts to the Lord." When I stop for a red light or wait for an appointment, that pause reminds me to turn my thoughts toward God, to thank Him or intercede for someone. When I hang up my telephone, I pray for the person to whom I have been talking. Often, something will surface in the phone conversation that is a prayer need. At times, as the Father prompts me, I pray aloud with the person before I hang up. Prayer alerts are the response of a heart for prayer and the life that prays.

• *Journaling*
Writing down prayers, thoughts, feelings, and reflections can be very meaningful, revealing, and growth-producing. I have had ebb-and-flow experiences with this strategy, but it does contribute to a focus on the day and on the Lord. It is invaluable in looking back to see how God has answered prayers and how spiritual growth has occurred. Often I find I want to move faster than I can write. At other times I want to be deliberate and I choose to put my thoughts on paper or computer. I wish I had more inclination to be consistent in journaling. Many find it a most profound exercise.

Do you see how the concentric circles of prayer fall so naturally into place? I was already following this general pattern when I realized there was a progression, beginning with God and my relationship with Him and moving outward, in a circular pattern, from my own family to my close friends, my pastor, fellow believers, neighbors, co-workers, acquaintances, random persons whose paths I cross, my country, other countries, missionaries, local believers around the world, mission strategists, the unreached.

There is no shortage of options for a personal prayer strategy. You do not have to fit anyone's pattern other than the Lord's pattern for you. Simply ask Him to give you the strategy He wants you to follow. He will not overwhelm you. More than anything, He wants to draw you to Himself. He will grow you in your heart's capacity for prayer and relationship with Him. Listen to His heart carefully and sensitively, and follow Him obediently and faithfully.

THE REACH OF PRAYER

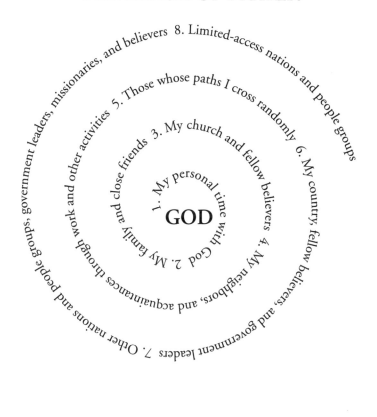

1. My personal time with God
2. My family and close friends
3. My church and fellow believers
4. My neighbors, and acquaintances
5. Those whose paths I cross randomly
6. My country, fellow believers, and government leaders
7. Other nations and people groups, government leaders, missionaries, and believers
8. Limited-access nations and people groups

GOD

Questions for Reflection

Have you determined the best time for you to regularly meet with God?

Are you faithful to Jesus' instruction concerning private time with the Father?

Do you have an intentional prayer strategy—although you may not call it that?

Is there need in your life to develop one?

What components of a prayer strategy is God leading you to include in your life?

After discerning His leadership, will you sketch out in writing a possible prayer strategy?

[1]S. D. Gordon, *Quiet Talks on Prayer* (Grand Rapids: Baker Book House, 1980), 12.
[2]Quoted by Joyce Huggett in *The Joy of Listening to God* (Downers Grove, IL: InterVarsity Press, 1986), 57.

5

A Family Prayer Strategy

Every Home a House of Prayer

"Be very careful, then, how then you live—not as unwise but as wise, making the most of every opportunity" (Eph. 5:15 NIV).

"Only be careful, and watch yourselves closely so that you do not forget the things your eyes have seen or let them slip from your heart as long as you live. Teach them to your children and to their children after them" (Deut. 4: 9 NIV).

"What we have heard and known, what our fathers have told us. We will not hide them from their children; we will tell the next generation the praiseworthy deeds of the Lord, his power, and the wonders he has done" (Psalm 78:3–4).

"The strength of the family may well be determined by how well family members support each other as prayer partners."—Dan R. Crawford[1]

Family Structures
One of the most dramatic changes in our nation lies in the structure of the American family. Through many generations, the typical family was considered to be a working

dad, a mom unemployed outside the home, children, and no stepchildren. That structure of the American household continues to diminish. Statistics reveal a distressing picture. For example, from 1960 to 1990, the number of children living with a divorced parent increased 352 percent.[2] In 1970, 3.2 percent of the nation's population over 18 was divorced. By 1996, that figure rose to 9.1 percent.[3] A relatively small percentage of families now adhere to the formerly "typical" pattern. Not only is this a phenomenon in our nation, it is also is a reality in our congregations. Many church families struggle with the same complexities of broken and blended families.

Lifestyle Issues
A fast and harried lifestyle adds to the problem of fragmentation in many homes. Combine soccer, baseball, gymnastics, tennis tournaments, ballet, Brownies, Scouts—plus all the church and school activities—and you have a collage of a few of the children's involvements. Then add to the mix the complex schedules of their parents. According to my own informal survey (two daughters, two sons-in-law, and three grandchildren; plus the Bible study class of mostly young mothers I teach), praying together tends to get lost in all the wonderful opportunities and awful stresses families have today.

In the midst of the wild and wooly atmosphere prevalent in too many homes, what is the place of prayer in the lives of families? My own experience reminds me how difficult it is to be a praying family. It was challenging enough in my day. Today the complexities are accentuated. Yet what could be of greater importance?

I have a fear that very few families, even churchgoing families, take the time and focus to pray together. The daily parade of events and activities keeps some families from having conversations with one another, much less with God! I have a dream—and a prayerful burden—that

Christian families will see and grasp the essentiality of consistently coming together before the Father in humility, repentance, and receptivity to His tender, loving grace. Surely, our Lord wants every home to be a house of prayer. To this end, every Christian family can benefit from having a prayer strategy—intentional prayer experiences that are a regular part of life together.

Consider the following suggestions for prayer experiences and disciplines for Christian families as they live their lives together with an intentional inclusion of God in their midst. These come from my own family's efforts to keep prayer central and vital in our home. In those days, we did not call our various experiences of praying together a prayer strategy, but in retrospect that is what we had.

Husbands and Wives Praying Together

The most obvious need is for husbands and wives to pray together. But apart from a quick prayer at mealtime (maybe), how many do? Even deacons, Sunday School teachers, and pastors often find prayer with a spouse missing from their daily commitments.

In homes where communication is a basic problem in the marriage, praying together, if it happens at all, is surface, rote, routine. Open communication and trust of one another must be inherent in the relationship for authentic prayer to come from the heart. Yet going to the Lord together is, in itself, a step toward redeeming a strained relationship. Wherever a couple is in their relationship with one another and with Christ, prayer is essential.

When a husband and wife come with authentic humility and contriteness to one another and to the Lord in prayer, God can and will do a work of grace within the relationship. This can open up new vistas of vulnerability and intimacy with one another, as well as with Him. Prayer should never be approached as a manipulative cure-all, but the God of prayer is ready and waiting as a loving Healer and

Redeemer. The couple who prays together naturally and invariably develops a closeness with each other and with the Father that brings joy and stability to the marriage and to the children. The best gift parents can give their children is a loving husband/wife relationship. Recently, I was part of an occasion honoring a pastor friend. His daughter, speaking for the family, said, "Of all the things I love about my dad, the thing I love the most is the way he loves my mother."

Recently, in the middle of the night, my daughter, Meme, had an emergency appendectomy—her appendix had ruptured. I made a hurried trip to the hospital, arriving shortly before the surgeon. Even as Meme and her husband, H. W., briefed me on her condition, they told me of the prayertime they had already experienced together. Then they asked me to lead in yet another time of prayer. As the three of us clung to one another, first I thanked the Lord that they had already spontaneously been to Him. What a bond this reveals about a husband and wife and their God.

Why is it essential for a couple to come to the Lord in prayer together in addition to the family prayertime? Truly honest prayer brings to the relationship an openness that melts barriers and creates greater closeness within the marriage. Those tender moments together before the Lord result in a special bond of intimacy.

But when can this depth of prayer together take place? If we do not nail down our intentions with a scheduled time, no matter how good our intentions, this prayertime likely will not happen at all. Some couples begin by planning to pray together every day. Certainly this is ideal. If they fail in that ambitious intention, though, they can become discouraged about their inability to be consistent. Those just beginning this commitment might start with a once-a-week plan, with both seriously committed to carrying through. As the prayertime becomes an ingrained and meaningful part of life, the couple can add other times during the week. Couples should be consistent but flexible as they seek the most realistic schedule for their time together with the Father.

As they realize the benefits of praying together, a prayerful couple will want to pray at spontaneous, unscheduled times as well. When making decisions together, they realize their need to have the mind and wisdom of God. At times of crises or times of thanksgiving, how crucial to go together to the Father. During the many times of concern about their children and other worrisome matters, how important for husband and wife to come before the Lord together in prayer.

In some instances, one or both may insist they are uncomfortable in praying aloud. A fact of human nature is that those with a basic shyness tend to be self-conscious about hearing their own voices in prayer. If a couple needs to grow into the comfort zone of shared prayer, they can first sit together, hold hands, and pray silently about the agreed-upon concerns. Usually, if they persist, they will gradually come to the place of praying aloud together. God's hearing is never restricted to those prayers spoken aloud. He hears our faintest thoughts directed to Him.

A positive factor in our praying aloud is that it gives more focus and discipline to our praying and an increasingly lesser concern for the words we use and the way we sound. Specifically ask the Lord to grow you, as you do your part in the growth process, to enjoy praying aloud with others. Seek to become comfortable in talking to Him conversationally, without concern for the way the words take form and shape.

When a couple prays together, they include many of the same elements that are part of one's personal prayertime. Pray the matters the Holy Spirit brings to your minds and hearts. Do not be concerned about your wording. God is not impressed with eloquent or spiritual-sounding words.

He is impressed only by the expressions that come from our hearts.

Parents Praying for Children

Rearing a family is an awesome responsibility. A significant element in children's development is for them to hear the voices of their parents in prayer, especially for them. In some homes only one parent is Christian. Even so, or especially so, the children need to hear the voice of that one Christian parent praying earnestly and regularly for him or her. This contributes to preparing the soil of the young child's heart for spiritual matters. It helps the child or grandchild to grow comfortable in his or her own personal prayer life, a basic and urgent goal of the Christian home and family. For heaven's sake—and your children's sake, and for your grandchildren's sake—give your children memories of your praying earnestly for them. These memories, of course, must be created now.

Family Worship

Family worship may almost be obsolete. Certainly it is a missing element in too many Christian homes. Churches have an important ministry in encouraging families to make valiant efforts to pray together.

Perhaps the most practical time for families to pray together is at a shared meal. A prayer of gratitude or blessing before *every* meal is simple and basic. Our girls, and now our grandchildren, love to sing the blessing that was often sung at the table as I was growing up, making it now a third-generation blessing.

Our family prayertime came at the breakfast table, after we finished eating. In Meme's and Debra's early years, we used a Promise Box, purchased at a Christian bookstore. Each day we read the promise Scripture verse from the box. The girls alternated in removing the promise, and yes, at times they argued about whose turn it was! Later, as they learned to read, they took turns reading each day from the Bible. We always included the missionary prayer calendar and the daily missions prayer request, again taking turns and often mangling names and locations. Many times we laughed together over mispronunciations and convoluted prayer needs. Isn't it wonderful that our Father in heaven savors our enjoyment of our time with Him and with one another! We each learned more about the world as we located the nations and discussed together what we knew about the missionaries, their countries, circumstances, and needs.

Then we each shared a personal request for that day. We prayed, each for the others, and we covenanted together to pray during the day for one another at the stated time of need. We made an effort to keep that commitment. As each daughter left the house for school each morning, her parting words were, "Bye. I love you. Pray for me."

Learning that prayer makes a difference is an important truth children (and adults!) need to recognize. Help children and grandchildren to acknowledge the yes answers and to express gratitude to a personal God Who knows and cares for them. Also help them understand that a loving God says, "No" and "Wait" at times, just as loving parents and grandparents do.

Bedtime Prayers
Bedtime is traditionally a meaningful time for family praying. Many sweet and tender bedtime prayers with my daughters and now my grandchildren fill my memories. Another ritual, after we have prayed at bedtime, is our saying in unison, "Good night, sleep tight, wake up bright, in the morning light, to do what's right, with all your might. Gooood night!" (Kiss. Hug.) Bradley, of course, long ago outgrew this little ritual; no doubt, Emily and Lauren, one of these days, will also. Hopefully, each will carry this and other childhood prayer experiences into their relationships with their own children and grandchildren.

Many parents do a good job of praying with their children in those young years when they must put them to bed. When the children outgrow this need, some parents unfortunately assume that they have also outgrown the need for prayer together. At this point, establish prayertime with your children in another, more grown-up way. Keep praying with your children!

Praying for Children As They Sleep
Many times, as our daughters were growing up, I went into their bedrooms as they slept, touched them lightly, and poured out my heart to the Lord for them. Especially during those worrisome times in their struggles toward maturity, I found myself at their bedsides praying silently late at night.

Long-Distance Family Praying
As our daughters went off to college, they continued to want us to know of their specific concerns and to have assurance of our personal, informed prayer involvement with them. It meant extra telephone bills, but it was worth the cost as it produced added closeness with the Lord and with one another. They still want me to be aware of their prayer burdens and concerns. They want to know I am praying currently and specifically for them. It is one of the most blessed privileges of my life.

Special Occasions for Worship
Meme and Debra suggested I include one of their favorite family worship memories. While this one relates to Thanksgiving, you can find opportunities throughout the year for special times of family worship.

Traditionally, at our Thanksgiving dinner table, Huber would place five kernels of corn at each plate. At the conclusion of our bountiful meal, he would tell the wonderful story behind the custom of the grains of corn. No one could tell it like he did, but here is the essence.

When the 107 passengers stepped off the Mayflower on a cold November day in 1620, life was extremely hard. The winter was devastating as the Pilgrims settled into the New World. They endured hunger and deprivation. Half of them did not survive the winter. Probably all would have starved to death had it not been for a few bushels of corn Indians had hidden in a cave. The story goes, that at one time, the Pilgrims were rationed to only five grains of corn a day. A young Indian named Squanto befriended the pilgrims, taught them how and where to fish, and showed them how to plant corn when spring came. He was a key person in helping them survive that first winter.

Squanto's role in the story adds considerable pathos to the account. He had been captured in his earlier years by a boatload of foreign opportunists who had landed briefly on the shores of the New World. Transported from his homeland to Spain, he was sold as a slave. A kindly priest befriended him. The Native American boy yearned to return to his family. Touched by the boy's smartness and fineness, the priest decided to help him return. He arranged for Squanto to go to England, and eventually, back to the New World, his homeland. When he arrived on the shores of the New World, eagerly, Squanto made his way to his family's village, only to find they had all been killed in an ambush.

Remarkably, when the Pilgrims came ashore, Squanto was a key person in their resettlement, for he was the only Indian who could speak their language! Talk about the providence of God! He had learned English while in England, and that proved to make a key difference in the lives of the Pilgrims. Squanto was a most special friend to them, and a part of the early history of our nation.

The first harvest in 1621 was bountiful. Overwhelmed with gratitude to their Creator and Sustainer, Pilgrim governor William Bradford called for a special feast to give thanks to God. The Pilgrims invited 100 Indians (of course, Squanto was among them) to join them as they celebrated for an entire week.

At some point along the way, the people of colonial New England began the custom of placing five grains of corn at their plates as they sat down to Thanksgiving dinner, symbolizing their thanksgiving to God and to those who blazed the trail before them. And so do we in our home.

A meaningful way to observe this simple custom is to move from person to person around the table with each holding a kernel and saying, "This represents God's blessing to me." Each one then describes a blessing in as much or as little detail as desired. In going around the table five times, with each person depositing one kernel of corn in the middle of the table and sharing one blessing at a time, there are tears, laughter, cheers—a kaleidoscope of meaningful memories shared and gratitude to the Lord expressed for each blessing. My family is certain your family will love this sweet, joyful time, as we do. It works well, regardless of the size of the group. It creates a true thanksgiving celebration.

Suggestions for a Family Prayer Strategy
1. Make prayer a part of the atmosphere of your home. Acknowledge to one another consistently, naturally, the goodness of God and His desire for His children to have abundant life. Express gratitude to God for His provisions as you count your blessings together. Take stock even now. Regardless of whether you live alone or with many family members, *is* prayer a part of the very atmosphere of your home?

2. Make prayer a daily overt experience in your home. Be prayerfully involved with one another. The timing of praying together, of course, depends on the individual family and its lifestyle. However, the principle is the same. The bonds that come from honest, open, earnest prayer with

and for one another and for family concerns are well worth the investment of effort and time.

3. Create a family prayer strategy that will accomplish the first two goals above. Keep it simple and brief. Be flexible. Strive for a balance between routine and variety.

a) Select a regular time and place for family prayer. Pray about everything that touches family members.

b) Spouses, pray with one another at special times, as well as routine times.

c) Parents, pray with your children at special times, as well as routine times.

d) Share prayer requests with one another, and pray aloud together concerning these specific requests.

e) Discuss and pray together about matters you hear on TV newscasts and read about in the newspapers. Make these a part of your prayer list.

f) Include reading the Bible together, discussing its applications to everyday life and specific situations.

g) Many families read together from a daily devotional book. Many books are available.

h) Adopt a missionary family. Learn about them, their country, their ministries, the people with whom they work, their needs. Send cards, email, and occasional gifts to them.

i) Adopt a people group as a family commitment. Learn about them and pray for them in the light of that information.

j) Prayerwalk your neighborhood together. See chapter 11 for more information.

k) Make your home a lighthouse of prayer. Read about Mission America's plan in the resources section.

l) Be creative. Be open to variety in prayer experiences.

Of course, a family cannot experience all of these at any given time. But as you prayerfully keep Christ central, include daily worship, Scripture reading, family concerns, and world awareness.

A Christian Home Week emphasis can provide an excellent time for families to make new resolves and commitments related to their family unit praying together. Well-planned observances provided by the church can be very influential and motivational in guiding the Christ following family into closer spiritual relationships with God, His church, His kingdom, and one another.

Now—how does a family begin to become a praying family? Begin by reading and discussing this chapter together. Plan together how best you can create and implement a family prayer strategy. Begin very simply and add to your experiences as time unfolds. Do not let your own intentions and the nudges from the Lord and His Word go unfulfilled. The years of family life evaporate all too quickly, believe me! Cherish your opportunities to have an impact on the lives of your family now. Be intentional. You will never regret your efforts. And you will regret (later) any and every lack of effort.

May your family taste the wonder of the difference the God of prayer makes in your relationship with Christ, one another, and the rest of the world.

Questions for Reflections
Can you recall a time when your parents prayed aloud for you by name?

If not, how would prayer have made a difference in your life if one or both had prayed in that manner?

Have your children heard you pray aloud for them?

If you are married, do you pray with your spouse?

Are you willing to work toward a family time of prayer together?

Will you consider working together on a family prayer strategy?

[1]Dan R. Crawford, *The Prayer-Shaped Disciple* (Peabody, MA: Hendrickson Publishers, Inc., 1999), 20.
[2]Bureau of the Census, "Marriage, Divorce and Remarriage in the 1990s," *Current Population Reports,* no. 180.
[3]Bureau of the Census, *Statistical Abstract of the United States: 1993* (Washington, DC, 1993), and *Statistical Abstract of the United States: 1997* (Washington, DC, 1997), comparing total number of divorced people over 18 to the total population over 18.

6

A Church's Prayer Strategy

Jesus' Intention: Every Church a House of Prayer

"Before they call I will answer; while they are still speaking I will hear" (Isa. 65:24 NIV).

"We need to realize that prayer is not just for personal use. Prayer is a ministry. Many matters are piled up in heaven, many transactions remain undone, simply because God is unable to find His outlet on earth. If the church does not have this ministry, she is not much use on earth."—Watchman Nee[1]

Watchman Nee's statement is very strong! Paul Billheimer is even bolder: "Any church that does not have a systematic prayer program is operating a religious treadmill."[2] Ouch!

Jack Hayford wrote, "It is staggering to even begin to realize that the whole process by which God's will is done on earth depends on an interceding church."[3]

Most importantly, Jesus said, "My house will be called a house of prayer" (Matt. 21:13 NIV).

Every church of Jesus Christ's needs to deal straightforwardly with the priority of becoming an authentic house of prayer. The issue is obedience to our Lord.

Is your church known as a house of prayer? In your town or city, do people have the impression that prayer is a vital priority in your congregation? Or is it better known for something else? A beautiful facility? Great music? Outstanding preaching?

How can your church more fully carry out Jesus' intention? How can prayer truly be the spiritual lifeblood of your congregation?

When there is physical health, lifeblood flows freely through all the arteries into all parts of body. When there is spiritual health, prayer flows through all arteries of the life of the church, into every area. How can prayer be the central core of the class you teach or of which you are a member? The deacon board? The choir? The praise team? The women's and men's organizations? Every committee, council, and board of your congregation? Your particular area of ministry?

God calls *every believer* to a ministry of prayer, not only those few considered to be prayer warriors. Jesus said to His followers, "When you pray" (Luke 11:2), not "If you pray." He also said His followers "should always pray and not give up" (Luke 18:1). Paul, Silas, and Timothy wrote to the Thessalonians, "Pray continually" (1 Thess. 5:17). Do the people in your congregation really understand how serious Jesus' intention is for them, both in terms of personal prayer and corporate prayer?

Every Sunday School class, every committee meeting, every ministry, whatever the activity, faces the challenge to place prayer at the center. Every time Christ followers gather for any event or session, our Father calls us to experience authentic corporate prayer. As we come together as God's people, we are meeting with Him. What a tragedy, a missed blessing, when we fail to fully acknowledge Him, commune with Him, and listen to Him. After all, this must be our main reason for coming together.

How can your church become more fully a house of prayer? Where do we begin? One way to approach this challenge is to create a church prayer strategy. Although you may not use the term *prayer strategy*, the concept inherent in the term is essential.

Adopt a Churchwide Prayer Strategy

A church prayer strategy is simply a plan that includes a variety of prayer involvements, experiences, and events designed to broaden the base of those participating in the church's prayer ministry.

Ideally, the prayer strategy comes out of the church's mission statement. Every congregation needs a mission statement—an expression of the church's motivating vision.

My church's mission statement is one example:
Enter the world and
Invite people to
Embrace God and
Instruct believers to
Obey Christ in every area of life.

Theoretically, at least, everything we do as a congregation comes out of that mission statement. To me, the mission statement not only calls for, but yells for a prayer strategy!

How does a church develop a prayer strategy?

First, ask God to reveal how He wants your congregation to partner with Him in ways that will involve as many members as possible in prayer. Ask Him to provide the strategy.

Your prayer ministry must have a leader. Many churches call this person a *prayer coordinator*. The pastor needs to be involved in the selection of this leader because they will work closely together. Importantly, the prayer coordinator must have a heart for prayer.[4] He or she needs to be a respected pray-er, one whose love for God, people, and the lost world is unquestioned by those who know him or her well.

A *prayer council* serves an essential purpose. Made up of representatives from across the spectrum of the congregation, it represents every area of the church: Sunday School, deacons, choirs, youth, women's organizations, men's organizations, etc. Such a group enhances the possibility that the churchwide plans and emphases the council adopts will receive support and participation from each area of the congregation. Members of the prayer council serve in a liaison role, bringing the work of the council back to those whom they represent. Additionally, they promote participation in the emphases, activities, and events of the church's adopted prayer strategy.

What are some possible elements of a prayer strategy? Even before giving consideration to any specifics, come together as a congregation and ask God to reveal the components He chooses. Listen carefully to Him. Select only those components He leads you to incorporate into the life of your church. Many possibilities exist. Be creative. Emphasize simplicity. Almost always, people respond best to the doable, that which is relatively free of complexities. A lengthy or complicated strategy will not endure. These suggestions are designed to give realistic help to any congregation desiring to be an authentic house of prayer, regardless of size.

Realistically, some churches may not be open to forming and implementing a churchwide prayer strategy. In such a situation, units within the congregation—a Sunday School class, a prayer group, or any organization of the church—may formulate their own prayer strategy, following some adaptation of the same components.

If neither your church nor any unit within it follows any of these possibilities, you can still make one or more of these elements a part of your own personal prayer strategy.

Some of the most effective intercessors have not had the benefit of a corporate approach to prayer. *One person's earnest prayers make a difference in the kingdom.* If there is no way for you to be a part of a congregation or group committed to strategic prayer, be encouraged to keep on being obedient to Jesus' intentions for you.

Ideas for Your Church's Prayer Strategy
Following are a variety of ideas for components of a church's prayer strategy. Some require commitments or levels of participation not possible for every church member. Others provide opportunities for everyone to participate. If you have or plan to begin a 24-hour prayer room ministry, keep it operating full speed, and add other prayer opportunities that will bring response from various levels of member involvement. This is a necessity if the church is to be a house of prayer.

•*Promote a daily moment of united prayer for your pastor*, a spot of time designated for *every* church member to intercede for him every day. Encourage church members to pray specifically for him wherever they are at that time, regardless of what they are doing. Some will be able to pray longer than that brief moment, but everyone, even children, can learn to pray daily, focused prayers for your pastor. Encourage him to communicate his specific requests for the people to cover with prayer.

•*Plan intercession for your pastor before and during worship services*. History says that when Charles Haddon Spurgeon was preaching in his pulpit, a group of men gathered in the boiler room of the church to pray for him. Spurgeon was convinced this group was key to what took place in the worship service. Churches today can follow this example, organizing special prayer attention upon their pastor while he preaches and on the congregation while they worship. Use this time to pray for the lost, for visitors seeking a church home, for God's touch on each person present at the point of their need, for revival. A rotating team, praying in a designated place during the worship hour, can fill this prayer role. You can also use a variety of groupings to pray with the pastor *before* the services, such as deacons, a rotation of members at large, church council, etc.

•*Maintain a prayer room ministry.* A comprehensive, 24-hour, 7-days-a-week prayer room ministry is the spiritual backbone of a church. This plan calls for intercessors to come to the church's designated prayer room (where prayer needs and requests are collected) and spend 1 hour each week in intercession for the matters administered by the prayer coordinator and prayer council. Some churches operate prayerlines or answering machines to receive prayer needs from all over the city and beyond. This strategy proves effective in numbers of churches—both for the intercessors and for those for whom they pray. An outstanding prayer room ministry represents the ideal. However, the logistical realities of safety in the middle of the night, weather conditions, and limited numbers of persons able to participate bring challenges for even the finest ministries to maintain the full 168-person complement necessary for round-the clock operation. The good news is that God honors consistently a fully operational 24-hour prayer ministry with thrilling results that come from such a level of commitment. Many manuals are available giving details for setting up and maintaining 24-hour prayer ministries.[5]

Prayer consultants are available who will, at the invitation of a church, work with congregations over a period of time in setting up the prayer room and its ministry. Donna Dee Floyd of Houston, Texas, and Elaine Helms of northwest Atlanta, Georgia, are two excellent consultants who have personally guided many churches in this process.

•*Organize a prayer vigil.* A simple but potentially dynamic prayer event is the prayer vigil. My church implements a 24-hour prayer vigil the first weekend of every month. Our time frame is 8:00 A.M. Saturday to 8:00 A.M. Sunday. With our congregation largely comprised of young families, we do things very simply, including a large sign-up board in our main hall, divided into 30-minute segments. Multiple names can occupy each segment. As the church's prayer coordinator, I create a prayer vigil guide each month suggesting how to spend the 30-minute period—two pages of prayer needs, Scripture passages, and directed meditation. During the week prior to the prayer vigil, those who will participate receive the guide in the mail. Many members have expressed spiritual fulfillment about their involvement. Some have said they had never before spent a half hour in continuous prayer.

Our vigil allows those who sign up to keep this 30-minute commitment wherever they are, even if they are out of town. This plan works well for any size church and represents another way to involve a larger percentage of the congregation, including new believers, in meaningful prayer.

•*Conduct a prayerwalk of your church building.* Recently our people came throughout the day on a Saturday for such an experience. We walked through the classrooms of our church, praying for those who would be there the next day studying God's Word. Some teachers had displayed pictures of class members and their prayer requests, giving prayerwalkers opportunity for specific praying. We walked and prayed throughout the worship center, asking God for His powerful presence to fill the room and to have an impact on the people who would gather the next day. We interceded for our pastor, praying that God's message would be proclaimed through him with power and love. We prayed for the music and the praise team, the congregation, the visitors, and especially, we prayed for those present who did not know Christ. Sitting down in some of the seats, we prayed for the person who would sit there the next day. We prayed for all the people and places around the world where Christ's love and salvation would be proclaimed and heard on the Lord's Day. We asked for the hearts of people to be open and responsive to the Holy Spirit. Your church can implement such a prayerwalk with minimum effort and realize positive participation and results.

•*Conduct prayerwalks* of your church's neighborhood. Chapter 11 gives information and a brief orientation.

•*Organize a prayer chain among your congregation*—those willing to be called and committed to pray for needs and requests brought to their attention. Immediately upon being contacted, each link calls the next link in the chain. The prayer coordinator or the pastor activate the chain by calling the first link.

•*Offer studies of books on prayer*. As a churchwide event, ask someone to teach or review one of the outstanding books on prayer. Include both some current authors and classic writers. See the selected bibliography for suggestions.

•*Offer prayer retreats at least once a year*. Retreats have strong potential as spiritual growth stimulants. Often a class, department, or some other unit of the congregation has its own retreat. A prayer retreat usually ranges from 2 hours to 2 days. Consider adding a silent retreat to the church prayer strategy each year.

•*Select a prayer leader in every Sunday School class*. Life-Way Christian Resources provides a helpful booklet for prayer leaders of every Sunday School class/Bible study group, *Lord, Teach Us to Pray*, by James E. and Val D. Harvey. This booklet gives specific suggestions for creative ways to take class/group prayertimes and prayer relationships beyond the routine and bring the Holy Spirit's vitality into them.

•*Conduct real prayer meetings on Wednesday nights*. If we call the Wednesday night service a prayer meeting, it stands to reason that a set-apart period of time during the service be given to prayer. Dividing the larger group into small groups enhances the experience of from-the-heart prayer. Prayer testimonies also make a vital contribution. Real prayer meetings are a cornerstone to a church that is a house of prayer. In the recent publication *A House of Prayer: Prayer Ministries in the Church,* compiled by John Franklin, a chapter is devoted to "Keys to Dynamic Prayer Meetings." This helpful chapter is written by Gregg Frizzell, pastor of Georgian Hills Baptist Church in Memphis, Tennessee. John Franklin is the prayer/discipleship specialist at LifeWay Christian Resources.

• *Conduct a churchwide concert of prayer periodically.* David Bryant is one of our day's outstanding prayer leaders. Continuing the call of Jonathan Edwards and others from the 1700s for concerts of prayer, Bryant challenges and motivates believers to join the current worldwide movement of prayer. Bryant suggests a format for a 2-hour concert of prayer appropriate for small groups, churches, citywide rallies, etc. You can obtain brochures from Concerts of Prayer International, Pentagon Towers, Box 36008, Minneapolis, MN 55435; telephone: (612) 853-1740. Check resources section for additional helps.

• *Maintain prayer groups.* Your church can form prayer groups around specific ministries of the church, such as worship, discipleship, evangelism, missions, ministry to the homebound, etc. A group praying for specific requests turned in by church members can have a significant role in the life of the church. Especially vital in this context is a group praying for the church's adopted unreached people group. Men's prayer groups and women's prayer groups can contribute so much to the spiritual life and outreach of the congregation.

• *Emphasize family worship.* Once a year, place a churchwide emphasis on family worship. Find creative ways to call the congregation to commit to regular family worship, giving opportunity for response and commitment. See chapter 5 for more ideas.

Assign prayer partners or triplets. Make assignments of partners or triplets for a limited amount of time—two months or six months, for example. Suggest how frequently they should ideally meet to pray. At least once a month, ask several participants to report on their experiences during prayer meeting time, sharing ways God has been at work within them and through them as they have agreed in prayer.

Use CompassionNet. This worldwide computer-based prayer network contains prayer folders for countries where Southern Baptists have work, as well as for megacities, unreached people groups, and population segments. It is updated daily, Monday–Friday. To subscribe, visit the International Mission Board's Web site at www.imb.org or call 1-888-462-7729.

Stay in touch with the International Mission Board PrayerLine. For up-to-the-minute prayer needs from around the world, regularly contact the IMB PrayerLine (1-800-395-PRAY), available toll-free, 24 hours a day. The prayerline also serves as a worldwide emergency prayer network. When crises arise, the prayerline is the first line of response. Report one or more prayer requests from the prayerline to your church during a Sunday service, Sunday School classes, Women on Mission® group meetings, Wednesday night prayer meetings, prayer group meetings, or other appropriate times. Ask someone to lead in prayer for each request when it is shared. The prayerline message is available also on email (email: prayeroffice@imb.org).

Call the North American Mission Board PrayerLine regularly: 1-800-554-PRAY. You will receive (1) a North American missions prayer request, (2) a spiritual awakening request (3) a Watchman request, and (4) a special request. Visit NAMB's Web site (www.namb.net/prayer).

Adopt a missionary. This plan has proven effective for many years in relating to a missionary or missionary family and establishes meaningful and often lifelong relationships.

108

Church members may already know the missionary you adopt, but not necessarily. The church pledges, as individuals and as a part of corporate gatherings, to take on the concerns of the lives and work of their specific missionary or missionary family. Most missionaries are constantly working on the maintenance of a personal prayer network, thus longing to be adopted. They will provide updated prayer needs and requests for the adopting church, group, or family. Also meaningful is for the adopting church to celebrate in special ways the birthdays of the MKs, the children of the adopted missionaries. For information about international missionaries, call toll-free 1-888-462-7729 or visit the IMB Web site (www.imb.org). For information about North American missionaries, call (770) 410-6000 or visit the NAMB Web site (www.namb.net).

•*Observe weeks of prayer.* The Week of Prayer for International Missions, the Week of Prayer for North American Missions, as well as weeks of prayer for state missions have long been highlights for missions praying in churches. Your church can hear testimonies of missionaries throughout the year, but they have special meaning during these weeks. For information about the Week of Prayer for International Missions, visit the IMB Web site at www.imb.org. For information about the Week of Prayer for North American Missions, visit the NAMB Web site at www.namb.net. For information about weeks of prayer for state missions, contact your state Baptist convention office.

•*Tap into daily worldwide prayer needs available by email*—about 30 each weekday, year-round. Prayer requests come from around the world daily and are distributed by the International Prayer Strategy Office at the IMB to those committed to specific intercession. Call 1-888-462-7729, or email prayeroffice@imb.org.

•*Adopt an unreached people group.* Churches and units within the church can make a difference for the people group and for the kingdom through committed prayer.

This commitment provides opportunity for the church to learn about a people completely beyond our personal worlds and involves them in praying into the kingdom people whom God loves and wants to love Him. Missionaries currently are seeking to enlist individuals and groups to adopt the people with whom they work and become a part of their prayer network. For example, my Bible study class adopted the Mandinka people in West Africa. We receive regular communication by email from missionaries Karen and Chris Austin. For more information and/or an assignment, call the International Prayer Strategy Office (1-888-462-7729).

•*Enter a Last Frontier PRAYERplus partnership.* More than 2,000 unreached people groups are in the Last Frontier of global evangelization. Long-term commitment to faithful praying is required to reach these people. Churches can enter this advanced partnership and involvement by committing to several years of prayer focus on a specific group. The plus part means the adopting church pledges obedience to God in whatever else He directs them to do in coordinated effort with the IMB toward evangelization of the adopted group. Members of PRAYERplus congregations go overseas to relate directly with the people group in some meaningful way that often involves business skills, professions, and/or spiritual gifts. For information, call toll-free 1-888-462-7729. Or email resource.center@imb.org.

•*Become a Global Priority church.* Churches qualify for this designation by committing to missions as a major thrust of the church. Missions praying, missions education, missions giving, adopting an unreached people group, participating in short-term overseas missions projects, and finding creative ways to further personalize missions for the congregation are among the priorities of this program. For information, call the IMB toll-free (1-877-462-4721).

•*Take part in a national prayer partnership between your state convention and missionary work in open, traditional fields.* Emphasis on Last Frontier people groups does not replace long-term efforts to win the lost to Christ, disciple believers, and plant churches in those places where missions work is already established. Large-scale prayer partnerships between an association or convention and the Mission in an open country are extremely productive. Many forms of direct ministry and witness involvement grow out of these partnerships that begin with foundational prayer needs. For information on this kind of prayer partnership, call toll-free (1-888-462-7729), or contact your state Baptist convention office.

• *Observe the annual Day of Prayer and Fasting for World Evangelization.* This emphasis takes place on Pentecost weekend, which falls in May or June. It began in 1988 during a meeting of executives of mission boards who have major plans related to world evangelization. These missions leaders agreed to promote this annual prayer emphasis simultaneously. The IMB, through the International Prayer Strategy Office, makes available information on a specific people each year as the focus of united prayer. This has continued to be an effective way for a church, or group within a church, to employ prayer as strategy and to make the church more fully a house of prayer. For information or to place an order for materials, call 1-888-462-7729 or 1-800-866-3621.

• *Read and make use of* the COMMISSION, Missions-USA, *and* Missions Mosaic *as prayer guides.* These excellent magazines have a world of interesting, stimulating missions coverage of various ministries in our nation and overseas. Many articles include prayer needs at the conclusion to assist intercessors in knowing how best to pray in light of the information. *Missions Mosaic* contains Prayer Patterns, a daily missions devotional and prayer guide that includes the missionary prayer calendar.

To order *the COMMISSION*, visit the IMB Web site (www.imb.org). To order *MissionsUSA*, visit the North

American Mission Board Web site (www.namb.net). To order *Missions Mosaic*, visit the WMU Web site (www.wmu.com) or call 1-800-968-7301.

•*Make use of* Operation World: A Day-by-Day Guide to Praying for the World, *by Patrick Johnstone.* This outstanding work was first published in 1974. *Operation World* is a unique prayer manual portraying the world's spiritual needs and leading the intercessor through the nations of the world alphabetically day by day in one year's time. The information highlights cogent facts and figures plus prayer requests, all designed to stimulate intercession. *Operation World* was the first publication to give complete denominational and religious population breakdowns for every country in the world. It is a monumental work.

Operation World has enhanced and blessed my own personal intercession and has contributed daily to the work of the IMB's International Prayer Strategy Office. Individuals, groups, Wednesday night prayer meetings, all can use *Operation World.*

Johnstone's wife, Jill, wrote a children's version, entitled *You Can Change the World.* Ill with cancer, she finished the excellent, attractive book dealing with people groups only a few weeks before her "homecall" (her husband's lovely term). Zondervan Publishing House published both books as companion volumes in 1993.

•*Consider going on a prayer journey.* God calls Christ followers specifically to go to destinations in the United States and overseas to pray on-site in the teeming megacities as well as the remote places of the world. If you are interested in information about overseas prayerwalking journeys, call toll-free 1-888-462-7729.[6]

•*Establish neighborhood lighthouses of prayer.* This plan is sponsored by Mission America, an interdenominational group representing 200 parachurch ministries and 200,000 churches and is joined in sponsorship by the North American Mission Board and many other organizations. It enlists

112

Christian homes willing to commit to pray regularly for each individual in the neighborhood. A lighthouse consists of at least two people, a couple, a family, a group of families, prayer partners, or groups. Participants can pray at home or while they stroll the streets of the neighborhood. The ultimate goal is for every person in America to be lovingly prayed for by name, cared for, and the gospel shared with each of them. The Lighthouses movement is also a part of Celebrate Jesus 2000. For information, call NAMB at (770) 410-6000 or 1-800-448-8032 or fax (615) 251-5983; or call Mission America at 1-800-995-8572. Email: missionamerica@compuserve.com. Visit www.missionamerica.org and www.lighthousmovement.com.

Link up with World Prayer Center. Located in Colorado Springs, Colorado, the World Prayer Center links together national prayer networks currently in more than 30 nations. It is a hub for receiving and distributing prayer requests from Christian bodies globally. When a church in one nation sends a request for prayer, the center distributes it automatically by fax and Internet to other prayer networks worldwide. Located in a command center called the Observatory, a database contains information about each country, its regions, and its ethnic groups, giving background information so prayer can be more specific and thus, more effective. For information, call (719) 536-9100; email: info@wpccs.org. Visit www.wpccs.org.

The USA National Prayer Network office is also located in the World Prayer Center. This ministry is seeking 5,000 USA churches with 24-hour-a-day, 7-day-a-week prayer room ministries to join the network. Each church's prayer room will be required to have a phone, fax machine, and computer to link up with the center. If your church is interested, email info@wpccs.org or call (719) 262-9922.[7]

* * *

Many more possible components exist for a church's prayer strategy. This list provides a beginning point. Start with those elements your congregation can implement effectively, and gradually add as God leads you to do so. See the resources section, page 253, for more information on prayer initiatives, movements, and involvements that can become a part of your church's strategy. *A House of Prayer: Prayer Ministries in Your Church* has a chapter entitled "99 Creative Ideas for Prayer Ministry." The author is Phil Miglioratti, head of the National Pastors Prayer Network and member of the National Prayer Committee.

Even before your church begins to develop a prayer strategy, remember that the strategy must come from the mind of God—the elements must be His ideas—or else it is possible those prayer efforts will be largely futile.

Remember: a prayer strategy is a means to the end of being obedient to Jesus' intention that your church and mine will be a house of prayer.

May it be so.

Questions for Reflection

How does your church measure up to Jesus' intention that His church "will be called a house of prayer"?

Does your church have anything comparable to a prayer strategy?

Would your congregation be open to developing a prayer strategy?

Ask God His desire for your church in this regard.

List two components of a prayer strategy that will work in your church.

114

Think with the Lord about ways you may become a catalyst that will move your church more in harmony with His intention that your church "will be called a house of prayer."

[1]Watchman Nee, *The Prayer Ministry of the Church* (New York: Christian Fellowship Publishing, 1973), 27–28.
[2]Paul E. Billheimer, *Destined for the Throne* (Fort Washington: Christian Literature Crusade, 1975), 34.
[3]Jack Hayford, *Prayer Is Invading the Impossible* (Plainfield, NJ: Harper and Row Publishers, 1975), 84.
[4]See "Afterword: Lingering Reflections."
[5]A list is included in the resources section.
[6]See further information in resources section.
[7]The World Prayer Center operates under the auspices of Global Harvest Ministries, a large network of prayer ministries headed by Peter and Doris Wagner.

7

A Deepening Understanding of Kingdom Praying

"May the peoples praise you, O God; may all the people praise you. May the nations be glad and sing for joy, for you rule the peoples justly and guide the nations of the earth" (Psalm 67:3–4 NIV).

"Your name and renown are the desires of our hearts" (Isa. 26:8).

"But seek first his kingdom and his righteousness, and all these things will be given to you as well" (Matt. 6:33 NIV).

"Mission . . . is seen as a movement from God to the world; the Church is viewed as an instrument for that mission. There is a church because there is mission, not vice versa."—David Bosch, quoting Anna Maria Aargaard[1]

"Prayer is a conduit through which power from heaven is brought to earth."—O. Hallesby[2]

God makes us covenant partners in the working out of His purposes in the world, and yet we are not equal partners. God is the senior partner and must therefore be approached in awe and reverence."—Donald Bloesch[3]

115

116

The earliest, clearest word on prayer as strategy comes
from God Himself. The psalmist quotes our Lord: "Ask of
me, and I will make the nations your inheritance, the ends
of the earth your possession" (Psalm 2:8 NIV). Acts 1:14
provides the New Testament pattern: "They all joined together constantly in prayer." Then, Pentecost happened.
Biblically, we see a direct connection between the prayers
of God's people and breakthroughs in accomplishing God's
purposes in the world.

This chapter explores the second major purpose of
prayer. Recall that the first major purpose is to know God
in Christ intimately, to love Him increasingly, and to become more like Him. The second purpose is to partner
with Him, through intercession, in what He wants to do
in this world.

Moses, Joshua, and the Amalekites
Exodus 17 records a familiar incident in the expansive history of God's people (17:8–13). It caused me to see with
fresh eyes that prayer must be the priority strategy in all we
are and do as God's people today. In our personal lives,
homes, churches, conventions, agencies, institutions, and,
certainly, in our missions efforts in our own country and
around the world, prayer must take priority.

Recall this familiar account. Moses was leading the children of Israel to the Land of Promise. But there were ob-
stacles in the way. One of them was a fierce, pagan army of
Amalekites poised near Israel's camp ready to wipe out the
Israelites.

Picture the events as they unfold. Moses called in Joshua
and they formed a strategy. Joshua chose the men to do the
fighting, and sometime after sunrise the next morning he
led them to the battleground. Moses took Aaron and Hur
with him up the mountainside overlooking the field below.
As the armies clashed below him, Moses lifted his hands
toward heaven, holding his staff in his right hand, in inter-

cession for the men below. Joshua's troops began to prevail, driving back the enemy.

After a while, Moses' arms grew weary. He relaxed them to his side and walked back and forth, no doubt keeping his eye on the battle below. To his dismay, he saw the tide of battle shifting. Could he believe his eyes? Yes, the Amalekites now were striking down the Israelites.

When Moses realized what was happening, he quickly raised his hands again, holding high the staff, in intercession to the Lord. Immediately the momentum of battle changed, and the Israelites again prevailed.

Can you imagine the instant when this magnificent truth dawned on Moses? He must keep his hands lifted to heaven in prayer if the Israelites were to have God's power. In that instant, he saw clearly that God responded to his intercession. Aaron and Hur stepped in and held up Moses' hands so that his intercession would be consistent until the Israelites won the battle. In verses 15 and 16, we read, "Moses built an altar and called it The Lord is my Banner. He said, 'For hands were lifted up to the throne of the Lord.'"

This passage is loaded with truths for us as the battle rages with the enemy's spiritual forces in our lives, cities, and world. As we absorb God's truths, keep in mind that differences and similarities exist between the Exodus event and now. For example, today God leads us to pray that people groups such as the Amalekites will be redeemed, not slain. He has revealed to us that the enemy is Satan, not the Amalekites or their descendants. God wants, even requires in His master plan, the earnest intercessions of His people lifted on behalf of others. This is employing prayer as strategy—a primary strategy in the work of God's kingdom. This strategic dimension of prayer is *kingdom praying*.

Kingdom Praying

What does kingdom praying entail? What does it mean to employ prayer as strategy in the life and work of God's kingdom?

Kingdom praying includes that dimension of intercession that reaches beyond our immediate surroundings. Praying about personal, local matters often happens more naturally and more consistently for most of us. My problems, my work, my family, my needs, and the concerns of those close to me—these tend to come more spontaneously to my heart and mind. Of course, personal, local praying is valid. In fact, it is essential. God longs for us to bring our personal burdens to Him. Yet kingdom praying is a level of prayer that reaches beyond us.

Kingdom praying, then, seeks to discern what God wants to happen in His kingdom, and prays for that to take place. In kingdom praying, we seek to attune our hearts to His heart's desire and pray for its fulfillment.

God's Heart's Desire

What is God's heart's desire? He expresses it throughout the Scripture: "that His ways may be known on earth, His salvation among all people" (Psalm 67:2). God wants all people saved! Peter expressed it very plainly that our Lord is "not wanting anyone to perish, but everyone to come to repentance" (2 Peter 3:9 NIV). Our Lord's heart's desire is for all people to love and worship Him and become a part of His kingdom. Thus, His heart's desire, according to His Word, must become the mission of every follower of Christ, the mission of every church.

Patrick Johnstone writes in *The Church Is Bigger Than You Think:* "For Christians, mission is not an optional extra for the fanatical few or for the specially anointed, it is a fundamental definitive of who we are in Christ and why we are in Christ."[4]

Many of us, individuals and congregations, have missed this understanding. As a result, we have missed, as Johnstone expresses it, "God's purpose, God's intimacy, and God's blessing."[5] The desire of God's heart is that all peoples of all nations will have opportunity to know and love His Son. The Great Commission is simply, but profoundly, to every believer and to every church.

The staggering fact before us is that at least two-thirds of the world's population does not know and love God's Son—close to 4 billion people. What can God's people do? Throw up our hands? As a matter of fact, yes, like Moses did—in intercession.

Hear again the psalmist quoting our Lord: "Ask of me, and I will make the nations your inheritance" (Psalm 2:8 NIV). In one of the most astounding statements in the Bible, God makes a connection between our asking and the nations being saved. He declares a direct link between the prayers of His people and the accomplishment of His heart's desire. He reveals that kingdom praying is a priority strategy in making Christ known and loved.

With this biblical truth freshly before me, I began the adventure of seeking to grasp more and more about kingdom prayer as strategy and bring together some understandings. While neither the concept of prayer as strategy nor our understandings are new, they must become an integrated part of the fabric of the life that prays.

Understandings of Kingdom Praying

•Prayer begins with God.
Prayer is God's idea. He prompts us to pray. We tend to think prayer is our idea, but prayer is our response to His initiative. God places it in our hearts to pray, and that's what we are to pray for—those matters that are His requests, His priorities. Have you thought of God as having

prayer requests? We may think we are the only ones with prayer requests, yet there are many matters for which He wants us to pray!

Everything we believe about prayer should begin with God and with what He wants. What are God's priorities for you? Your family? Your church? Your work? The world? How can your praying, individually and corporately, become more focused on His kingdom priorities? Every individual and every church needs to consider carefully and prayerfully this foundational question. Prayer begins with God and His priorities—with what He wants to take place in your life, in your church, and in the world.

• *There really is power in our praying.*
God has chosen to accomplish His purposes in this world in response to the prayers of His people. Does this mean He is powerless without our praying? Not at all. God can do anything He wants at any time in any way He chooses—with or without our prayers. Yet He has made a holy decision to release His power in response to the prayers of His people. Thus, He gives us this awesome role of dynamic partnership with Him. His power does the work that makes the difference, saves, and transforms. But our prayers release His power. T. W. Hunt often says, "God refuses to act alone." We do our part; He does His. This is His plan—partnership with Him.

The nation of East Germany provides a dramatic example of God releasing His power in response to the prayers of His people. I will never forget the November morning in 1989 when I heard the early morning news exclaiming—not just announcing—that the Berlin Wall had crumbled into souvenirs. It was the most shocking news of the decade. No one saw it coming. Commentators and columnists scrambled to find factors that brought down that remarkable wall and all it represented to the world. Consider one of those factors:

More than a decade earlier, Christians, distressed by conditions in their nation, had begun gathering on Monday evenings at a church in Leipzig, East Germany, to pray for their land. They prayed faithfully, earnestly, asking God for freedom to worship Him openly, for freedom from godless Communism. Believers gathered each week in increasing numbers to pray for revival in their land and for the very officials who were restricting their freedoms. They pleaded for the touch of God upon their people and their land.

Eventually the Monday night crowds overflowed the church. A neighboring church opened its doors, and soon that church filled to overflowing. The prayer gatherings spread throughout Leipzig and to the next city. In time, churches in many cities were open for prayer on Monday evenings. Spontaneously, the people began to bring candles with them. They left the churches each Monday evening and walked with lighted candles through the streets of East Germany in throngs, in quiet demand for freedom to worship God and for other basic freedoms.

And the Iron Curtain fell.

What caused the breakdown of Communist control? Some called it people power. But we know Whose power it was. Even some secular writers and commentators brought into the equation the pressure created by those Monday night prayer meetings, with people filling the churches and then the streets, carrying lighted candles of hope. *Christianity Today* reported the account in an article entitled, "Revolution by Candlelight."[6] The subtitle noted that "the streets of Leipzig are all marked with candle wax, not bloodstains." The candle wax symbolized the prayers of God's people.

Is God calling *us* to prayer and intercession in new and bold and extraordinary ways? The history of revival, spiritual awakening, and renewal reveals that concerted, united, extraordinary prayer has always preceded a major move of

God's Holy Spirit. Can we grasp this simple, profound, essential, powerful truth?

•*The reach of prayer is total.*

Prayer can reach into every life and every home in your neighborhood, into every town, city, state, and nation— even into all 237 nations of the world. In response to our intercession, God can turn the hearts of people toward the gospel. Through our partnership with Him in prayer, He will encourage believers we have never seen. Our prayers can reach into places we have never been and never will go and impact them for Christ. God *is* able!

A well-known classic story from missions history illustrates this truth. It involves J. O. Fraser, a pioneer missionary to the Lisu tribe in southwest China. Fraser had gone to China in the early 1900s with the China Inland Mission. Laboring hard in the mountain villages, he preached and ministered with very little response. Depressed and suicidal, he almost gave up.

In desperation, he wrote to his home country (England) and enlisted a prayer group to pray specifically and unitedly for him and for the people with whom he worked. Even as he wrote, he renewed his own faith and began praying with new earnestness for several hundred Lisu families to come to Jesus. Eight intercessors responded, pledging to God and to Fraser to pray faithfully.

Later Mrs. Fraser wrote the account of their lives and labors. She gave this description of the remarkable differences she observed before and after the intercessors began to pray: "He [Fraser] came to the place where he asked God to take away his life rather than allow him to labor on without results. He would then tell me of the prayer forces that took up the burden at home and the tremendous lifting of the cloud over his soul, of the gift of faith that was given him and how God seemed suddenly to step in, drive back the forces of darkness and take the field."[7]

Thousands of Lisu people accepted Jesus as Savior and Lord.

Later, in retrospect, Fraser wrote his intercessors: "I used to think that prayer should have the first place and teaching the second. I now feel that it would be truer to give prayer the first, second and third places and teaching the fourth."[8]

Indeed, the reach of prayer is total. It was then, and it is today.

•*Every believer can have impact for Christ through prayer.* Through kingdom praying, every Christian of every age, every race, and every circumstance can have great effect for Christ where we live and around the world. Everyone cannot go to another country to personally introduce people to Jesus. Some can and do, but everyone cannot. Everyone cannot financially have impact for Christ. Some have that ability, but not all. Yet every believer can *pray* and make a difference for Jesus near at hand and around the world. Imagine the extraordinary release of God's power that would take place if all believers of all ages were mobilized in united prayer!

In Bangladesh I met with the leaders of the Baptist Union and urged them to bring to their churches an emphasis on kingdom praying. Carefully, through an interpreter, I laid out the challenge of joining with believers around the world in praying for the salvation of those outside the boundaries of their own country, as well as for those within. I could see they were responding with growing excitement as they envisioned themselves joining with many other intercessors worldwide and praying lost people into God's kingdom.

In the time of discussion, the president of the Baptist Union responded first, "We desperately need that vision of praying beyond ourselves." He continued sadly, "Recently I was participating in the worship service of one of our churches when someone asked for prayer that his sick goat be made well." The union leader expressed his concern that believers grow in their concept of prayer, develop a burden for the lost of the world, and see themselves as making a difference for Christ and the gospel through their intercessions. I replied, "My brother, we have that same need in my country. We may not pray for a sick goat, but we pray for the Americanized equivalent of our sick goat." We agreed that the tendency to be focused on our own personal, local burdens is the same the world over. After a moving time of repentance and testimonies, our group had a meaningful prayertime of dedication and rededication to kingdom praying.

Every believer, through prayer "in the Spirit" (Eph. 6:18) can have an impact for Christ, and thus be obedient to the Great Commission—in Bangladesh, in your town or city, and in mine.

● *Kingdom praying takes us into the realm of spiritual warfare.*
"Our struggle is not against flesh and blood, but against the rulers, against the authorities, against the powers of this dark world and against the spiritual forces of evil in the heavenly realms" (Eph. 6:12 NIV).

Surely, no one would argue with Paul about the existence of spiritual forces of evil in the world. Daily we encounter and observe some degree of the unseen, sinister, divisive, deceptive, destructive forces that demonstrate the power of Satan's presence. The "powers of this dark world" constantly clash with the love, power, and will of God. There is no doubt but that Satan seeks the destruction of the people of God and the work of God. There really is a war.

While Satan intends destruction, God intends the spiritual *con*struction of His people. Our loving Lord envisions and desires joyful worship of Himself and transformation of the worshipers. Satan, at the same time, envisions leading each and all who will follow him into disobedience and rejection of God.

God wants to transform us, remold us. He desires to remake our characters to be like Jesus. He wants us to be holy. He promises those who respond to His work within that He will supply all we need for life and godliness (2 Peter 1:3–4).

Peter advises the believers spread throughout Asia Minor, and throughout our world today, "Be self-controlled and alert. Your enemy the devil prowls around like a roaring lion looking for someone to devour. Resist him, standing firm in the faith" (1 Peter 5:8 NIV).

One way the devil devours us is to distract us from prayer. Not surprisingly, prayer is the very means God uses to give us the ability to resist Satan and thwart his schemes.

Paul offers straightforward instructions on how to prepare for the many battles of this war. To be ready for battle, he says, we must have spiritual armor and spiritual weapons: "Therefore put on the full armor of God, so that when the day of evil comes, you may be able to stand your ground, and after you have done everything, to stand. Stand firm then, with the belt of truth buckled around your waist, with the breastplate of righteousness in place, and with your feet fitted with the readiness that comes from the gospel of peace. In addition to all this, take up the shield of faith, with which you can extinguish all the flaming arrows of the evil one. Take the helmet of salvation and the sword of the Spirit, which is the word of God" (Eph. 6: 13–17 NIV).

S. D. Gordon observed, "Now mark the keenness of Paul's description of the man who does his most effective work in praying. There are six qualifications under the figure of the six pieces of armor. A clear understanding of truth, a clean obedient life, earnest service, a strong, simple trust in God, clear assurance of one's own salvation and

relation to God, and a good grip on truth for others—
these things prepare a man for the real conflict of prayer.
Such a man is invincible in his Chief, Jesus."[9]

In preparing for war, never underestimate the enemy.
We must be alert and keep our spiritual armor ready. With
spiritual armor in place, the Christ follower reports for
duty prepared. Expectation builds as the time approaches
for the battle. What is the next command? Fight? No. The
command is "Pray!" Indeed, we are on a battlefield, and
the appropriate action is prayer.

James joined Peter in admonishing us to resist the devil
(James 4:7). He added the reassuring words "and he will
flee from you." We must claim the promise of God's Word
when Satan moves into a realm that has been turned over
to God. What a great and comforting promise! But we
must resist him and not let him establish a beachhead.

Even when he fails in his attempt to lead us into disobedience, Satan does not surrender. When other approaches
are rebuffed, he seeks to lure us into procrastination and
complacency. He never gives up. He is cunning. Even
when believers have spiritual successes, he tempts us with
pride. Recognizing his strategies is important!

In the light of these truths, we must not blame our every
downfall on Satan. Certainly, he is the author of all evil,
and so we are tempted to shift to him responsibility *we*
should acknowledge for ourselves. The Satan-made-me-do-
it syndrome may be, in reality, a rationalization for our
own faulty decision making. Or it may be a failure to
claim the resources God offers every one of His children.
As we receive and draw on the strength and energy of the
Holy Spirit, "Christ in us," and keep our eyes on Jesus, we
have a power Satan cannot penetrate. After all, He Who is
in us is so much greater than Satan. This power of Christ
within creates our ability to resist the evil one. This power
causes him to flee.

Yet some Christians give inordinate attention in their thoughts and conversation to Satan. Some share the words Satan has spoken to them personally. My own goal is to refuse flatly to listen in my mind, heart, or soul to anything that might faintly resemble his thoughts, attitudes, or words. Any time we allow his influence to linger in our awareness, we get into trouble.

Keep in mind that addressing Satan is not prayer. Addressing Satan is addressing Satan.

Satan is darkness and lies and master of all things deceitful. When we step out of the circle of God's truth, we become vulnerable to the evil one's invasion of our perspective, attitudes, relationships, and behavior. Christ is light and life and reality and love, joy, peace, patience, goodness, kindness, faithfulness, gentleness, and self-control. Life in Him counters the enemy's influence and vitiates his power.

With our attention fixed on Jesus, we are in the safest place. He wants us close to Him in order to protect us from the enemy. He is true to His every promise to be with us always.

The warfare is real. But God's power is indescribably superior to Satan's power. We can stake our lives on this fact.

•*Kingdom praying calls forth laborers to go into the fields.* Jesus Himself instructed us: "'Ask the Lord of the harvest, therefore, to send out workers into his harvest field'" (Matt. 9:38 NIV). We desperately need laborers where we live and to the ends of the earth to witness, teach, and live out Christ's love and redemption obediently and faithfully. Surely God is calling more laborers than are hearing and responding. Through employing prayer as strategic kingdom praying, we can do our part in praying forth those whom God is calling.

Have you prayed for God to call forth laborers from your church, and from your family?

•*Kingdom praying is the most crucial work we can do.*
Kingdom praying is work! It demands our time, our energy, our intentional attention, our focus, our self-discipline. We must recommit ourselves to it every day. Prayer is work, but prayer *works*. More accurately, God works in response to the work of prayer, in response to the prayers of His people.

Oswald Chambers said, "Prayer does not just fit us for the greater work. Prayer *is* the greater work."[10]

T. W. Hunt stated, "Prayer is the shaping force of history. God used Moses' prayers to preserve Israel through the wandering years. He used Nehemiah's prayers to make possible the rebuilding of the wall around Jerusalem. Jesus' prayers shaped His disciples and helped to develop them into the kind of people that would populate a new kind of kingdom. Paul's prayers were God's instruments for shaping the personality and destiny of the new church as it spread across the Mediterranean world."[11]

God's Word, as well as history and our own experiences, teach us that the most powerful work we can do is to be obedient and faithful in the work of prayer.

For Whom and for What Do Kingdom Pray-ers Pray?

Employing prayer as strategy involves all that concerns the heart of our Lord. We can be sure these include:

1. *The lost—beginning with lost family members in our own homes, moving to those in our neighborhood, and reaching out in concentric circles around the world.* Every day we encounter personally those who do not know and love our Lord. Does it enter your mind and heart to pray for them to come to Him?

2. *Missionaries—those serving in our own country and those assigned around the world.* The main purpose of kingdom praying for missionaries is to release God's power and divine energy in their lives, families, and ministries as they

seek to bring others into the kingdom. Missionaries desperately need and desire our united, specific praying.

3. *Believers around the world.* While we have traditionally emphasized prayer for missionaries, we have more recently emphasized our responsibility to pray for the growth, development, courage, and boldness of fellow believers in other nations. World evangelization will not take place unless and until local Christ followers take responsibility for evangelizing their own people group and/or nation and discover their role in sharing the gospel even beyond their own borders.

4. *Leaders of our nation and officials around the world.* The Scriptures clearly mandate intercession for our own leaders and for government officials in other lands, for officials' decisions can either impede or enhance the spread of the gospel. We must pray increasingly for the leaders of the world, asking God to use for good even those influences that are intended for evil. We can pray strategically when we pray for leaders to do that which will enhance the gospel, knowingly or unknowingly.

5. *More laborers, here and around the world.* Jesus specifically directed prayer for laborers as a part of a disciple's responsibility. Pray that those whom God is calling will not only hear but also respond.

6. *Mission strategists.* Missions leaders request prayer for God to give them vision and wisdom as they make crucial decisions impacting many lives and lands. Pray they will discern and know God's heart and plans for reaching the lost. Intercede for leaders of all evangelical missions agencies and prayer movements.

7. *Worldwide revival and spiritual awakening.* A sweeping, incredible movement of prayer has preceded every spiritual awakening throughout history. One of our greatest prayer burdens is to *pray* that people will pray.

8. *Bible translators.* Another key strategy in fulfilling God's heart's desire is producing the Scriptures in the heart language

of the people. Bible translation agencies are working together with a goal of publishing portions of the Bible in every language spoken by more than 250,000 people. With Scriptures another essential strategy in discipling believers and planting churches, pray earnestly for this essential missions ministry.

9. *The* Jesus *film.* First produced in 1978 and considered the most effective single tool of world evangelization, more than a billion people worldwide have seen the *Jesus* film (originally the vision of Bill Bright of Campus Crusade). Close to 50 million people have made some form of commitment to Jesus after viewing it. Pray for its continued and even heightened effectiveness.

10. *Christian radio and television broadcasts.* The goal of Christian broadcast agencies is to give opportunity to every person on earth to hear the gospel in a language they can understand. Pray for the agencies pursuing this goal, and ask God to supply the translators they need. Pray for those who even now are hearing the gospel by radio and television.

11. *Persecuted Christ followers.* Believers living in various parts of the world today suffer persecution, even to the point of death, because of their faith. Family and former friends often ostracize them. Pray for Christian sisters and brothers around the world who daily face not just the threat but the reality of persecution.

When We Pray

When we pray, we link hands with Jesus and the Holy Spirit, a powerful threefold linkage.

The role of the Holy Spirit is well known: "We do not know what we ought to pray for, but the Spirit himself intercedes for us" (Rom. 8:26 NIV). We are to pray and have confidence that the Holy Spirit will interpret our heart's cry. "Pray in the Spirit on all occasions with all kinds of prayers and requests" (Eph. 6:18 NIV)—meaning pray in the presence and power of the Holy Spirit.

Jesus also has a role in interceding for us at the right hand of the Father. Our part is to pray for the release of His power. God's part is to do the work. What a privilege to be included on this dynamic team!

Missionary Ed Pinkston, representing a lifetime of missionary work in West Africa wrote: "When we get to heaven and are able to read God's history book, I believe we will see that the people really responsible for many of the miracles are the unseen, unsung believers who lift to the Father their intercessions on behalf of His people and His work."

Prayer is the ultimate strategy for releasing God's power into our lives, our families, our churches, our world.

Our Lord declared, "Call to me and I will answer you and tell you great and unsearchable things that you do not know" (Jer. 33:3 NIV). But we must call unto Him.

God said, "Ask of me, and I will make the nations your inheritance" (Psalm 2:8 NIV). But we must ask.

Paul wrote to the Ephesians that our God "is able to do immeasurably more than all we ask or imagine" (Eph. 3:20 NIV). But we must ask.

Prayer is *God's* strategy.

Questions for Reflection
We often think of prayer as resource and as support. How was prayer a valid strategy in the experience of Moses and Joshua?

How can prayer become a possible strategy in your life?

Why do you think God has chosen to make us His partners in the accomplishment of His purposes in the world?

What makes prayer so powerful and crucial?

Are you a kingdom pray-er?

In reviewing the areas of concern of kingdom pray-ers ("For Whom and for What do Kingdom Pray-ers Pray?"), to which of these areas do you give your strongest prayer attention? Your weakest prayer attention?

Will you now make a recommitment—or perhaps a first-time commitment—to kingdom praying?

[1]David Bosch, *Transforming Mission: Paradigm Shifts in Theology of Mission* (Maryknoll: Orbis Books, 1991), 390, quoting German writer Anna Maria Aargaard.

[2]O. Hallesby, *Prayer* (Minneapolis: Augsburg Publishing House, 1931), 117.

[3]Donald Bloesch, *The Struggle of Prayer* (San Francisco: Harper and Row, 1980), 55–60.

[4]Patrick Johnstone, *The Church Is Bigger Than You Think* (Great Britain: Christian Focus Publications, 1998), 23.

[5]Ibid.

[6]Clayton Bell Sr., "Revolution by Candlelight," *Christianity Today*, April 23, 1990.

[7]Mrs. J. O. Fraser, *Fraser and Prayer* (London: Missionary Fellowship, 1963), 11.

[8]Ibid., 47.

[9]S. D. Gordon, *Quiet Talks on Prayer* (New York: Gossett and Dunlop/Revell, 1941), 11–12.

[10]Oswald Chambers, *My Utmost for His Highest* (New York: Dodd, Mead and Company, Inc., 1935), 291.

[11]T. W. Hunt, *The Doctrine of Prayer* (Nashville: Broadman Press, 1987), 15–16.

Rediscovering Prayer As Strategy

"I stand in awe of your deeds, O Lord. Renew them in our day" (Hab. 3:2 NIV).

"The greatest impact any of us can have on Christ's global cause is to be involved in consistent prayer for the whole world and to teach other Christians how to pray this way."—David Bryant[1]

Although the phrase *prayer as strategy* does not appear in church history, a number of historical examples express and employ the concept. Early pioneers of this approach to prayer revealed their deep conviction by their modus operandi and even by their quaint words. They expressed clear, sensitive understanding of God's desires and intentions that the prayers of His people would impact every generation and every nation. We owe a debt to those who went before us, for the trails they blazed for the kingdom and for us—with their intercessions. Somehow, they understood the strategic nature of prayer.

As early as 1723, Presbyterian minister Robert Miller, in his book *A History of the Propagation of Christianity and the Overthrow of Paganism*, put forth the premise that *intercession* is the primary means of converting the heathen. He did not call that primary means of prayer a strategy, yet that was his major premise. Many others also upheld this concept.

Count Zinzendorf and the Moravians

At approximately the same time as Robert Miller, the story
of the Moravian Brethren, descendants of John Huss, sur-
faces in the pages of church history. A colony of brethren,
fleeing persecution in Austria, was established at Herrnhut
in Saxony, Germany, in 1722. Led by Christian David, the
community settled on a portion of the baronial estate
owned by Count Nikolaus Ludwig von Zinzendorf. By
1727, Zinzendorf, a devoted believer with a burden for the
salvation of the world's peoples, had moved from Marien-
bourn to join the group. Additional believers representing
a variety of theological bents came from near and far to
Herrnhut for refuge. Instead of the love and understanding
Zinzendorf expected to characterize the community, strife
and argument over secondary issues surfaced. He felt great
frustration because some of those he befriended failed to
comprehend his understanding of the believers' main
marching orders: "Go into all the world and preach the
gospel." Zinzendorf and others in the community spent
many long nights in prayer and intercession.

Zinzendorf felt led to conduct a communion service and
invited all to participate. During the service, a most unusual visitation from God took place as the believers were
on their faces before Him. When at last they arose from
their knees, they had been transformed.[2]

This marked the beginning of the Moravian 100-year
prayer meeting and, in the unfolding of time, the Moravian missionary movement. As they prayed around the
clock—24 hours a day, year after year—revival swept
through Moravian churches and spilled over into many
places of the world.

Soon after the beginning of the continuous prayer meeting, Zinzendorf, on a visit to Denmark, met a West Indian
slave and two Eskimos from Greenland. They pleaded for
missionaries to take the gospel message to their people.
The count's serious concern for the lost caused him to

envision Moravians responding to the plea. Extraordinary prayer nurtured his vision into reality.

In 1732, the Moravians sent two of their own as missionaries to St. Thomas in the West Indies. In 1733, a mission was begun in Greenland. In the next 28 years, Moravians commissioned 227 missionaries to other countries as additional fields were opened: the Arctic, Algiers, China, Ethiopia, North America, Persia, South Africa, Suriname, West Africa. From the launching of their missionary enterprise until 1930, the Moravians sent 3,000 missionaries to the nations of the world with the gospel of Christ.[3]

A Surprising Influence

The Moravians had a profound effect on Christian history in surprising ways. On May 24, 1738, 11 years into the prayer watch, a young Anglican priest, struggling with doubt and despondency, wandered into a Moravian prayer meeting at Aldersgate in London. Later, he described that night as a spiritual milestone in his life. He described his heart as strangely warmed, and he gave his life in deep commitment to Christ. He considered this to be his conversion experience. The man was John Wesley.

Only three weeks later, Wesley took seven companions and traveled to Herrnhut to see with his own eyes and heart what God was doing there, and to experience the remarkable prayer meeting. He stayed until September before returning to England. Evidently, he did not agree with all he found within the community. Yet, at the end of his visit, he wrote in his journal, "I would gladly have spent my life here, but my Master calling me to another part of the vineyard, I was constrained to take leave of this happy place."[4]

"Their ministry was bathed in prayer by a whole denomination committed to world evangelization," wrote Patrick Johnstone about the Moravians. "Ordinary Christians without much education or theological training gained a vision which was very simple—to win the heathen even if they had to give time to secular pursuits for survival. The Moravians started more missions in ten years than the whole of Protestantism over the previous 200."[5]

Although Zinzendorf, one of history's great missionary statesmen,[6] did not use the terminology, he led the Moravians to employ prayer as strategy, and thus launched one of the outstanding evangelistic thrusts in history.

The Little Book with a Long Title
Meanwhile, in Scotland in 1744, John Erskine helped organize concerts of united prayer in the major cities of the nation. Jonathan Edwards, a powerful preacher in Northampton, Massachusetts, was in correspondence with Erskine and other Scottish evangelicals. Edwards was impressed by what he heard from Scotland, wanted to support the concept of Concert for United Prayer drawn up by the Scottish ministers, and longed for a similar prayer movement among his own people. In 1748 he wrote and published *A Humble Attempt to Promote Explicit Agreement and Visible Union of God's People in Extraordinary Prayer, for the revival of Religion and the Advancement of Christ's Kingdom on Earth.* (Actually, this is a shortened version; the original title is said to have been 187 words!)

Thirty-six years later, in April 1784, a copy of the book reached England and the leaders of Northamptonshire Baptist Association. The book was a motivating factor in the association's historic June 1784 "call for regular meetings, on the first Monday of every month, for concerted prayer for the general revival and spread of religion." Historian Charles Deweese gives Edwards's book and this association's call for prayer the credit for "both accelerating the momentum toward regular prayer meetings in Baptist life and eventually helped to move the course of Baptist history toward a higher consciousness of responsibility for missions."[7]

The prayer meetings spread to other associations, and may have been the major influence for a similar prayer call made in the United States through a circular letter written by 23 New England ministers of various denominations. Addressed to "the ministers and churches of every Christian denomination in the United States," the letter called for them to unite "in extraordinary prayer for the revival of religion and the advancement of Christ's kingdom on earth." The New England ministers suggested the first Tuesday of every quarter as the focal point of the united prayer. Evidence exists that Dutch Reformed, Methodist, Moravian, Presbyterian, and Baptist churches became a part of this united effort.[8]

William Carey

Another of those greatly influenced by Edwards's book was William Carey. This young rural pastor/cobbler in England had an amazing passion for the evangelization of the whole world. In the midst of his consuming attention to the Great Commission, Carey managed to secure reports and information about other parts of the world from British trading companies that had representatives scattered in distant lands. He made a hand-sewn leather globe that reflected an up-to-date (at that time) survey of the nations. He also created a wall map before which he would kneel to pray for the lost people represented by the map. Strategic praying from his burdened life was a significant link in the missionary movement begun by the Moravians. Indeed, Carey is said to have embodied the first wave, or era, of missions.

In 1789, during his ministry as the young pastor of the Baptist chapel at Moulton, Carey attended a meeting of ministers at Northampton. John Ryland Sr. suggested to his colleagues that day that one of them propose a topic for discussion. When no one spoke up, Carey rose and offered for consideration, "The duty of Christians to attempt the spread of the gospel among heathen nations." Ryland Sr. is said to have thundered, "Young man, sit down. When God pleases to convert the heathen, He can do it without your aid or mine."[9]

Carey was persistent in his convictions and actually was a latecomer to a group of men already praying for a return to evangelism in the midst of a hyper-Calvinistic climate. The vision of Andrew Fuller, Samuel Pearce, and John Sutcliff matched his own.

In 1792, Carey published a small booklet, *An Enquiry into the Obligation of Christians to Use Means for the Conversion of the Heathens*.[10] It sold for 35 cents. Called "the charter of missions" and "the distinct point of departure in the history of Christianity,"[11] researcher Johnstone describes it as a world survey, "a masterpiece of factual accuracy, balanced assessments and global comprehensiveness."[12] The last chapter carried the heading, "An Enquiry into the duty of Christians in general, and what *means* (author's italics) ought to be used, in order to promote this work." Carey wrote, "One of the first and most important of those duties which are incumbent upon us is fervent and united prayer." The book presented six means for getting the gospel to the heathen. Prayer was the first.[13]

Even better known is Carey's famous sermon from Isaiah 54:2 with the theme Expect Great Things [from God]; Attempt Great Things [for God] preached at the Baptist associational meeting in Nottingham, England, May 31, 1792.[14] The message had an electric effect and made a difference for all eternity. Carey expressed in the sermon, as in his book, his passion for the world and his visionary ideas of what *means* were needed for obedience to the Great Commission. Again, the first of these means was prayer.

John Ryland Jr. had baptized Carey only 9 years earlier. Ryland Jr. said of Carey's sermon, "Had all the people lifted up their voice and wept, as the children of Israel did at Bochim, I should not have wondered, so clearly did he prove the criminality of our supineness in the cause of God."[15]

Finally, out of the 1792 meeting in Nottingham, came a resolution that "a plan be prepared against the next Ministers' Meeting for forming a Baptist Society for propagating the gospel among the heathens." The modern missionary movement is often said to have begun at that time and place. But wherever Carey and others went from 1792 forward, the Moravians were already there.

The first missionary appointed by the new society was John Thomas, and the young Carey was appointed to accompany him as his assistant. Carey invested four decades of his productive, fruitful life in India. Thus, he has often been called the father of modern missions. Perhaps Zinzendorf could be called the grandfather.

Response to Carey's book was widespread. A second missionary society was formed in London. Then two societies took shape in Scotland, followed by another in Holland, and another in England.

The Missions Movement in America
Carey's influence reached to America and inspired women in Boston to form prayer groups for missionary endeavor. The first group, formed in 1800, was led by Mary Webb, a tiny 21-year-old paralyzed woman, who called together seven other Baptist women and six Congregationalist women to form the Boston Female Society for Missionary Purposes. Their purposes included praying and collecting money for the work of William Carey and others.[16]

The missions movement in America is said to have begun in 1806 in a haystack. Five students from Williams College, a Congregationalist school in Williamstown, Massachusetts, were caught in a rainstorm. Taking refuge under a convenient haystack, they used the time to pray for spiritual awakening of the students and for the lost of the world. Led by Samuel J. Mills, each student made a

140

commitment to the Lord and to foreign missions. This
began a sequence of events that included the formation of
the first Student Volunteer Movement that later found
those young men influencing the world as they poured out
their lives for the sake of the gospel. A small marker recognizing the location of the haystack prayer meeting still
stands on the campus, quietly representing the monumental role of strategic prayer.

In the midst of this first wave of mission awakening, a
dozen missions agencies formed on both sides of the Atlantic, and by 1812, about 20 women's missionary societies
existed. That same year, the Boston Female Society for
Missionary Purposes called for other women to organize,
to pray, and to give. A bold call! In that era, women's involvement in anything outside the home was frowned
upon. Mary Webb wrote, "We are not ashamed to acknowledge that we pray, that we meet in praying circles."
They were the women about whom an early reporter said,
"They feared God more than men." This group inspired
more than 100 similar groups in the 18 states of the US.

The assistant pastor of the First Baptist Church of Richmond, Virginia, was one who heard Mary Webb's call. His
wife, sister, and other women responded by forming a
women's praying society. Some expected the pastor to op-
pose the society. He surprised them by making a statement
that has reverberated through the years, "I never heard of
praying doing anybody any harm. For my part, the sisters
may pray on." Thus, the first Female Missionary Society in
Virginia began in 1813.[17] The sisters led the way in employing prayer as strategy!

The Second Wave of Missions: Inland
Slightly ahead of the second wave, Robert Morrison was
the first Protestant missionary to go to China. He reached
Macao in 1807 and made an important contribution in his
translation of the Scriptures.

Congregationalists Adoniram and Ann Judson and
Luther Rice sailed from American shores for Burma in
1812 as the first American missionaries. Unable to book
passage on the same ship, the Judsons arrived ahead of
Rice. While making the long sea voyage, Judson studied
and worked on his project of translating the New Testament. Gradually, he found himself coming nearer and
nearer to the Baptist position on baptism. Ironically, Rice
also arrived in Calcutta unsettled about his beliefs on the
same subject. Less than three months later, each having ag-
onized through to his or her own decision, all three were
baptized by one of William Carey's associates. Integrity required them to resign from the Congregational Board,
leaving them without support. Carey offered to support
the Americans through the English Baptist Missionary Society. However, they all agreed the best plan would be for
American Baptists to provide the support.

Rice returned to America to stir up the Baptists and encourage the formation of organizations for the support of
foreign missions in general and the Judsons in particular.
He was eloquent and drew large crowds. Significantly, he
encouraged the involvement of women, astutely aware of
their potential in the cause of missions. His vision proved
to be accurate.

Rice's efforts helped lead in the formation of the Triennial Convention in 1814, the first national body of Baptists. Organized primarily as a foreign mission society, the
convention's main purpose at first was to support the Judsons. Soon, their purposes expanded. In 1817, the convention voted to recommend to its churches that they observe
the first Monday of every month as a day of prayer for missions.[18] For many years, this remained an important emphasis.

Commissioned by the Triennial Convention, J. Louis and
Henrietta Hall Shuck sailed for China in 1835. As a youth,
Shuck had attended a missions rally where an offering was

received. Having no money, he wrote on a slip of paper, "I give myself," and placed it in the offering plate. The Shucks were powerful missionary influences in China and in America.

The Southern Baptist Convention

Formed in 1845 with missions a major priority, the Southern Baptist Convention immediately created Domestic and Foreign Mission Boards, promoted the monthly Concert of Prayer meetings for missions, and sent missionaries to China and Africa.

By the 1880s in the SBC, however, interest in missions had waned, and the prayer emphasis had fallen into serious decline. A report of the convention's Committee on Progress and Prayer in 1881 attributed the decline of interest in missions primarily to the abandonment of the monthly Concert of Prayer and urged the reestablishment of the monthly event in each church throughout the bounds of the Convention.

Meanwhile, Lottie Moon, destined to become a legend among Southern Baptists, was one of the earliest single women appointed by the Foreign Mission Board (now International Mission Board). Harriet Baker was the first, in 1849, but her career was brief, and she "served to confirm the board's opinion that single women were not suited for foreign missionary service."[19] Finally, with a change in policy in 1872, Edmonia Moon was appointed to China. The following year, on July 7, 1873, Lottie Moon, Edmonia's sister, was officially appointed by the Foreign Mission Board meeting in Richmond, Virginia.

Arriving in China, Lottie immediately enveloped herself in love for, and work with, the Chinese people. She wrote many challenging, chiding letters to Henry A. Tupper, corresponding secretary of the FMB and her trusted friend, asking Southern Baptists for helpers, money, and prayers for the sake of the gospel and the people in China. She described the massive numbers of lost souls around her in the Shantung Province. "Thirty million lost people," she wrote in one of her letters, "yet the one million Southern Baptists at home can barely muster enough through their giving to send only three women and one man to win all of those people to our Lord. I don't know how that looks in heaven, but it certainly looks peculiar in China."[20]

In 1883 the Foreign Mission Board called for special services of prayer for missions, and in 1888 the Convention adopted a committee report urging a return to the establishment and maintenance of the monthly concert of prayer for missions.

The founding of Woman's Missionary Union in 1888 greatly enhanced the focus of prayer on missions in Baptist life. Lottie Moon had pleaded, in her many letters, for the forming of such an organization. Through her inspiration and intense devotion, a special day of prayer and offering for foreign missions was observed each year 1888 to 1891. Beginning in 1892, the prayer emphasis was lengthened to include an entire week. In the meantime, many women's missions organizations of other denominations also organized for the purposes of supporting missionaries with their praying and giving.

China Inland Mission

Perhaps more than any other single person, Hudson Taylor epitomizes the second era of missions. Like Carey, Taylor studied maps, charts, and statistics. His concern was that, while missions organizations had their missionaries assigned to the coastlands, those lost people in the inland portions of the world were not hearing the gospel. In the progression of events and God's use of this young man, Taylor founded the China Inland Mission. The organization fostered a total of over 6,000 missionaries stationed mostly in the interior of China.

Other missions agencies came to embrace Taylor's vision. About 40 missionary-sending organizations took shape and the deployment of personnel to the inland of other nations became a major thrust of the gospel.

The Student Volunteer Movement
While the earlier student movement had come out of the haystack prayer meeting, the Student Volunteer Movement for Foreign Missions came into being in 1886. This later organization was much larger and was supported by prayers and funds from many sources. Eventually, the movement sent 20,000 missionaries overseas. Eighty thousand other members of the movement were active in reinforcing the foundation of mission support in local churches. The movement is credited with the effectiveness of the Laymen's Missionary Movement and with strengthening the proliferating women's missionary societies.

Presbyterian pastor A. T. Pierson was a well-known missions advocate. He joined evangelist Dwight L. Moody, and others in insisting that the Great Commission could be fulfilled and the world evangelized by the end of the century. However, 1899 concluded with much still needing to be accomplished among the peoples of the world.

The 1900s
In 1910, the historic World Missionary Conference was held in Edinburgh, Scotland. Delegates were convinced that the 1900s would be the century providing "worldwide opportunity to make Christ known."

All too quickly came a sequence of staggering deterrents to missions plans and projections: World War I, Communism, the global depression, World War II. Missions subsided in the overwhelming events of world conditions and restrictions. However, after the end of World War II, missions fervor was reborn and came back stronger than ever before.

Strategic prayer played a significant role in many places around the world in the eventful decades of the last part of the twentieth century.

China

In 1951, China's Communist government began intense oppression of the Chinese Christians. Eight thousand missionaries had been forced to leave the country in 1949–50. Church services were outlawed. Bibles and all Christian literature were destroyed. During the tragic days of the cultural revolution (1966–76) led by radical communists, an all-out effort was made to eradicate Christianity altogether. Reports from China indicated that all pastors had either been killed or were imprisoned. The future of the Chinese church looked bleak. But Chinese Christians regularly met secretly in homes to worship God and pray for their nation, with laypersons as leaders of those Christ followers who dared to defy the restrictions.

When missionaries serving in China had been reassigned to other countries, they took with them their burden for the Chinese people and called the Christians of the world to pray intensely for China. Many intercessors around the world responded to their appeals.

Meanwhile, in China, Chinese Christians came together in home groups in growing numbers. The church planters of many of the new unregistered congregations were often pairs of unmarried women.[21] Quietly, believers shared the gospel with neighbors and those with whom they worked. They generously shared their meager food and clothes with the needy, especially the families of those who had been killed or incarcerated. Many who were caught witnessing or worshiping suffered merciless mistreatment.

Intercessors worldwide kept apprised of the situation. In fact, China has been called the most prayed-for nation in history. Moved by the calls for prayer for Chinese Christians living, and some dying, in the midst of constant persecution, I read everything I could find about Chinese Christians and listened for reports. Daily I joined with other intercessors to pray for the believers' protection and boldness and for God's sustaining power upon them day by day.

On my first trip to China in 1984 (China had begun to open in 1979), I had the privilege of meeting with a Chinese medical doctor, a devoted believer. Even as she shared her story, her courage and humility shown through. During the cultural revolution she had been forced to scrub floors and toilets on her knees all day every day in the hospital where previously she had served on the medical staff. She was a radiant, irrepressible Christ follower, a bold witness through it all. I was moved to tears as I looked into the eyes of one who represented the suffering people for whom I had prayed. Indeed, it seemed as though I had seen her before.

As I prayed for the people of China in the 1950s, 1960s, and 1970s, I confess that I did not have the faith to ask for all that actually took place. One of the amazing stories of the twentieth century is the fact that when China began to open, Christians numbered in the multimillions—perhaps 50 million believers. This took place at a time when Chinese believers had no church buildings in which to meet, no trained pastors, and faced constant harassment and persecution. Astounding!

For many years it had seemed to the world as though Satan had gained the victory in China. Doors were closed to traditional mission strategies. But doors cannot shut out the prayers of God's people or the power of the Holy Spirit. Years of faithful prayer by Christ followers inside China and prayer as the only strategy that could be employed by many intercessors outside China relentlessly released God's power in strategic ways that only He can explain. God honors prayer as strategy.

South Korea

Christian believers in South Korea are known for their extraordinary prayer. Presbyterians planted the first Protestant church there in 1884. Today, there are 30,000 churches, with 35 percent of the Korean population now Christian. The story behind the story of continual revival in South Korea is the faithful, intense prayer permeating the lives of believers and their churches, and their intercessions for the lost in their families and among their neighbors and co-workers.

Seoul, the capital, is almost 40 percent Christian. Ten of the 20 largest Christian congregations in the world are located in Seoul. Pastor Paul Cho's Full Gospel Central Church is the world's largest. Seoul is also home to the world's largest theological seminaries. Sixty-five percent of the Republic of Korea Army is now said to be Christian. On average, more than 20 churches are planted there each day. Using indigenous principles as the foundation, Korean Christians now send missionaries abroad. Their goal is to have a total of 10,000 missionaries, with at least one Korean missionary working in every nation of the world.[22] And we think our goals are ambitious! We have much to learn from them.

The best known and most powerful characteristic of the Korean churches is their daily, 5:00 A.M. prayer meetings. An impressive number of intercessors attend. I have taken part in some of the early morning sessions, and the experience is incredible. The Full Gospel Central Church sponsors a prayer mountain with thousands of members spending every Friday night in all-night prayer and fasting, a pattern other churches have followed.

Other Nations

In the former Soviet Union, many believers are convinced the stunning changes took place in the collapse of the Soviet bloc because of the prayers of the faithful *babushkas.*

Those grandmothers never wavered in their earnest intercessions for their nation and their families. No doubt, they
did not understand the theory of prayer as strategy, yet
they experienced it. Although the babushkas had no way of
knowing, praying believers around the world undergirded
their earnest prayers.[23] Dramatic new opportunities developed for getting the gospel into the hearts and minds of
people previously closed off from Christian witness. The
intercessions of God's people faithfully preceded and accompanied these developments. The new opportunities
brought with them an added level of strategic prayer as
more and more of God's people grasped His view of prayer
as the ultimate strategy.

Latin America, parts of Africa, and Asia also show evidences of this spiritual phenomenon. Even in the Islamic
world, as the love of Christ is being lived out and communicated, response is remarkable.

The Third Wave of Missions: Unreached Peoples
Missiologist Ralph Winter of the US Center for World
Mission and editor of *Mission Frontiers* observed that 90
percent of missionaries from North America were working
with national churches overseas that had been in existence
for some time.[24] Although unnoticed at the time, another
wave in missions was forming—the third wave.

The names most associated with creating this third wave
are Cameron Townsend and Donald McGavran. Both
came out of the Student Volunteer Movement and served
as missionaries in different fields, Guatemala and India.
For almost half a century, Townsend waved the flag for the
overlooked tribal people. His passion led him to found
Wycliffe Bible Translators, dedicated to reaching into the
new frontiers with the Bible translated into the heart language of the people. At the same time, McGavran was dis-
covering a category of lost people he called homogeneous
units. Today we call them people groups. Slowly, but

surely, these two turned the attention of the missions world to the hidden, unreached peoples who did not know Jesus, nor had they been given opportunity to know Him.

International Conferences
Under Billy Graham's dynamic, inspiring leadership, the historic 1974 meeting of the International Conference on World Evangelization in Lausanne, Switzerland, drew 4,000 leaders from 150 countries. An exciting discovery was that half of the delegates were from the Third World. The conference focused attention on giving opportunity for *all* the world to know and worship Christ. The Lausanne meeting has proven to be extremely influential in the flow of attention to the unreached peoples of the world.

In 1980, a World Consultation on Frontier Missions was held in Edinburgh. Delegates from 57 Third-World missions organizations attended the consultation alongside delegates representing other missions agencies. An International Student Consultation was held simultaneously. Another significant meeting that same year was the Consultation on World Evangelism in Thailand.

In 1976, the Southern Baptist Convention Missions Challenge Committee asked the Convention to "set as its primary challenge that every person in the world shall have the opportunity to hear the gospel of Christ in the next twenty-five years." In 1977–78, the SBC approved and made ambitious plans for Bold Mission Thrust, a world evangelization effort for fulfilling the Great Commission by the year 2000. Convention agencies went all out in preparation, projecting 5-year planning cycles and setting performance goals. Churches were challenged to enlarge their giving by 15 percent annually.[25] The Bold Mission Thrust launch took place during the 1979 meeting of the SBC in the Astrodome in Houston, Texas, with Billy Graham as speaker. Twelve hundred responded to an impassioned invitation.

These gatherings and others like them brought attention to the new era in missions. A dramatic focus became giving opportunity for all peoples of all nations to know, love, and worship Jesus. The 1980s were splashed with the new wave of awareness and burden for people living in the uttermost parts of the earth in need of the Savior. Churches increasingly saw their God-intended role in fresh new ways that go back to the Scriptures—becoming a part our Lord's plan and intention that His people make disciples of *all* nations, thus bringing glory to God and joy to His people.

Prayer Leaders Team

Evidence suggests that a worldwide prayer awakening—or at least the beginning of such an awakening—is taking place. We see signs of it in our own land and hear many inspiring reports from around the world. For years I have had a special interest in, and a commitment to pray for, spiritual awakening to take place in our day.

In the 1980s a group comprised of those who had responsibility for providing prayer leadership for the SBC agencies for which we worked, began to pray together for such an awakening. Henry Blackaby of the Home Mission Board (now North American Mission Board) and T. W. Hunt and Avery Willis of the Sunday School Board (now LifeWay Christian Resources) and I, representing the Foreign Mission Board (now International Mission Board), came together for the singular purpose of seeking God in extraordinary ways and praying for the revival and spiritual awakening many were longing to see the Holy Spirit bring to His people and to the world. Earnestly, we prayed and envisioned such a time. Immediately we requested representatives from Woman's Missionary Union and the Brotherhood Commission to become a part of the group. Barbara Elder and Douglas Beggs joined our newly formed team.

An early emphasis (strategy) we agreed upon was the solemn assembly. Convinced God wanted us to encourage this biblical format of coming before Him in confession and repentance, we prepared a suggested plan for agencies, churches, and conventions to follow. Members of the team presented the concept to the executives of our own agencies as well as to the president of the Southern Baptist Convention and the chairman of the SBC Executive Committee. Each leader was receptive and affirming.

The Foreign Mission Board (now International Mission Board) was the first of the agencies to experience a solemn assembly, and other agencies held observances as well. Our team led a solemn assembly for the SBC Executive Committee in Nashville.

The most moving solemn assembly of all took place in Atlanta in 1992 as a part of the Southern Baptist Convention, when the entire Wednesday evening session was given to the experience. Twenty thousand people filled the hall to overflowing. Most importantly, God filled the hall with His Holy Spirit. Our earnest desire and prayer was that pastors and churches adopt and adapt the experience for use with their congregations. This happened in a number of churches across the nation.

We also worked with the implementation of the Bold Mission Prayer Thrust, a plan to support with specific prayer the accomplishment of the goals of Bold Mission Thrust (BMT). Our prayer leaders team requested each state convention to elect or select a Bold Mission PRAYER Thrust coordinator. These coordinators came together each year for prayer experiences and training for leading the churches of their states in implementing Bold Mission Prayer Thrust. In addition to attention to the BMT goals of global evangelization as a guide for prayer, there was a constant focus on prayer for revival and spiritual awakening in our land and around the world. A number of states caught the vision and implemented Bold Mission PRAYER Thrust among their churches.

Another part of our team's agenda was a series of national teleconferences focusing on prayer. Through SBC-Net, we connected with sites set up to interact with those gathered in the studio in Nashville—the prayer team and invited guests. This gave opportunity for interaction around the country with committed intercessors that resonated with the need and potential of God-ordained prayer and worldwide spiritual awakening.

For several years, a national prayer conference preceded the Southern Baptist Convention meetings in New Orleans, Atlanta, Indianapolis, and Houston. These conference sites have special meaning because of those who gathered to meet with God and one another and to give themselves to extraordinary praise and intercession. The prayer leaders team gathered at Glorieta and Ridgecrest, often in Nashville, but also in Richmond and Memphis for intensive times of prayer and seeking to discern God's heart and His directions.

Our work also led us to relate to the prayer leaders of other denominational and parachurch missions agencies and organizations. It was inspiring, challenging, and stretching to interact with those who were giving leadership in their agencies and organizations to many of the same goals to which we gave our hearts' attention concerning prayer for global evangelization.

Worldwide Prayer Movements

Today, more than ever before, many outstanding movements of prayer exist. Vast numbers of earnest intercessors in the non-Western world are mobilized and praying. Many organizations whose mission is strategic prayer for the world are based in the United States and work worldwide. Among them are Concerts of Prayer International; Lydia Fellowship; Esther Network; March for Jesus Movement; Youth with a Mission's Prayer for the Muslim World During Ramadan; Praying Through the 10/40 Window (now under the auspices of the Great Commission Global Roundtable); Global Harvest Ministries Network; Intercessors International. These represent extraordinary prayer efforts linking massive numbers of intercessors in united prayer.[26]

All missions organizations with initiatives related to global evangelization have prayer plans to support their initiatives and to employ prayer as strategy in reaching toward their goals. Indeed, evidence exists that we are on the front end of seeing extraordinary results from the cumulative power of massive strategic prayer involvement.

A Call to Another Level of Prayer
This brief overview is important in our context because the third wave of missions called God's people to another level of praying. Research data identified more than 10,000 unreached people groups, each needing, first of all, to have prayer lovingly and earnestly focused upon them—with very little information about them—except that they had no opportunity to know the Savior.[27] It is possible that many of those people groups had never before been prayed for. Millions were living behind doors closed to the gospel, doors which needed to be prayed open. In some situations, a new kind of missions personnel was needed for unique assignments. Strategic prayer was needed for bringing into the missions mix the appropriate strategies to draw the people to Jesus.

Yet, in a sense, how different is this level of prayer from that which the Moravians experienced? And William Carey? And Mary Webb? And the "sisters'" in Richmond? And Paul? No doubt, we have only rediscovered a dimension of prayer that has been discovered and rediscovered again and again since the days of Moses.

The next chapter will discuss the third wave, specifically in Southern Baptist missions, and the place of strategic prayer in its unfolding. To be a part of this era has been,

154

and continues to be, one of the cherished spiritual markers of my life. May we, with unified hearts, fully experience the joy of loving Christ devotedly, working closely with Him, and obediently praying toward the fulfillment of His greatest commandment and His Great Commission.

Questions for Reflection
What influence did the Moravians have on the development of prayer as strategy?

What was William Carey's view of the role of prayer in getting the gospel to the lost world?

Describe two nations in the twentieth century where prayer has been a major factor among its people.

What place does prayer have, generally, in American life today?

What are you doing in terms of strategic praying for revival and spiritual awakening in our nation and throughout the world?

[1]David Bryant, *In the Gap* (Ventura, CA: Regal, 1979), 155.
[2]F. J. Huegel, *Prayer's Deeper Secrets* (Grand Rapids, MI: Zondervan Publishing House, 1959), 72–74.
[3]Patrick Johnstone, *The Church Is Bigger Than You Think* (Great Britain: Christian Focus Publications, 1998), 78.
[4]Robert Southey, *The Life of Wesley* (London: Oxford University Press, 1925), 147.
[5]Johnstone, *The Church Is Bigger Than You Think,* 79.
[6]Ibid., 78.
[7]Charles W. Deweese, *Prayer in Baptist Life* (Nashville: Broadman Press, 1986), 35.
[8]James Leo Garrett Jr.,"Prayer," *Encyclopedia of Southern Baptists* (Nashville: Broadman Press, 1958), 2:1103.
[9]Timothy George, *Faithful Witness* (Birmingham, AL: New Hope, 1991), 53.
[10]Published first in Leicester, UK, 1792: Anne Ireland.

[11]Basil William Miller, *William Carey: Cobbler to Missionary* (Grand Rapids, MI: Zondervan Publishing House, 1952), 36.

[12]Johnstone, *The Church Is Bigger Than You Think,* 28.

[13]Miller, *William Carey,* 59–60.

[14]Herbert C. Jackson and Lynn E. May Jr., "Carey, William," *Encyclopedia of Southern Baptists* (Nashville: Broadman Press, 1958), 1:231.

[15]George, *Faithful Witness,* 32.

[16]Catherine Allen, *A Century to Celebrate* (Birmingham, AL: Woman's Missionary Union, 1987), 16.

[17]Ibid., 17.

[18]Proceedings, Triennial Convention, 1817, 133–34.

[19]William R. Estep, *Whole Gospel Whole World* (Nashville: Broadman and Holman Publishers, 1994), 119.

[20]Allen, *A Century to Celebrate.*

[21]Johnstone, *The Church Is Bigger Than You Think,* 31, quoting from Jonathan Chao, *The China Mission Handbook* (Hong Kong: Chinese Research Center, n.d.), n.p.

[22]Patrick Johnstone, *Operation World* (Grand Rapids: Zondervan Publishing House, 1993), 337.

[23]See chapter 7's account of the role of prayer in the fall of the Berlin Wall.

[24]Printed first in an article in 1981 in *Mission Frontiers* and reprinted in the November-December 1997 issue of the same magazine.

[25]Jesse C. Fletcher, *The Southern Baptist Convention: A Sesquicentennial History* (Nashville: Broadman and Holman Publishers, 1994), 264.

[26]See resource section for a more comprehensive list.

[27]Some use the number 12,000.

9

The Converging Streams of a New Paradigm

"But you are a chosen people, a royal priesthood, a holy nation, a people belonging to God, that you may declare the praises of him who called you out of darkness into his wonderful light" (1 Peter 2:9 NIV).

"All the nations . . . will come and worship before you, O Lord; they will bring glory to your name" (Psalm 86:9 NIV).

"Prayers have no boundaries. They can leap miles and continents and be translated instantly into any language."—Billy Graham[1]

From the dawn of Southern Baptist missions, prayer for missions has received major emphasis. Every president of the Foreign Mission Board (now International Mission Board; IMB) has exerted leadership in varying degrees in calling for prayer to be the foundation of missionary call and work. Significantly, Woman's Missionary Union (WMU), for more than a century, has continually raised high the flag of earnest prayer for missions.

When R. Keith Parks became president of the Foreign Mission Board (FMB) on January 1, 1980, one of his top leadership priorities became an intensification of prayer as a key component in missions. At the same time, he proposed to develop his vision in a unique way. He established an office of intercessory prayer and enlisted Catherine Walker, newly retired from a distinguished career as missionary to Indonesia, to direct this work. Parks and Walker had served together in Indonesia, and he knew firsthand of her humble and deeply prayerful spirit. Walker became special assistant to the president for intercessory prayer.

Her mandate was to create a process for receiving specific prayer requests from overseas missionaries and getting them into the hands and hearts of praying people in the United States. At the same time, she was to guide intercessors to pray in ways that God's work in a certain situations could be recognized and acknowledged as His response to the prayers of His people. Many overseas Missions (organizations of missionaries serving on the same field) already had prayer coordinators in place, but Walker systematically encouraged every Mission to select a prayer leader. Then she worked with these prayer coordinators, encouraging heightened communication of needs and a greater number of specific prayer requests more closely related to the details of missionaries' lives and work.

Walker also developed new and comprehensive ways to enlist pray-ers in committed intercession for overseas missions. Under her leadership, prayer requests from around the world were organized and filed electronically by country and by topic. Attempting to personalize requests, she also listed the missionary's home state and/or the missionary who sent in the request. A monthly mailout, "Called to Pray," communicated prayer needs and requests to praying people far and wide. A new era of getting personalized missionary prayer requests into the homes and churches of intercessors began. "Called to Pray" also included answers to prayer. Churches soon had access to taped prayer requests spoken by missionaries. Walker was, and continues to be, an inspired motivator of prayer for missions. "The rationale of prayer is obedience, not great answers," she declared again and again.

At the end of her 5 years of service on the Richmond staff, Walker retired (again!) in 1985. At that point I was asked to take her place. It was a bolt-out-of-the-blue thought to me—another of God's surprises. When I had come to the Board 3 years previously as assistant to the executive vice-president, I had assumed I would continue in that position as long as I remained with the board. However, even in my surprised state, I felt irresistibly drawn to the new place of service. It was work I believed in with all my heart—calling Southern Baptists and Baptists around the world to a life of prayer involvement with God and missionaries and a lost world. I resonated with the intensity of the prayer focus before me.

A New Paradigm
A new paradigm is a new model, a different way of seeing and doing things. Some of us did not know the word at that time. However, we would soon experience the concept, for several streams were destined to merge and to create a new paradigm—a new way of doing missions praying. This new paradigm related to employing and implementing prayer as strategy, the primary strategy, the first strategy to be employed—before any other strategy was brought into being. It related to specific, intentional, united praying for people living beyond the reach of the gospel.

Bold Mission Thrust
The first of the streams that would eventually merge to create the new paradigm was Bold Mission Thrust. In 1976, the Southern Baptist Convention adopted a world evangelization emphasis for the remainder of the century. The plan became known as Bold Mission Thrust and had the overarching goal that every person in all the world by the year 2000 would have opportunity to hear and respond

to the gospel of Jesus. Goals for the agencies and churches were developed and became the measuring rods for the years to come. During the Southern Baptist Convention meeting in Houston, Texas, in 1979, a challenging appeal was made for commitment to the ambitious goals of Bold Mission Thrust.

A New Leader

Keith Parks, elected in 1979 to succeed retiring Baker James Cauthen as leader of Southern Baptist overseas missions efforts, already was known for his passionate, single-minded burden for a world desperately in need of the Savior. His leadership became the second of the converging streams. Church historian William Estep, author of the most recent history of the Foreign Mission Board, believed it significant that in Parks's first official address to the board as president January 7, 1980, he used the term *global missions* five times and alluded to the concept repeatedly. "Therefore, virtually every action Parks attempted to lead the board to take was in the interest of his concept of global missions," Estep observed.[2] Parks's monthly column in *the COMMISSION* was entitled World in View, another constant reminder of his passion.

One of the specific Bold Mission Thrust goals assigned to the FMB was to have missionaries at work in 125 countries by the year 2000. Only a few years into the emphasis, Southern Baptists, led by the FMB, were already on course to reach that specific goal, ahead of schedule.[3] Yet Parks remained concerned that many of the 237 nations in the world were closed to the presence of missionaries. As matters stood then, there was no avenue for getting the gospel to the people behind the closed doors. At least 1.2 billion people had no opportunity for hearing and responding to the eternal life offered by a loving Savior.

Parks took no comfort in the assurance of reaching the goal of being in 125 countries. That would fall woefully short of the overarching goal to make the gospel available to all peoples of all 237 nations in their heart language. With his vision of global evangelization constantly in focus, Parks led FMB staff, trustees, and missionaries to seek ways to deal with the formidable task of "doing our appropriate part in fulfilling the Great Commission and Bold Mission Thrust."

A significant issue was the fact that the missions world was not divided neatly into nations. More accurately, it was divided into groupings of peoples who spoke the same language and had similar ethnicity, yet flowed across country borders. Many of these groupings of peoples were out of reach of the gospel. Ralph Winter had passionately communicated this perspective to the Lausanne Congress on World Evangelization in 1974 as he challenged the Christian world to give attention to the globe's hidden peoples. In 1980 the Edinburgh World Consultation on Frontier Missions focused attention on forgotten groups. The Lausanne Strategy Working Group reported further understandings of the unreached people groups and their unique, urgent need for the gospel in 1982.

Missions Research Data

David Barrett created the third converging stream. A noted British missions researcher and missiologist working in Nairobi, Kenya, Barrett had done major research on the peoples of the world for the purpose of missions advance. His data documented the validity, from a missions perspective, of relating to the lost world in terms of ethnolinguistic people groups rather than country borders. Barrett's tedious, trailblazing work, begun in 1969, was published in 1982 in the influential volume *World Christian Encyclopedia*.[4] His research is considered a key factor in today's encompassing emphasis on the unreached world by virtually all worldwide missions agencies.

The FMB brought Barrett to Richmond, Virginia, as a

consultant, making available his vast reservoir of data to their researchers and strategists. His computerized database contributed significantly to heightened information about and understanding of unreached people groups and closed countries. He noted more than 10,000 people groups and more than 300,000 large cities where the gospel was not being publicly proclaimed—virtually all of them behind closed doors.

Of course, we had known all along that multitudes of peoples were out of reach of the gospel, but our view of them was fuzzy. Now, with this valuable information available, we wanted and needed to know who they were, where they lived, and how they could be reached. We longed for them to know and worship Jesus. Our intense praying reflected that concern.

Indeed, the specific identity and locations of these unreached peoples were coming to light. Although unreached peoples can be found throughout the world, 85 percent of them lived in what Barrett called World A, the unreached world-areas stretching across North Africa, the Middle East, and Asia. The term *10/40 Window* is also a general designation for that part of the world, meaning from 10 degrees north to 40 degrees north of the equator, reaching from the Atlantic Ocean to the Pacific Ocean. Today the IMB's term for unreached peoples is the *Last Frontier.*

Shocking facts emerged. Sixty-five percent of the world's population lives in World A. Ninety percent of the world's poorest people live there. Residents of World A comprise 95 percent of those who have never had the opportunity to hear the gospel. Less than 1 percent of money given by Christians was going to efforts to get the gospel to the people of World A. Of the 51.4 million Bibles and 100 million Christian books printed, .01 percent went to the vast expanse of World A and its people groups. It follows that prayer attention to that large segment of the population was minuscule.

Information about the unreached peoples began to flow—the Kurds, Beja, Uzbeks, Kazakhs, Biharis, Kashmiris, Wolofs, Uighurs, Huis, Zhuang, Achenese, Sundanese were among the earlier peoples we "met." Among the closed countries upon which we focused our early attention were Mongolia and Albania.

One of the clearest facts before us was that, as things then stood, our traditional strategies had no way of touching those masses of peoples closed off from the gospel. Missionaries, Bibles, Christian radio broadcasts, the *Jesus* film—none were allowed. God dealt with us at a level that burdened and moved us at the core of our beings. We went to our knees, struggling with the role of prayer in the midst of crisp, new information that sharpened our vision and enlarged our burden.

Already we knew and experienced prayer as an absolute necessity in missions. Now God was revealing to us that in this radical missions world of unreached peoples, prayer is a strategy to be employed in opening closed doors and closed hearts. Equally significant, prayer is a strategy in calling responsive Christ followers to go into those restricted places as soon as doors are prayed open. Additionally, prayer is a strategy in praying for the preparation of the spiritual soil for the time when the gospel would be prayed into the midst of a people group.

The Father was teaching us! Prayer was not just a strategy in a list of strategies. Prayer was the first strategy to be employed—before any other strategy. In many locations at that time, prayer was the *only* strategy that could be employed, for all other strategies were banned. Yet there was no way anyone, not even the evil one himself, could ban our praying and the release of God's power into the midst of the people for whom He was directing us to pray.

A major development in the Southern Baptist missions picture took place in 1985 with the establishment of Cooperative Services International. Created to respond to exciting new opportunities to provide teachers and health and social services workers to China, this new arm of the FMB would also, in God's timing, become the means for sending personnel into many otherwise inaccessible countries. The concept of nonresidential missionaries (NRM) (later called strategy coordinators [SC]) was first articulated in 1986. Nonresidential personnel would soon be assigned to unreached people groups among whom they were not permitted to live because of local restrictions, yet they would be responsible for developing creative strategies for relating to, and providing services and ministries to, World A people groups. Their highest priorities were: (1) to develop a prayer network to focus specifically on the opening of the closed doors, the people, and their need for Christ; (2) to see that the Bible was translated, if not already available, in the group's heart language; (3) to determine the best means of sharing the gospel; and, in time, (4) to form a church with the new Christian believers. Evangelism That Results in Churches was more than a theme in Parks's leadership. The phrase captured the thrust of every strategy. The birth of NRM/SC would prove to be a challenging vision and have incalculable impact on the missions world.[5] These programs were birthed under the direction of Cooperative Services International.

On July 31, 1987, in a memo to Keith Parks and Bill O'Brien, I proposed that the Board's recently formed Global Strategy Group "officially declare that, in addition to being the most significant resource for the support of missions, prayer is the first and foremost strategy in world evangelization." The memo included mention of the strategic prayer plan soon to be launched. The plan called for enlisting churches willing to adopt and pray strategically for a specific, assigned closed country or unreached people group. The memo concluded with these words: "We are on holy ground as we deal with this awesome potential. May God in Christ reveal His plans for us to follow."

A major staff reorganization in 1987 geared the Board for global strategy. Many changes emerged for the purpose of "developing a deliberate global strategy to enable Southern Baptists to have our appropriate part in presenting the gospel to everyone in the world by the year 2000."[6]

As a part of the flow of the changes, the name of our office, the Office of Intercessory Prayer, was changed to the Office of International Prayer Strategy in order to more accurately reflect the new prayer approaches already in motion. Terri Willis, associate director, and Joanie Marsh, administrative secretary, not only did their jobs well but also brought much joy in the midst of our serious burdens and soul-stirring work. Often, I said, "We should not be having this much fun in the prayer office!"

Adopting People Groups

God had given us a strategic prayer plan. Foreign Missions Week at Glorieta Baptist Conference Center (now Glorieta, a LifeWay Conference Center), WMU Week at Ridgecrest (now Ridgecrest, a LifeWay Conference Center), and the FMB's 24-hour PrayerLine offered vehicles to implement the plan. Through these channels, Parks called for 100 churches to make a yearlong commitment to adopt and pray for a specific unreached people group or a closed country "where prayer is virtually the only strategy that can be employed."

More than 300 churches responded. The Office of International Prayer Strategy made adoption assignments of a closed country or an unreached people group to each responding congregation and began sending these churches monthly prayer bulletins, prepared by the Office of Communications, related to their assignments. Each church's commitment included united prayer that doors closed to Christian personnel would open and that God would call workers who would prepare themselves to go to that specific people group or restricted country, as soon as a crack in the door had been prayed into being. A crucial part of the assignment was prayer that the people's hearts would be readied for the gospel we envisioned they would hear one day.

Each month for a year, fresh information went to each church concerning their adopted people group or closed country, offering suggestions of how better to pray for their assignment. We suggested ways a church could make this an important emphasis in the life of the congregation. We stressed united, specific prayer, for we were committed to these two simple, but profound prayer principles: (1) the more united we pray, the more the power of prayer—God's power—is intensified; (2) the more specifically we pray, the more the power of prayer—God's power—is intensified.

The following year the call was sounded for 500 churches to receive a prayer strategy assignment of an adopted unreached people group or restricted country. Our office was covered with responses from congregations.

A new paradigm was taking form and shape. Indeed, God was leading us to pray in new ways. To our praying for missionaries and for the people with whom they worked, God was leading us to add a full-fledged emphasis on prayer for people with whom missionaries could not work. Thousands of intercessors began praying for people in remote parts of the world whose names we could not pronounce. Bringing praying people and praying churches into a dynamic partnership with God by employing prayer as strategy—His strategy for getting the gospel to all peoples—became our magnificent obsession. The streams had converged and created a new paradigm. It was to us a new way of doing prayer.

With awed excitement we began to see God bringing dramatic changes in those places and among those peoples for whom His people were praying and earnestly releasing His power. The next chapter provides three examples. As you read those accounts, keep in mind that today there is

no place on earth capable of remaining completely free of
Christian influence. Some other tactics of the early prayer
strategy follow.

The PrayerLine

The toll-free Foreign Missions (now International) Prayer-
Line, already in service during each year's Week of Prayer
for International Missions, was expanded and extended to
a 24-hour, every-day-of-the-week, all-year-long instrument
to communicate specific current prayer needs to committed intercessors. For the first time, crisis needs could get
into the hands and hearts of praying people immediately.
When an emergency need developed overseas, we immediately replaced the current message on the PrayerLine with a
description of the crisis and suggestions as to how to pray
for it. We urged groups and churches to tape-record the
messages and play them for worship services and other
gatherings of the congregation. Churches also printed
PrayerLine messages to distribute in handouts and place on
bulletin boards. The PrayerLine continues to be an effective lifeline between international prayer needs and intercessors at home.

Global PrayerGram

This monthly mailout of prayer needs served those who
preferred to have prayer requests in written form. The
Global PrayerGram lent itself for use especially by prayer
groups. Missionaries, and later strategy coordinators,
around the world provided the needs, requests, and reports
of answered prayer.

Prayer Networks

A prayer network, important for *every* missionary, was (and
is) an especially critical part of preparation, training, and
on-the-field relationships of those nonresidential personnel/
strategy coordinators assigned to unreached people groups.

In the early stages of training and orientation, I met individually with each NRM/SC personnel to pray and explore ways to establish a viable prayer network of intercessors for them, their families, their assigned people, and for God's guidance in bringing together all these meaningful components. This was one of my favorite parts of my work.

Prayer Alerts

Prayer alerts were designed to communicate, confidentially and safely, urgent prayer needs that could not be revealed openly. Because of possible negative repercussions to personnel and/or believers in restricted areas, we faced the tension of sharing as much information as possible in order for intercessors to pray as intelligently as possible.

Although our original system of prayer alerts seems painfully slow today, it was speedy for the 1980s! Faxes and mailouts of crisis prayer needs immediately went to a list of individuals and churches committed to give priority prayer attention to the urgency of the prayer alerts. FMB trustees and many other intercessors were kept aware and updated concerning the confidential crises.

One example of a dire crisis developed when a volunteer was directing a large, comprehensive program designed to improve the living conditions of the people in a restricted-access nation. Serving as his translator was a young American believer who lived in a neighboring country, also a restricted-access nation. As the project drew to a close, with no warning, the two men were kidnapped and held as hostages. Caught in a complex web of local political and ethnic infighting, they were pawns in the hands of totally unpredictable captors.

Prayer was desperately and instantly needed; yet we could not give out the information that would explain the seriousness of the situation. Revealing the facts could possibly mean disaster—even death—to those two men. We dared not place them in more jeopardy than they already faced.

168

Tedious, sensitive, and scary negotiations lasted for six months. We activated the Prayer Alert system to ask in vague terms, as clearly as we dared, that intercessors in this network pray more earnestly than ever before for a situation we could not describe in a country we could not reveal. The only information we made clear was that these prayer alerts represented an extremely volatile situation and could not be shared publicly. Twelve vagued-up prayer alerts were sent during this time of crisis. What a challenge to frame the messages in terms that would truly alert the pray-ers to the need for extraordinary prayer without using words that would incite retaliation if they were discovered by the wrong people! Many intercessors became involved; some of them were so attentive to the situation that they called our office for more frequent updates.

There was much praise to God when the workers finally were released unharmed. Those who took fuzzy prayer alerts into their hearts and prayed faithfully and earnestly made the difference. More accurately, God made the difference in response to the extraordinary intercessions of His people.

First Sunday Concert of Prayer for World Evangelization
The monthly concert of prayer for world evangelization called for churches, Sunday School classes, missions and prayer groups, and individuals to declare the first Sunday of every month a concert of prayer, joining with believers around the world in a prayer focus on global evangelization. We used the PrayerLine to communicate a major current prayer need each month and to share specific ways to pray for that need. We invited all Great Commission agencies and groups to participate by calling our PrayerLine's toll-free number and communicating the emphasis to their constituents.

Day of Prayer and Fasting for World Evangelization
In 1987, Keith Parks, attempting to develop a network of
Great Commission agencies, invited leaders of missions organizations with world evangelization plans to gather for
prayer and dialogue around their common goals. Although
there was little lead time, executives representing 20 missions agencies attended. This historic meeting signaled
forthcoming efforts to link with all other evangelical
groups committed to completing the Great Commission.

As the leaders gathered, a prayer meeting spontaneously
happened. Moved by the experience, the group agreed the
agencies they represented would issue a call for an annual
day of prayer and fasting for world evangelization. They
further agreed to call their constituents to pray specifically
for a designated unreached people group each year—one
that had little or no access to the gospel. They set the date
for the Saturday of Pentecost weekend. Thus the annual
Day of Prayer and Fasting was born, cosponsored by the
missions groups represented at the historic meeting.

Another outcome of the meeting related to research. Because of the work of David Barrett, the FMB had the
largest missionary database. Parks offered to share the vast
information with other agencies. More than 100 missions
organizations can now access the database for missionary
purposes.

The third result of the historic gathering was an agreement to find ways to work together more effectively. All
three developments have gained continuous momentum.

Through the years of promoting the Day of Prayer and
Fasting, after each year's prayer focus on a specific people
group, significant developments have taken place to create
opportunities for the gospel. Without exception, the featured unreached peoples are difficult, needy, hard-to-reach
groups. Even as we pray, we claim the biblical promise that
"nothing is too hard for Him" (Jer. 32:27).

Prayer Focus on Peoples of World Religions

An early effort in united praying for the peoples of the world was to focus love and prayer attention on the Muslim world. The FMB Communications Office created resources to support the emphasis. This became, and continues to be, an annual emphasis. In years since, the IMB has also encouraged prayer focus on other world religions.

The FMB also appointed a Muslim Ministry Task Force for the purpose of "raising Southern Baptist awareness of the Muslim world and to give focus to the needs and challenges of witness and ministry." Out of this task force came a recommendation that the FMB and the Home Mission Board (now North American Mission Board) cosponsor a Muslim Awareness Conference at Ridgecrest Baptist Conference Center (now Ridgecrest, a LifeWay Conference Center). Leaders of all Southern Baptist Convention agencies were invited to participate.

A resulting prayer strategy contained a variety of components, including a year of prayer for the Muslim peoples; quarterly prayer guides focusing on a different region of the Muslim world; video resources; and a 30-day prayer focus booklet.

Use of Prayer Pins

An attractive prayer pin, distributed to at least 200,000 individuals, served as a symbol and reminder for those making an intentional commitment to pray daily for global evangelization. Featured on the small pin was a pair of praying hands symbolically lifting up the world to God. The pin spoke volumes and opened many opportunities for witness in America and overseas and was especially appreciated by Christians in other lands. It may be a stretch to call prayer pins a strategy, but without a doubt, they created interest in the larger strategy of drawing the world to the Savior and the role of worship and intercession in such a worthy aspiration.

Adoption of Missionary or Missionary Family
Asking families, individuals, churches, and groups to adopt
a specific person or family as their prayer commitment
continues to be a meaningful endeavor. Not only is it reassuring and comforting to the missionaries, who give heartfelt testimonies concerning remarkable answers to prayer,
but also many intercessors express the joy of daily involvement in the lives and work of those on the front lines of
sharing the good news of Jesus in far-flung places.

Missionary Prayer Calendar
This simple but important strategy involves intercessors all
over the world in praying for missionaries specifically on
their birthdays. One amusing testimony came from a longtime missionary friend serving in East Africa who claimed
he preferred to play golf on his birthday. He would schedule his tee time as intercessors in America who lived in the
eastern time zone would arise. Then, he declared, as those
in the central time zone added their prayers for him, his
game always improved. When mountain time folks arose
and prayed for him, he would be at the top of his game. By
the time the sun came up Pacific time, he would be having
his best game of the year!

Seriously, endless examples exist of remarkable "happenings" on the birthdays of missionaries. One relates to Ivory
Coast missionaries Travis and Kim Forsythe and their 2-
year-old son, Nathanael. Travis and Nathanael were traveling home to Dabakala when they stopped for food in a city
on the way. Bandits, at gunpoint, descended on the
Forsythe car. Travis clung to the open door, trying to con-
vince the gunmen to let him get Nathanael out of the vehi-
cle. The driver shot and wounded Travis, who chased the
car as it sped away with his son in the backseat.

Kim Forsythe was home in bed with complications in her
pregnancy. Their 5-year-old daughter, Gloria, was with her.
It was Kim's 30th birthday, which meant that thousands of

Southern Baptists were praying for her even as the gunmen attacked her husband and kidnapped her son.

Meanwhile, within an hour after the carjacking, the gunmen put Nathanael out of the car and left him alone on a dark road in a village. Villagers found him and placed him in the care of a midwife, who fed and bathed the child and put him to bed while authorities located and notified his parents.

By 1:30 A.M. Nathanael was back with his family. Travis's injury was miraculously superficial, as the bullet had passed through his right side between the ribs without hitting any vital organs.

Even without knowing their specific circumstances and needs, faithful intercessors make a difference in the lives of missionaries through their prayers. We cannot humanly calculate the power released by the prayers of God's people. Many missionaries declare that they take on difficult spiritual challenges and tasks on their birthdays, knowing they are being specifically covered with prayer on that day.

Creative Access Project

Another, more extensive form of the adoption model developed under the leadership of Bill O'Brien, former executive vice-president of the FMB. A group of large churches from across the nation, representing a variety of perspectives on denominational matters but having a clear response to God's call to be on mission with Him, was asked to partner with the FMB in focusing on an agreed-upon people group in a "creative access project." This meant developing a relationship with a people group that would be open to involvements with the adopting church in America. The church's first commitment was to a strong prayer emphasis on behalf of the assigned people. The second goal was for members of the church to go overseas, relate directly to the leadership of the people group, and seek ways the church's laypersons could offer, on-site and in

person, their professional skills, business acumen, gifted-
ness, and talents to the people group.

One of the participating churches was Johnson Ferry
Baptist Church in Marietta, Georgia. The congregation is
a vibrant example of a people of God who received a vision, embraced it, and would not let it go. They were
asked to adopt the Kyrgyz people of Kyrgyzstan in the former Soviet Union.

Johnson Ferry's prayer coordinator, Elaine Helms, led
the prayer involvement. One Sunday every month, the
church bulletin included an insert giving the latest news
and prayer needs from the FMB prayer office about the
Kyrgyz.

At a point well into the prayer portion of the project,
Alex Thompson, international *Jesus* film coordinator for
Campus Crusade, heard of the church's involvement with
the Kyrgyz. Thompson was soon to leave for the former
Soviet Union to work on arranging further translation of
the *Jesus* film into the language of the Kyrgyz and to seek
permission and plans for its distribution. At that point,
conditions were unpredictable, for it was not long after the
fall of the Berlin Wall. Aware that the Johnson Ferry congregation would give special prayer attention to the project, Thompson contacted the church and asked them to
pray for him, for the work being done on the translation of
film project, and the important arrangements for distribution. When he arrived in Kyrgyzstan, Thompson found
that the translation of the film into the heart language of
the people had been completed already! Arrangements for
distribution went smoothly.

Thompson reported back to the church upon his return.
The congregation was excited to hear of the obvious hand
of God upon the project. They were thrilled by the part
they had contributed through their work of intercession.
Their personal and corporate prayers became more intense
and specific for the Kyrgyz people. In February 1992, a

team from the church made a mission survey trip to
Bishkek, Kyrgyzstan's capital, to seek ways God wanted to
use their church in relating to this people located ten time
zones away. A major breakthrough developed when the
Kyrgyz minister of health allowed the Johnson Ferry
Church to fill the position of coordinator for reorganizing
health care for the entire country!

Working with other churches and organizations, the
Johnson Ferry Church provided humanitarian aid ship-
ments including medical/dental equipment, warm cloth-
ing, and curriculum for the medical institute. They established a business development program to help Kyrgyz
believers achieve economic self-sufficiency, which in turn
bolsters the needed resources of the local church. The
Johnson Ferry Church also provides a monthly mail service, manned by volunteers, to ensure that field workers in
Kyrgyzstan will receive mail and packages from friends and
loved ones at home.

Over the years, about 100 members of the Johnson
Ferry congregation have traveled to Kyrgyzstan. On the
home front, approximately 1,000 members have been personally involved in some way with the project.

Prayer coordinator Elaine Helms says, "These are only a
few of the ways God has led us to minister to the Kyrgyz
while He is drawing them to Himself. We give Him all the
praise for including us through prayer. We stepped out in
faith, never dreaming of all that God had in mind when
He called us to pray for the Kyrgyz people."

Today the Johnson Ferry congregation remains intricately involved with "their" people—with continuing joy.
It all began when they agreed to a God-breathed assignment and went to the Lord in consistent, focused, specific,
united prayer for the unreached people and for open doors
to their land and their hearts.

The basic strategy has remained intact: connect
churches with a specific unreached people for adoption,

and first bring to bear the strategic nature of loving intercession. Today's PRAYERplus commitments promoted by the IMB bring missions alive for many of God's people in similar ways.

Evangelism That Results in Many Churches

David Garrison, associate vice-president of strategy coordination and mobilization of the IMB, documents the phenomenon of today's current church planting movement.[7] Defining a church planting movement as "a rapid and exponential increase of indigenous churches planting churches within a given people group or population segment," Garrison gives illustrations of "startling accounts of hundreds, thousands, even tens of thousands coming to faith in Christ, forming into churches and spreading their new-found faith."[8] Many of the following examples from Garrison's work are from areas that once were classified as restricted, or even closed.

In a southeast Asian country, a strategy coordinator found only three churches and 85 believers among a population of more than 7 million lost people. Four years later there were more than 550 churches and nearly 55,000 believers.

In a city in China, more than 20,000 people came to faith in Christ, resulting in more than 500 new churches.

In Latin America, two Baptist unions grew from 235 churches in 1990 to more than 3,200 in 1998.

In central Asia, a strategy coordinator told of estimating about 200 believers in the churches in the area. The following year, the number of baptisms added up to 15,000.

In western Europe, a missionary reported starting 15 new church cell groups before leaving for a six-month stateside assignment. When he returned, there were at least 30 churches.

A missionary strategy coordinator in Ethiopia commented, "It took us 30 years to plant 4 churches in this country. We've started 65 cell churches in the last six months."

Amazing! How can we understand such a phenomenon? Garrison believes universal elements are present in every church planting movement, the first of which is prayer. "Prayer has been fundamental to every church planting movement we have observed. Prayer typically provides the first pillar in a strategy coordinator's master plan for reaching his or her people group. However, it is the vitality of prayer in the missionary's personal life that leads to its imitation in the life of the new church and its leader," he says.

The third wave of missions, to borrow a term from the previous chapter, splashes over into this chapter, and it is larger and more encompassing than we dared to dream. God is more powerful, in response to the prayers of His people, than we know how to comprehend. We are seeing daily evidences of His perfect love and spectacular glory.

Current Leadership
Under Randy Sprinkle's capable leadership as director of the Office of International Prayer Strategy since 1994, strategic prayer emphases have been enhanced. Randy and Nancy Sprinkle served as missionaries in Ethiopia, Botswana, and Lesotho. Randy did pioneer work in prayer as he and Nancy opened work for Southern Baptists in Lesotho.

One morning back in 1986, I picked up my ringing telephone and heard Randy's greeting. Our conversation began with a warm exchange of catch-up news. Then he told of their assignment to open Southern Baptist work in Lesotho, in southern Africa. I resonated with his vision of prayer as the foundation of every aspect of the new work. He shared his conviction that God had revealed to him that He had prepared a whole state to have a strategic role in Lesotho involving informed, earnest prayer for each decision, each step, each emerging ministry even before it

came into being. "But," he said, "I do not have a clue
which state would be able to take on such a challenging
commitment." Even as he spoke, in the back of my heart, I
knew which state the Father had prepared. Randy was simply asking, "Can you help?"

Without knowing Missouri was his home state, I told
him of the effective statewide prayer network operated by
Missouri WMU, which included praying women, men,
and youth throughout the state. It seemed instantly clear
to me that the Sprinkles' work and the Missouri network
would be the perfect match. With the dynamic leadership
of Missouri WMU executive director Alberta Gilpin, I
knew before asking that Missouri WMU would be challenged and eager to lead in this strategic prayer involvement. Were they ever! Randy tells the story of the
Missouri/Lesotho Prayer Partnership eloquently in his
book *Until the Stars Appear.*[9] Imagine my joy when, upon
my retirement, Randy became my successor in the Office
of International Prayer Strategy.

A New Century and New Directions

As the new century approached, a major restructuring
under IMB president Jerry Rankin's leadership placed most
missionaries worldwide on strategic teams assigned to
people groups. Not only is the unreached world more naturally divided into people groups, but research and world
events also indicate that most of the rest of the world sepa-
rates itself more naturally in this manner rather than by
country borders. Thus, the team concept has been incorporated, and the people group principle is being given priority profile and responsibilities in current directions.

Prayer: The Continuing Essential

The use of email, the Internet, and other technologies have
greatly enhanced and broadened communication of daily
prayer concerns and crisis situations from all corners of the

earth. Prayer networks of intercessors are only a keystroke away from knowing how to pray in immediate terms for those missionaries and peoples to whom they have made one of the most important commitments in the Christ-following life—earnest intercession.

Thus, the goal continues to be to respond with humble, contrite hearts to the remarkable words of our Lord, "Ask of me, and I will make the nations your inheritance"(Psalm 2:8 NIV). How faithful God is to do what He says He will do.

Prayer carries an awesome role in missions and global evangelization. Yet even in acknowledging such a fact and emphasizing the power of God Himself released by prayer, we must be careful to communicate accurately the place of prayer as it relates to the Scriptures and to the communication of the gospel. John Piper makes this point best: "I am not comfortable with calling prayer 'THE work of missions.' I believe wholeheartedly that it is the proclamation of the gospel that is the work of missions. I do not say this from a desire to minimize the place of prayer, or to jeopardize its awesome indispensability. Rather I say it out of zeal for the place of the word of God in missions. Prayer is the power that wields the weapon of the word, and the Word is the weapon by which the nations will be brought to faith and obedience."[10]

Indeed, people are saved by their response to hearing and believing the word of God about Jesus. Yet it is prayer that releases the power of God and the gospel into lives. The salvation of the nations depends on the proclaiming of God's word. We must not fail in that proclamation. Neither must we fail in our praying.

Questions for Reflection

What is the role of prayer in global evangelization?

On a scale of 1 to 10, how do you rate your own awareness of strategic praying?

On the same scale, how do you rate your concern for those who do not have opportunity to hear the gospel?

Do your prayers reflect the degree (or lack thereof) of your concern?

Has your church had the experience of adopting an unreached people group?

If not, what can you do to help encourage such a commitment?

[1]Billy Graham, *Hope for the Troubled Heart* (Minneapolis: Grayson, 1991), 151.
[2]William R. Estep, *Whole Gospel Whole World* (Nashville: Broadman and Holman Publishers, 1994), 340.
[3]The goal was reached in 1990.
[4]David B. Barrett, *World Christian Encyclopedia: A Comparative Study of Churches and Religions in the Modern World, AD 1900–2000* (Oxford, England: Oxford University Press, 1982). A new, three-volume edition of this classic reference source has just come off the press, edited by David Barrett, George T. Kurian, and Todd M. Johnson. This work offers a fuller comparative scope, pays greater attention both to the other world religions and to the secular realm, and describes more fully the range of Christian attempts to relate to both.
[5]For more information on the nonresidential missionary concept, see V. David Garrison, *The Non-Residential Missionary: A New Strategy and the People It Serves* (Monrovia, CA: MARC, 1990).
[6]Estep, *Whole Gospel*, 355, quoted from FMB Minutes, October 9–11, 1987.
[7]Garrison served as the first director of the nonresidential missionary program.
[8]David Garrison, *Church Planting Movements* (Richmond, VA: International Mission Board, 1999). For copies, call 1-800-866-3621 or visit the IMB Web site at www.imb.org.
[9]Randy Sprinkle, *Until the Stars Appear* (Birmingham, AL: New Hope, 1994).
[10]John Piper, *Let the Nations Be Glad* (Grand Rapids, MI: Baker Books, 1993), 62.

Case Studies on the Role of Strategic Prayer

"See, I have placed before you an open door" (Rev. 3:8 NIV).

"How to multiply the number of Christians who, with clear, unshakeable faith in the character of God, will wield this force of intercession—that is the supreme question of foreign missions."—Andrew Murray[1]

God, when He wants to do something, first leads His people to pray, as the stories in this chapter illustrate.[2] This divine/human partnership brings together the intercessions of His people and the faithful release of His power.

Those churches first responding to the call to enter a prayer involvement with a closed country or unreached people group may not have realized it at the time, but they were pioneers in another dimension of Southern Baptist missions praying. They employed prayer as an intentional strategy at a time when prayer was the only possible strategy, for doors were closed to all other strategies among those peoples.

Today, no nation is considered completely closed. Some have entrance restrictions, but entry, under certain conditions, is possible. An amazing number of Southern Baptists, as well as Christian missions personnel from other denominations, currently work among the people groups for whom many intercessors first began to pray during the 1980s. An amazing number of unreached people now know Jesus as Savior and Lord. An amazing number of churches have been planted with local believers now preaching the gospel.

It is important to fully acknowledge that intercessors from many denominations and missions organizations were praying strategically also, and our prayers were lovingly intermingled before the Throne of God. In fact, Christ followers representing multiple missions agencies made significant contributions to the developments described in the three stories in this chapter. Only heaven knows the full impact of praying people and praying churches in opening doors once tightly closed to the gospel. We on this earth have the joy of seeing and celebrating some of the results. Each of these three stories is unique, illustrating, among other things, God's creativity in answering the prayers of His people for the fulfillment of His purposes.

The Kazakhs
In 1988–89, the second year of the prayer adoption strategy for closed countries and unreached people groups, a number of churches received the Kazakh people of the Republic of Kazakhstan as their assignment. Located in the (then) Soviet Union, Kazakhstan is four times the size of Texas with a population of 18 million people, 8 million of whom are Kazakhs. The remainder is made up of ethnic Russians, Ukrainians, and Koreans, as well as other central Asian people.

First Baptist Church, Pineville, Louisiana, was one of the churches who adopted the Kazakh people and agreed to pray for them in a focused way. Although the Kazakhs were a new name to this congregation, various individuals and groups and, most especially, the church's International Department, were faithful to lift the Kazakhs to our Lord. Earnestly and over a period of time they prayed for ways for the gospel to be communicated in the heart language of this faraway people. God placed a caring love in their praying hearts for the Kazakhs.

By now, it was March 1990, only a few months after the fall of the Berlin Wall. To the surprise of this congregation, they found as they read their local newspaper one morning a picture of several government officials from—Kazakhstan. They could not believe their eyes. Kazakhs were right there in Pineville! The accompanying article told of the delegation from Kazakhstan traveling to different locations in the United States, exploring the possibility of establishing linkages and exchange programs between Kazakhstan and the US.

Intercessors excitedly made contact with the visitors from Kazakhstan. Working hastily, they secured Bibles and presented them to their gracious visitors. If we could have foreseen the future and told those intercessors that representatives from the unheard-of people for whom they were praying would one day show up in their city, they could not have believed it. God is so creative when His people offer Him their earnest prayers!

Meanwhile, after years of veiled existence under strict Soviet rule, Kazakhstan was ready for new relationships with other peoples of the world. Different parts of central Asia had varied degrees of openness, but after the demise of the USSR, areas became open to Christians who were willing to offer economic and social aid and development to that part of the world.

The Central Asian Foundation, a nonprofit human and economic development corporation, initiated a Kazakh-American Cultural Festival to be held in Kazakhstan June 21–July 6, 1991. Kazakhstan's Golden Apple Foundation assisted the Central Asian Foundation. A major partner in the endeavor was the Baptist Convention of Pennsylvania/South Jersey. Three hundred thirty volunteers were enlisted to go to Kazakhstan to be a part of the humanitarian, cultural, and economic projects involved in the festival. Only the blessing of God upon a plan could have pulled together such a gigantic undertaking.

During opening ceremonies in Kazakhstan on June 21, Kazakhstan president Nursultan Nazarbayev described his republic as a crisis situation and told the Americans: "This festival was conceived as an opportunity to get closely acquainted with new friends. Your hand of help is a symbol of friendship which spreads to our people."

Through this effort the volunteers were the first ones in on the ground floor of a new beginning for the Kazakh people. Through forged friendships, the people shared hopes and dreams, as well as testimonies. Neither people would ever look at the other in the same way again.

The Americans dealt with the highest levels of government in this effort. Members of the volunteer team from the US had opportunity to meet with and witness to the leaders of the country.

The Golden Apple Foundation had requested the Americans to provide, among other things, a team to address issues of religion. Bringing together religious leaders of the region's major faiths—Islam, Russian Orthodox, Seventh-Day Adventists, Baptists—the gathering was the first of its kind in Kazakhstan. During the conference held in a large auditorium in Almaty, the capital city, Kazakh and American keynote speakers delivered addresses, followed by discussions. Television, radio, and newspaper reporters attended and reported the unusual event. Only a year earlier, Protestant leaders feared imprisonment for practicing their faith in Kazakhstan. Now their pictures appeared on the front pages of the area's newspapers with Islamic, Russian Orthodox, and Seventh-Day Adventist leaders! The climactic moment was the signing of a manifesto calling for laws to guarantee religious freedom and stating that the government should not interfere in any religious confession—either by restriction or favoritism.

Four other cities in Kazakhstan hosted activities. A host of team members including medical personnel (who brought footlockers loaded with medicines nonexistent in Kazakhstan), business and professional people, technical specialists, educators (all of whom led seminars in their fields), university students, construction workers, pastors, media producers, athletes, musicians, linguists, craftsmen, and performing artists worked across the land. Each morning on the front page of the local *Pravda* newspaper, the daily schedule of concerts, seminars, classes, sports events, and the array of activities available to the Kazakh people appeared.

One project took place in the city of Zaisan. The previous year an earthquake, with no warning of impending disaster, had ripped apart the foundations of homes and buildings, leaving 14,000 people homeless. Most of the people were outside their homes at the time of the quake, a local custom in the evening. One 2-year old child was killed. If the earthquake had occurred a few hours later, officials estimated that 7,000 would have died inside their totally destroyed homes. The disaster affected 80 percent of the town's population. News of the earthquake and its devastation never leaked outside Soviet Central Asia. Thus, no help came, either from international aid organizations or from the Soviet central government.

Cooperative Services International (CSI), on an earlier fact-finding tour, had learned about the disaster. Schools were unsafe. Many children were attending classes in makeshift arrangements. CSI appropriated $120,000 for the devastated city. A 15-man construction team came as a part of the festival to help with three projects: repair a boarding school dormitory; build a Kazakh-American Friendship

Center; and break ground for a new US-Kazakh school.

Local festival director Dusenbek Nkipov called the Zaisan project "the most humanitarian work of the festival." The construction projects in Zaisan became a focal point of humanitarian aid in Kazakhstan.

During the building projects, a city official asked the Americans to pray for rain for the drought-parched area. In the worship service that evening at the dormitory where the group stayed, the team prayed for the people of the city and then prayed specifically for God to provide the desperately needed rain.

The next morning dark clouds formed. By noon rain began to fall steadily. The Kazakh interpreter assigned to the visitors had witnessed the special time of prayer for rain the previous evening. In amazement he stopped everyone he saw and told the story: "The Americans prayed to their God for rain, and He answered their prayers!" The rain continued for three days.

Reliable estimates of Kazakhs attending and participating in various aspects of the festival were 100,000. Opportunities for witness abounded. Four hundred professions of faith were reported. Twenty discipleship groups began meeting. The first Kazakh-speaking church in the world was formed.

All expectations were exceeded, resulting in an array of continuing humanitarian, environmental, business, and social projects. The cultural festival marked the defining moment for the establishment of evangelical witness among the Kazakhs. Scores of the short-term volunteers who came from America to participate in the festival from several different evangelical groups have since moved to Kazakhstan as full-time workers.

The Kazakh-American International Business Institute opened November 18, 1991. The first courses included English, international trade, marketing, business ethics, accounting, and finance. The project was established in cooperation with the Kazakh government and supported partly through CSI.

In December 1991, the Kazakh-American Friendship Center opened in Zaisan. The friendship center was but one of the humanitarian projects funded in Central Asia through CSI.

A second Kazakh-American Cultural Festival was held May 10–15, 1992, in the United States at the invitation of the Baptist Convention of Pennsylvania/South Jersey. Virginia and other states assisted in hosting the group. Three hundred Kazakhs made the trip and participated in the multifaceted exchange.

The story of Kazakhstan is so extensive that an entire dissertation has been written on it. To do justice to those who had key roles, Cooperative Services International personnel need to be highlighted and interwoven throughout the account. There is no way to adequately describe their strategic involvement.

From the vantage point of the prayer strategy focus, this story began when intercessors in First Baptist Church, Pineville, and other churches adopted the Kazakh people and began praying earnestly for the release of God's power, love, grace, mercy, and salvation into their lives and land.

The concerted prayer effort for the Kazakhs began in 1988–89. Today there are 60 Kazakh churches with more than 4,000 believers.

Mongolia

All my life I thought Mongolia was the end of the earth. When I went there a few years ago, I became certain that it was.

History sets the fascinating stage. In 1266, Kubla Khan, leader of the most impressive empire of that era in world history, asked the journeying Marco Polo and his uncles to take a message to Rome requesting that the church send to Mongolia "100 men of learning devoted to the Christian faith, who would be able to prove 'to the learned . . . by just and fair argument, that the faith professed by Christians is superior to and founded on more evident truth than any other.'"[3]

Historian Stephen Neill asserts, "If attention had been paid to this request at the time, the results might have been considerable."[4] However, no one was sent to Mongolia for more than 20 years. When the church finally sent two teachers of the Christian faith, one died on the way. By then Kubla Khan had "grown too old in idolatry,"[5] the historian records, and the Mongol leader was no longer interested in anything new. In the meantime, Buddhist monks had arrived and had taught the court and the people Buddhism. As a result, Buddhism became the religion of the Mongolian people.

Beginning in 1920, a revolution supported by the Soviet army established a Communist government that dominated the land for 70 years. In 1990 Communism was renounced. A 1992 constitution adopted a multiparty democracy. In a recent election, in spite of the limited number of polling stations and vast distances between them, more than 90 percent of the eligible population voted. The population is surprisingly well informed and has a literacy rate of 90 percent.

Economically, Mongolia is curiously immune from full-fledged industrialization. However, the nation has important copper and gold mines and is the world's largest source of cashmere.

With this broad sweep of a historical brush of that far-away land, now come to Atlanta, Georgia. The year is 1986. The FMB began to focus prayer more intensely on those countries and peoples where the gospel was not allowed. We were drawn to Mongolia. Research revealed only five known Christians behind Mongolia's closed doors. We became burdened for the 2.5 million people of Mongolia, a people cut off from the rest of the world.

Attending a luncheon during the WMU Annual Meeting in Atlanta one June day, I sat at the same table with Maxine Bumgarner, executive director of West Virginia WMU. In the midst of our conversation, Maxine commented that she looked forward to the day when the West Virginia Baptist Convention grew large enough numerically and financially to have a country partnership, like many of the larger/older state conventions had with Baptist unions and conventions on established missions fields. I heard myself saying, "In the meantime, would you be interested in having a prayer involvement with a closed country, where prayer is the only strategy that can be employed?"

Maxine said she had already considered that possibility, knowing so well the praying hearts of West Virginia women. We discussed the potential adoption and parted with quiet excitement.

As I returned to Richmond praying to know our Lord's mind, the nation of Mongolia kept coming into my thoughts. I consulted with Lewis Myers, director of Cooperative Services International. Aware that he and his wife, Toni, would soon be going to China with the hope of getting into Mongolia for the first time, we discussed Mongolia as a possible prayer assignment for West Virginia. I reported back to Maxine. She was immediately captured by the challenging possibility. In fact, she called Lewis Myers and invited him to come to West Virginia to report his findings as soon as possible after his return.

As the Myerses made their way to the other side of the world, their own Sunday School class and other intercessors prayed that they would be permitted to enter Mongolia. They were able to get into the country; they made the trip as tourists from China to Mongolia by train. In an extraordinary development, Myers was permitted to meet personally with the nation's minister of education and asked if there were ways Americans could help him in his work. The answer was, "Yes. Send teachers!" Mongolia was desperately in need of English teachers and those qualified to teach in the medical field. Indeed, these were personnel needs the FMB would be able to meet without delay.

Upon his return from Mongolia, Myers went to West Virginia and reported to the assembled state WMU officers council. He described the wonder of the slightly open door to Mongolia. To give the women options from which to choose as they sought the Lord's leadership, Myers told of several unreached people groups who also needed to be adopted. Then, leading the discussion back to Mongolia, he explained that now, with God's opening the door to workers, there would be a special need to enlarge the base of prayer involvement with Mongolia. West Virginia could be significant in the future of the gospel in that nation, Myers told them, by becoming powerfully and prayerfully committed from the very beginning of the relationship. The response of the West Virginia women was electric. The officers council voted unanimously to adopt and pray for Mongolia.

The project quickly began to take form and shape. Maxine led the entire Baptist Convention of West Virginia to join WMU in taking this commitment seriously. We provided from the FMB all the information we could muster at that early stage, for it was scarce and sporadic. West Virginia WMU did outstanding work in creating excitement and burden for the Mongol people among churches throughout the state.

A remarkable level of prayer interest developed. With the scarcity of information, Maxine taught the churches to rely heavily on praying personalized Scriptures, such as Isaiah 60:15–16: "Although you, Mongolia, have been forsaken and hated, with no one traveling through, I will make you, Mongolia, the everlasting pride and the joy of all generations. Mongolia, you will drink the milk of nations and be nursed at royal breasts. Then, Mongolia, you will know that I, the Lord, am your Savior, your Redeemer, the Mighty One of Jacob."

Still, the project was not all mountaintop experiences. In the early days especially, before long-term workers were in place, it was difficult to see God's hand at work. Were the prayers making a difference? Inevitably, just when discouragement threatened, some word would come—a small group of volunteers returned from a three-month assignment of training English teachers in Mongolia—and they brought an encouraging report of positive developments. A group returned from helping to create an English curriculum for the Mongolian schools—another spurt of excitement and assurance that God was faithful in hearing their prayers. One reassurance even came in the *Charleston (W. Va.) Gazette,* when a small article on an inside page of the newspaper announced that a translation of the New Testament into the Mongolian language had been completed. "Imagine," the West Virginia women exclaimed, "God's announcement of His answering our prayers is in our newspaper!"

In 1991, a pharmacist and his wife were the first long-term workers God called and placed in Mongolia. After 2 years of teaching in a medical school (as well as English classes), they returned to the States for appointment as career missionaries. A busload of West Virginia Baptists made the trip to attend the appointment service. Only then did the intercessors learn the timing of the couple's call to Mongolia—shortly after the people of West Virginia had begun to pray for laborers for Mongolia. The couple was the first fruit of their prayers as other workers began to hear and respond to God's call.

West Virginia was the first of the smaller and newer state conventions that soon would be receiving assignments for prayer adoptions of unreached peoples. The churches in these conventions had significant roles in the early development of prayer as strategy. Their unheralded prayers have made, and continue to make, a tremendous difference in God's kingdom on earth.

Five years after that Atlanta conversation, with Myers's encouragement, I began to plan a prayer journey to World A. Eager to include Mongolia in our itinerary, I called West Virginia to ask Maxine if she would be interested in going. Was she ever!

Flying from Irkutz, Siberia, to Ulan Bator, Mongolia,[6] anticipation seemed to heighten as we landed. Our personnel working there met us at the airport. We had been told in previous communications that we would have opportunity to meet some Mongol believers who also had been told of our focused prayer interest in them. In addition, they had been briefed about the West Virginia/Mongolia prayer adoption led by Maxine.

The next morning, we met the first of our new friends, a beautiful young woman whose Christian name is Ruth. She wept as she was introduced to Maxine, and hugged her and held her hand all morning. Again and again she said, "Thank you for praying for me. Thank you for praying for my people. Thank you for praying for my country."

Sara, another new Christian, joined us for lunch and spent the remainder of the day with us. Again, bonding took place immediately. When they parted in the evening, Ruth said to Maxine, "Since you prayed for me for 5 years before I became a Christian, I feel you are my mother."

Meanwhile, as we prayerwalked and fellowshipped with personnel at work in Mongolia, the young women left Maxine's side only to sleep in their own beds at night. Maxine called them her daughters, and they glowed with joy. We hugged them, wept, laughed, prayed together, and hugged some more. In a very real way, these young women represented to us many unreached peoples for whom we had prayed strategically without knowing names and faces. They said again and again, "Thank the people of America for praying for us and for sending people to tell us about Jesus."

How we celebrated the release of God's power and the work of His hand in response to the prayers of His people! We rejoiced in the willingness of those workers whom God had called to come to this cold (even in May), difficult, remote end of the earth. We thanked the Lord for those who gave financially to provide means to make it possible for Mongolians to know, love, and worship Him.

Several years later, Ruth traveled to America and stayed for two months in Maxine's home in West Virginia. Only then did Ruth confide to Maxine that her mother had abused her because of her faith in Christ and then disowned her. Only then did Maxine understand the emotional depth of the statement Ruth had made to her in Mongolia. The two women prayed together, studied God's Word, sang, spoke in churches, met with women's groups, and had daily family time with Maxine's mom in a local nursing home.

One day Maxine described to Ruth how she had spent a certain period of time praying from Isaiah 60 for the Mongolian people. Ruth exclaimed that a new believer in her church in Mongolia had written a song that expressed the message of the chapter. The remarkable thing was that the new Christian had never read Isaiah nor had she ever written a song before. Together Maxine and Ruth tracked the timeline and discovered that the writing of the song coincided with Maxine's praying the Isaiah passage. Ruth began to call Maxine *Aja* (beautiful mother). The bonds had grown even deeper.

On February 24, 1994, the first church was constituted in Mongolia with government recognition. The historic group had begun as a Bible study in the home of volunteers Gary and Evelyn Harthcock (aged 77 and 75!). Government officials sat in the midst of the congregation. Some observers commented that the Book of Acts was being reenacted in Mongolia.

After centuries of darkness, now there are more than 35 missions agencies at work in Mongolia. Many Mongol fellowships and congregations meet every week. The number of Christian believers is estimated at about 5,000. Now Mongol evangelists are sharing the gospel. An estimated 1 million people in Mongolia have seen the *Jesus* film. The New Testament in the people's heart language is being widely distributed.

Indeed, God's deeds are marvelous when His glory is declared among the nations (see Psalm 96:3).

Albania

Albania was also among the closed countries we assigned to churches for adoption. In 1967, Albania's Communist parliament voted the nation a pure atheistic state, proudly proclaiming it to be the world's most atheistic nation. New laws made it a criminal offense to have any kind of religious affiliation. Christians were persecuted, some savagely. Bulldozers leveled churches, cathedrals, even mosques. Christianity almost disappeared.

Yet God already had placed Albania on the hearts of some of His people, exemplifying another of God's principles. J. Edwin Orr, prayer statesman and historian, is often quoted as saying, "When God is ready to do a new thing with His people, he always sets them a praying!" One whom God called to pray for Albania was a young pastor's wife in Arkansas. I did not know it at the time, but Sheila Everett later wrote me that she had asked God several years before for a prayer burden. In her Sunday School class one Sunday, she heard a Campus Crusade staffer describe the spiritual state of Albania. She had barely heard of the little nation, but her discernment was that God was giving her Albania as her prayer burden. She took her perceived assignment very seriously.

It was then that God led us at the FMB to create what turned out to be massive prayer involvements with closed countries and unreached people groups, and we called for churches to commit to such a prayer assignment.

The Everetts' church was one of the first to respond. Without knowing of the serious prayer involvement with Albania by the pastor's wife, we happened to assign that church Albania. Sheila wrote our office a letter saturated with excitement. "How like God to have you assign our church Albania," she wrote. She explained she felt this was confirmation that she really had heard God accurately when He gave her Albania in response to her request. She was thrilled that her entire church would be participating in prayer for Albania.

A year later, Sheila called our office and explained that God was moving them to Fort Worth, where her husband had been called to pastor University Baptist Church. She said the prayer involvement had meant so much to their Arkansas church that they wanted to lead their new congregation in the same prayer experience with Albania. She requested that we continue sending the monthly prayer material related to Albania to their new church.

Meanwhile, the plot thickens. A newly planted mission church in central Texas also received Albania in that first wave of assignments. A young lawyer and his family, temporarily on leave from their home church to assist in the establishment of the mission church, took the prayer project with Albania seriously. Earnestly, Mary and David Carpenter prayed daily for the people of Albania, as did their then 4-year-old son, J. T. "Dear God," J. T. prayed again and again, "please call someone to go tell the people of Albania about Jesus and open the doors so they can get in."

When the Carpenters returned to their home church, they found this church was also praying for Albania. They could not get away from Albania!

An incredible thing began to unfold. They began to feel God calling them to be the answer to their prayers. They contacted Foreign Mission Board, and in time, they began the missionary process. They were told, "The doors are still not open, but many intercessors are praying. Go to the seminary and take your required classes. By the time you are ready to go, perhaps there will be a crack in the door, and you may be able to get in."

They sold their lucrative law practice, left their affluent lifestyle, and moved to a rental house in Fort Worth. On Sunday, they went to the neighborhood church. When the invitation was given, they joined the church. Can you guess which church? It was, of course, University Baptist Church, already steeped in prayer for Albania and already loving its people. The Carpenters walked into the sweetest prayer embrace of any family on the way to the missions field I know about.

They fulfilled their requirements and training. By then, Albania had undergone radical government changes. One of these changes was a decision the government made to honor Mother Teresa, a native Albanian, and one of the world's best-known Christians. In a fascinating twist of circumstances, the award was presented to Mother Teresa by the widow of the president who had led the parliament to declare Albania an atheistic state years before!

The closed door cracked open. The Carpenters were able to get into the country. God soon gave them a vision for an evangelization plan that would touch the entire nation. They began praying profoundly about the development of His plan. They met Campus Crusade staffers in Albania, and learned that, amazingly, God had led them to the same plan and methods, and *they* were praying strategically for God's further guidance. Together, they prayed and worked on the vision God had given them.

The vision was to show Campus Crusade's *Jesus* film in 900 villages all over the little mountainous nation. The team would need helicopters; thus, the missions organization, HeliMissions, joined the project. They would need generators, huge screens, movie projectors, Christ-following volunteers from America, Europe, Albania—a mammoth undertaking. Twenty-seven missions organizations became involved.

But first, the workers sent word around the world that most of all, and first of all, they needed prayer. They needed people of God to lift up their hearts to the Father in intercession for the release of His power as they labored on the Albanian fields below. They sent out the word. One of their strategies was to enlist pray-ers in Baptist retirement centers to pray specifically and unitedly for Albania, and they used other means of creating a solid prayer base before any other action took place.

In Albania today, there are 160 congregations plus many Bible studies and discipleship groups with an estimated 7,500 to 8,000 believers. Now Albanians are preaching the gospel, even in the midst of most difficult times in their country. The nation's problems have been overwhelming. The Kosovo tragedy of 1999 brought disaster to thousands of lives and families in the Baltic States. David Carpenter and his teenaged son, J. T. (remember the 4-year-old praying so earnestly for the people of Albania?), returned to Albania to be a part of the ministry to the thousands of refugees pouring into the little nation from Kosovo.[7] As we grieve for the people and the tragic heartbreak, intercessors all over the world are praying. Prayer will be needed for years to come for those people torn from their roots and for those who are overwhelmed by the events thrust upon them.

Christ followers are praying that many will come to the Savior and experience God's love, strength, and comfort. We pray for strength, wisdom, and continuing compassion for those responding in Jesus' name to the indescribable spiritual, physical, and emotional needs. In it all, let us remember and be grateful: The gospel is there—active, thriving, planted deeply into the fabric of the lives of Albanian Christ followers.

The beginning of this story for Southern Baptists, from my vantage point, was when God reached down in Benton, Arkansas, and tapped Sheila Everett on the shoulder in response to her request and said, "Pray for Albania." Can one young woman's prayers in Arkansas be a vital part of opening closed doors and praying Christ followers into a land? Can one young couple make a difference in the evangelization of a whole nation? Can one church—or two or ten—be dynamic partners with God in releasing His power and changing a portion of the world? Oh, we have the promises of God that the prayers of His people are powerful and effective as we lift our hearts in kingdom praying.[8]

Questions for Reflection

Have you ever asked God for a prayer burden?

Will you, even now, covenant with the Lord to daily turn your heart toward Him in intercession for those who do not know Him?

Have you had a personal experience in employing prayer as strategy?

Do you pray for those persons affected in crises that appear in the pages of your newspaper or come to your awareness through news broadcasts?

Has your church adopted an unreached people group for a prayer involvement? Would it be a possible consideration now?

If your church is not open to this type of prayer commitment, consider another approach. A Sunday School class, or any group, may receive an assignment. What are some

options for you to be a part of experiencing strategic praying?

[1]Andrew Murray, *State of the Church* (Fort Washington, PA: Christian Literature Crusade, 1983), 13.
[2]This is a reference to J. Edwin Orr's classic statement.
[3]Stephen Neill, *A History of Christian Missions* (Middlesex, England: Penguin
Books, 1964), 107.
[4]Ibid.
[5]Ibid., 108.
[6]See chapter 11 for more description of this around-the-world prayer journey.
[7]The Carpenters now work bivocationally in the practice of law (David), as ad-
vocates for strong involvement of laity in missions, and as consultants (Mary
and David) to churches in becoming centers for world missions. Mary also
serves as minister of missions for their church, First Baptist Church, Wood-
way, Texas.
[8]A wonderful footnote to this story surfaced when God called the Everetts
from University Church, Fort Worth, to First Baptist, Pensacola, Florida.
There they found that a dedicated pray-er, Joan Peterson, a leader in the
church's prayer ministry, had received from God, in a way similar to Sheila's
experience, the assignment of praying for Albania. In comparing notes, they
discovered each had received their prayer burden from the Lord at the same
time. This illustrates again the truth of the principle stated by J. Edwin Orr.
Indeed, God called many intercessors of many denominations around the
world to pray for Albania.

11

Prayerwalking: A Strategy for All Pray-ers

"The earth is the Lord's, and everything in it, the world, and all who live in it" (Psalm 24:1 NIV).

"And what does the Lord require of you? To act justly and to love mercy and to walk humbly with your God" (Mic. 6:8 NIV).

"The great people of the earth today are the people who pray—not those who talk about prayer, nor those who can explain about prayer, but those who take time to pray."—S. D.Gordon[1]

Prayerwalking is sweeping the world. No one can pinpoint when or where it began. It is as though God whispered the idea to unrelated intercessors in different parts of the earth. Beginning in their own homes and neighborhoods and reaching worldwide, God's praying people are releasing His power and are finding their relationships with God and others enriched by this dynamic partnership. Of eternal significance, God is changing lives and situations in response to this strategic form of prayer.

Praying On-Site with Insight

The experience of prayerwalking is best defined by the subtitle of the book *Prayerwalking*,[2] by Steve Hawthorne and Graham Kendrick. Prayerwalking is "praying on-site with insight." It involves literally going to the place where our concerns are located and focusing our prayer attention on the life or situation before us. It means praying for the release of God's power, love, blessing, and salvation upon a person, home, neighborhood, town, city, nation. Prayerwalking is praying with insight, awareness, and sensitivity for the needs of the person or circumstance we encounter.

Many years ago, I read in a book by Frank Laubach that as he walked, he prayed for people he encountered. I was intrigued by the thought. I have dabbled with that experience through the years, interceding for someone before me whom I did not know. As I recall, Laubach did not use the term *prayerwalking,* but that is what he was doing.

The basic premise of prayerwalking is to pray as we go, wherever we go, for the people and situations immediately before us and for those whom the Holy Spirit brings to our minds. Prayerwalking prompts us to stay closely in touch with the Father about all matters that are a part of our daily lives and His kingdom work. Prayerwalking has reinforced my desire to pray my way through my days, literally and naturally. When we take prayerwalking seriously, it teaches us more about what it means to pray without ceasing, to stay connected to the Vine, to walk without fainting. Prayerwalking is a natural part of the life that prays. Conversely, the life that prays is a natural prayerwalker, whether one uses the term or not.

Who Prayerwalks, and Why

All serious Christ followers have done prayerwalking without knowing to call it that—and prayerdriving also! Prayerwalking is literally incorporating prayer into one's daily walk with the Lord. It can be as simple as walking for exercise and praying for the people we encounter and the homes we pass. Or it can be an organized, planned activity, where participants divide into partners and walk and pray through a portion of a neighborhood. A combination of churches can come together, divide up a larger area, and cover many neighborhoods with prayer, home by home. An entire state may emphasize prayerwalking, as Florida Baptists have done. An entire part of the world may focus on prayerwalking, as Christians in Africa are doing.

Prayerwalking covers the gamut of life. For example, I have prayerwalked university campuses in our country and on other continents, as well as hospitals, mosques, palaces, and parliament buildings. I have gone with prayerwalkers to areas where churches needed to be planted and covered the neighborhoods with intercession. I have met with prayerwalkers in elevated places high above a city. In some places in the world, the elevated location is a mountain overlooking a city. Where I live in Texas, it needs to be a tall building! Whatever the elevation, we pray for God to prepare the spiritual soil of the city for the gospel. We intercede for the people, praying they will be open and receptive to the transforming love of Jesus, asking the Holy Spirit to bring revival and spiritual awakening. I have driven through many high-crime areas, prayerfully asking the Father for the salvation of lives and for the transformation of troubled neighborhoods.

Some ask, "Why go out to pray? Why not pray in the quiet of my devotional place at home?" A part of the answer is that when we pray from a distance, people and situations tend to be fuzzy and vague. When we pray up close, "on-site with insight," people and situations come sharply into focus. We see them through God's eyes rather than our own. We develop clearer vision and deeper concern, a new intensity, a fresh burden. Prayerwalking is good for the prayerwalker!

Does Prayerwalking Make a Difference?
But does prayerwalking make a difference beyond ourselves? We have God's Word that "the earnest prayers of

His people are powerful and effective" (James 5:16). For example, a congregation desperately needed a building location for a new church site, but it was totally unavailable. It became available after prayerwalkers went to that lot, planted their feet upon it, and prayed. Permits that had been held up endlessly and hopelessly in a government office, seriously hampering missions work, have been granted when prayerwalkers gathered outside that government building and prayed. Tightly closed doors have come off their hinges when prayerwalkers have prayed on-site with insight.

Some would argue, "Those are just coincidences!" I love the words of Archbishop Temple, who said, "When I pray, coincidences happen."

The Proliferation of Prayerwalking
Prayerwalking is being called a phenomenon. A nationwide network morning news show did a special feature on prayerwalking. Promise Keepers has made prayerwalking an integral part of their rallies. The AD 2000 and Beyond movement has given tremendous impetus to prayerwalking through the huge Praying Through the Window initiative. For example, 607 prayer teams went to key Gateway Cities (the cultural, religious, and political centers for the region) in 1997 for prayerwalking. Simultaneously 35 million Christians in 102 countries prayed for unreached peoples in the 10/40 Window.

Increasingly, prayer journey teams are going to all parts of the world for the purpose of prayerwalking. Missionaries are inviting and urging volunteers to come to their overseas assignments and prayerwalk with them and the local believers. Many volunteer teams go overseas for other missions purposes and add prayerwalking to their agenda.

Prayerwalking especially seems to be proliferating in Africa. A yearlong emphasis in the West Africa region brought teams from America throughout the year to prayerwalk with missionaries and local believers. Operation Torch is enlisting hundreds of prayerwalkers to participate in prayer journeys to North Africa, with focus on the people groups of the region.

Learning As You Go

I became vaguely aware of prayerwalking some years ago in my work at the Foreign Mission Board (now International Mission Board) when newsletters and materials occasionally mentioning the experience crossed my desk. These captured my attention, and I wanted to know more. Yet at that point in the 1980s, I could locate no books or guides to answer my questions.

In conversation one day with Lewis Myers, then vice-president of Cooperative Services International, I found myself commenting, "Thousands of volunteers go overseas every year to do all kinds of work—digging water wells, teaching, construction work, medical and dental projects; many go to participate in evangelistic crusades. Since we believe prayer is the most crucial work we can do, why not send prayer teams on prayer journeys to do the work of prayer?" Myers was extremely responsive and urged me to develop the concept. Then he said, "I want the first team to go to World A."

And to World A we went. Lewis and Toni Myers and I took 18 prayerwalkers on an around-the-world prayer journey. A very special group, most of the team members were newly retired missionaries who had invested their lives in introducing people to Jesus and growing and preparing them for kingdom service. The group came to the prayerwalking experience with joy and spiritual energy, eager to enlarge their hearts and reach out to touch another part of the world through this dimension of prayer.

Our team went first to London where we received an intensive orientation. It was a challenging crash course in global missions, with an abundance of overview information and insight concerning the people and places for whom and for which we would be praying on-site. Even as we learned about them, we prayed earnestly for these people who still seemed at a distance. Our final session was a meaningful commissioning service. We left London for World A with a combination of burden, excitement, and anticipation.

From London, we went through Russia to Uzbekistan, to the cities of Tashkent and Samarkand. Then to western Siberia, to Urkutz, and into Ulan Bator, the capital city of Mongolia. From Mongolia we flew to China, to Beijing and Tianjin, and ended the journey in Hong Kong. In a real sense, we learned to prayerwalk as we went. We had remarkable experiences with God and one another, with our personnel, and with the few local believers in the places we were privileged to go.

Since that first prayer journey, I have been with many prayer teams in many places of the world, in America and overseas. Some of my thoughts growing out of these experiences follow.

As Old As the Scriptures

Prayerwalking may be a somewhat recent revelation to us, but it is as old as the Scriptures. In biblical times, there was a lot of walking; of course, walking was transportation! And God's people talked with Him as they walked, and vice versa. Enoch, Abraham, Moses, Joshua, the disciples, and many others walked and talked with God. Jesus, as He left His footprints on the paths and roads of the land, surely talked to the Father intimately about the people He encountered, and about His desire that they live life abundantly on this earth and into all eternity. He even prayed for us (John 17:20–23)!

The biblical base for prayerwalking weaves itself throughout Scripture. My favorite launch comes from the psalmist's words, "The earth is the Lord's and everything in it, the world, and all who live in it" (Psalm 14:1 NIV).

Prayerwalking calls us to do our part in humbly *reclaiming for Him*, through prayer in Christ's name, a portion of God's world—for it already belongs to Him—a person, a family, a neighborhood, a city, a nation.

Prayerwalking the Great Wall
During that first prayer journey to World A, it was important especially at that time in that part of the world that we not make any religious indication—no bowed heads or closed eyes in public. Going public could have jeopardized the continued presence of our personnel in some of the places on our itinerary.

In China, the largest nation in the world, populated by the greatest number of lost people in the world—well over a billion—we of course wanted to prayerwalk the Great Wall. Because of its dramatic, historic, symbolic nature, we wanted not only to prayerwalk a short portion of the wall (it is over 1,500 miles long) but we also wanted to share a special time of corporate worship and intercession for the masses of lost people in this huge nation.

By the time we had gathered our friends living and working in and around Beijing, our group grew to about 35 for our trek to the Wall. The Great Wall is always teeming with people, not just tourists, but many Chinese. The Chinese love the Great Wall and especially love to go there on Sunday afternoons. It so happened that Sunday afternoon was the *only* time our schedule would permit us to go.

As our bus approached the huge parking area, I could see that the Wall was especially crowded. I knew then that a time of corporate worship would be out of the question. Mentally, I made a scaled-down Plan B. As we came closer, I could see how iffy Plan B was. Plan C came into the mix: simply prayerwalking on our own in the midst of the masses (not all bad!). Plan C seemed more and more realistic as we moved along with the crowd, shoulder to shoulder.

We arrived at the spot where we would get on a cable car to take us near the place we would actually climb onto the Wall. The cable car was a new wrinkle since my earlier visit. My first thought was that a cable car to the Great Wall was some kind of technological desecration! Someone commented that Chairman Mao was no doubt spinning in his grave. By the time I reached the cable car, I welcomed the transportation.

A Reserved Chapel of Sorts

The cable car deposited us close to the point of literally stepping onto the Wall—the one spot where all the crowds were headed. We still had to climb a few steps further and make a 140-degree (approximately!) turn to get onto the Wall. As we began the final part of the turn, before us appeared about ten ledges of seats approximately 10 feet wide, carved into the side of the cliff. We could not believe our eyes, but the area was deserted. In that mob scene, this was a miracle.

We fit comfortably into the space. It seemed that God had reserved for us this spectacular chapel of sorts overlooking the beautiful mountains and valleys. Hosts of lost people streamed before our eyes as they made that turn and stepped onto the wall. In comparative quiet in that breathtaking spot, we had a beautiful time of praise of our awesome Lord.

As we gave ourselves to worship and intercession with our eyes open and our heads up, we could not help but notice that many Chinese were pausing and taking pictures of *us* as *we* prayed for them! It was as though the Holy Spirit were saying, "I want you to pray for this person, and this one, and now this one." It was a prayerwalk in reverse! They did the walking.

Our service under that big sky was most meaningful. The time went quickly. Reluctantly, we had an open-eyed benediction and left our little sanctuary. With a rush,

Chinese visitors poured into the spot we had found curiously empty. In seconds our chapel was completely occupied. Somehow God had graciously saved it for our time of worship of Him and intercession for these people in need of the Savior who walked before us.

We joined the hordes walking the wall as we continued the work of intercession from that spectacular perspective. We were confident our Lord took every step with us and heard every prayer lifted to His throne, in Jesus' name.

The World of Voodoo
Another unusual prayerwalking experience took place in a very different part of the world—in Togo, West Africa. There I was introduced to the most pervasive form of darkness I have encountered: the world of voodoo. Of course, I had heard and read about this darkness in our country, but I had never encountered it personally. The acknowledged birthplace and capital of voodoo is just a few miles away in the adjoining country of Benin. Voodoo maintains a strong hold on many people in West Africa and, in varying degrees, all over the continent. To be accurate, voodoo dominates many people all over the world, with Haiti and Brazil as further unfortunate examples.

Voodoo, which originated in Africa, combines aspects of witchcraft, ancestor worship, curses, and countercurses. Followers of voodoo attribute anything bad that happens to themselves, their family, or friends to some enemy's intentional curse. Consumed with desperate determination to identify *who* placed the hex on them, adherents consult a voodoo priest, or fetisher. This man supposedly determines the source of the curse by casting bones on the ground. From reading how they fall, the fetisher names the enemy involved, prescribes what must be done to counter the curse, and advises how to send another curse in retaliation. This involves securing the proper items from the fetish market, which offers a bizarre assortment of skulls of cats and monkeys, dried lizards and snakes, and various kinds of hair, bones, and teeth—plus other stuff! To us, it is an unreal world beyond our comprehension; but to those who subscribe to it, it is frighteningly real.

With our hearts in our throats, we put on our spiritual armor and prayerwalked the fetish market. Our group was comprised of missionary women and several African women believers. The market contains booth after booth selling the nightmarish items. At the back of the booths, the fetishers wait behind curtains to be consulted. Salesmen out front work aggressively to sell the services of the voodoo priests and the fetishes used to counteract curses. They even tried to sell *us* their wares and services!

We walked and prayed before the booths and throughout the market area. We prayed with the heaviest burden for these fearful, misguided people to be released from Satan's darkness and have opportunity to move into the wonderful light and marvelous freedom of Christ. We prayed that someone who speaks their language would tell them the great good news of Jesus in ways they could comprehend and respond to.

It was a very warm day in the fetish market, but I shivered as we walked and prayed. The sun shone brightly, yet I felt surrounded by darkness and evil. A certain heaviness has remained in one corner of my heart ever since that day. I continue to lift to the Father those who live in the oppressive grasp of Satan's deceptive power. I pray for the day to come when they will celebrate the victory of knowing Jesus as Savior and Lord.

Prayerwalking at Home
You may or may not ever prayerwalk on the Great Wall or in a fetish market, but you can make a difference for Christ by prayerwalking where you live.

After that first around-the-world prayerwalk, the Missions Committee of my church (at that time, First Baptist

Church, Richmond, Virginia) invited me to report to
them. By the time the meeting adjourned, the committee
had spent time in prayer and then voted, with excitement,
to sponsor a prayerwalk once a month, beginning in the
area of our church's location and spreading into the neighborhoods beyond.

The plan we discerned God gave us was to gather on
every first Sunday at noon, immediately after the late service, receive assignments of partners and prayerwalking
routes mapped out on index cards, and then spend 45 to
60 minutes walking and praying. We speculated that ordinarily those prayerwalkers who participated without their
families would be able to join their families for a slightly
late Sunday dinner.

On our prayerwalking launch day, however, our plan
called for us to come together for a quick lunch and briefing which explained the how-tos of prayerwalking. A longtime member of the church briefed us on the dynamics of
the area we were about to cover with prayer. The church is
located in an old, historic part of Richmond. Unique issues
exist related to the geographic, cultural, historic, and spiritual aspects of the community. For example, the immediate neighborhood is a combination of handsome, aristo-
cratic homes and run-down houses with rooms rented out
to an assortment of substance abusers and university students. Senior adults, many of them economically disadvantaged, also reside in the area. We received sensitive insights
into the people for whom we would be praying, their context, their needs, their longings.

Each of us received a partner and then our prayerwalking
routes mapped out on index cards. We agreed to gather back
at the church at a certain time to report our impressions, insights, and findings of situations where a ministry and/or
witness response from the church would be appropriate.

Before we left for the prayerwalk, we had a time of
prayer together. No bowed heads or closed eyes, for we

needed to become comfortable with praying in the prayer-walking mode. We asked the Holy Spirit to go ahead of us, to guide every step, every prayer, and every encounter. We asked Him to bring to our minds His thoughts of what He wanted us to pray. And we asked Him to fill us to over-flowing with His love for the people we would encounter.

Then we went to our assigned portions of the neighbor-hood. As we walked, we worshiped our Lord. We expressed our adoration and thanksgiving. We confessed our sin and asked Him for cleansed lives. We claimed the promises of God. We prayed the Scriptures as God brought them to mind, and we also used the printed page of Scriptures we had been given for that purpose. We felt a freedom to in-tersperse talking with God with talking with one another. At one point, my partner and I quietly sang a praise song.

Only the First Chapter
Shortly after we left the church on that initial prayerwalk, my partner and I encountered a woman selling flowers from a little stand at a major intersection. We bought a bouquet and chatted with her, learning that she lived in a distant suburb of the city. We told her what we were doing, and asked her if she had a personal need about which she would like us to pray. Her eyes teared immediately. There was a long pause. Finally, she told us she was not a religious person, but she would like for us to pray for her teenaged grandson. He had been gone from home for several days and the family did not know whether he had run away from home or had met with foul play—or worse. She ex-pressed her anxiety and said with emotion, "I believe God sent you to me to pray for my grandson and my family." We were thankful for the opportunity to pray with her, and we continued to pray for her after we parted. I asked per-mission to communicate the names of her family to a pas-tor in her area. She consented. I followed through with calls to her and found the boy had returned home after the third

day. Meanwhile, the pastor near their home was already in touch with the family, and the church was ministering to them. Often, prayerwalking is only the first chapter!

We continued our assigned route, pausing to visit with Sunday afternoon walkers as the Holy Spirit prompted us. We prayed for the people quietly as we encountered them, asking God to make them aware of His loving presence in a real and personal way. We prayed for His love, blessing, and salvation to become realities in their lives. We appeared to be just strolling, but in actuality, we were engaged in the powerful act of intercession.

We returned to the church at the appointed time to share our experiences. One young man reported to the group words to this effect: "I am a member of the Missions Committee, but I was out of town on business when the committee heard the report and planned this event. I came today because I wanted to support the work of the committee. However, I was leery. I had never heard of prayerwalking. Today, when I heard the explanation for the first time, I thought, 'This is weird, but I must go through with it.' When my partner and I began our assigned walk, I did not want to be the first to pray. But as soon as my partner started talking to God so naturally and warmly, I knew God was right there, walking with us. I have never had such a strong sense of His presence."

Emotionally, the young man described the special time with the Lord he had experienced. He continued, "I have been a member of this church for years, and I have driven through these streets countless times. However, I saw things today I had never before noticed. I have been oblivious to the people right around us. Indeed, I realized today that I was seeing, for the first time, this neighborhood and these people as God sees them. And it broke my heart. Pray for me as I sort through what God is teaching me and doing within me." That young man became our best enlister of prayerwalkers.

When we prayerwalked the next month, we had new prayerwalkers in attendance, so we had an abbreviated briefing. The third month the briefing was not necessary. Those joining us for the first time received an experienced prayerwalker as a partner.

We prayerwalked when it was hot and humid. We prayerwalked when we nearly froze stiff. We did shorter routes under those conditions.

While our prayerwalking was a churchwide activity sponsored by the Missions Committee, any group can sponsor a prayerwalk: Women on Mission groups, Sunday School classes, deacons, youth—even children make excellent prayerwalkers.

The Flexibility of Prayerwalking

Prayerwalking can also bring together many churches sharing mutual concerns about their town or city. They may join forces in assisting one another in praying through each church's community, eventually covering the entire area with prayer. Prayerdriving is a way to involve those who are not walkers. Intercessors who, because of limited mobility, need to stay at the church, can be a part of the prayerwalking experience by praying from a designated place there.

Prayerwalking offers much flexibility. Before the young women come to my home each week for Bible study, I prayerwalk my own living room, praying that God will fill the room to overflowing with His vivid presence. I kneel before the sofa and before each chair and ask God to touch the life of the young woman who soon will be sitting there and stir her heart with His love, His Word, and His conviction. Prayerwalking has a way of adapting itself into many facets of our days and our schedules.

Prayerwalking can happen at any time, like today, with me, unexpectedly. This afternoon, I dashed to the grocery store to get an onion to make spinach balls for the Bible study group meeting at my home tonight. I quickly purchased my onion, jumped back into my car, turned the key—and nothing happened. Not having time for a problem, I went into denial, thinking if I tried it one more time, the car would start. I tried again and again. Reality began to set in. Finally, I called the auto club and they promised to rescue me within an hour. I resigned myself to (1) a long wait, (2) a time-consuming ride in the tow truck to my automotive service, and (3) the complexities of a broken-down car with no alternative transportation. What to do? Usually, I have something with me on which I can work, but today I had nothing. I had not taken time for my usual exercise as yet—I could get my exercise by walking while I waited. Then it hit me. One place I have never prayerwalked is a grocery store parking lot! That was about to change. I took off. The Holy Spirit brought countless intercessions to my mind as I covered the perimeter of the large parking lot many times in the 55 minutes it took the auto club representative to arrive. During that period I also prayed for a kaleidoscope of people hurriedly going into and coming out of the grocery store. I was amused at the good time I had with the Lord on the grocery store's parking lot! Frustration never came.

As a bonus I had not thought to ask from the Lord, the service representative, when he finally arrived, was able to repair my car on the spot in 10 minutes, and I was quickly on my way home in my very own operational car.

Be creative. Prayerwalking can take place anytime, anywhere, everywhere, planned and unplanned. Find ways to turn blown plans into opportunities to meet with God and to focus your intercession on those around you. You will find ways of adapting prayerwalking that I have not yet discovered.

I have shared with you from personal experiences so that you will see clearly how simple and doable prayerwalking is for anyone who desires to have fellowship with God and longs for others to have that same privilege. As something of a review, consider these spiritual nuts and bolts of prayerwalking.

Prayerwalking and the Two Major Purposes of Prayer

Prayerwalking relates closely to both major purposes of prayer. Like all authentic prayer, prayerwalking has as its foundational purposes: (1) an intimate love relationship with God in Christ. It provides another way to better know Him and His heart. Also (2) prayerwalking places us in dynamic partnership with God. It brings the releasing of His power, blessing, and love into a specific life, home, area, situation, or even nation. Prayerwalking relates directly to God and His kingdom.

Preparing for a Prayerwalk

1. In preparing for a group of prayerwalkers in a location where some of the participants are unfamiliar with the area, provide insight into the local dynamics of the neighborhood and its people. Make it possible for them to pray in the specific light of current understandings and insights.

2. Before you prayerwalk, pray together as a group. Welcome the Lord into the very midst of this time with Him. Invite Him to be an active participant. "'For where two or three come together in my name, there am I with them'" (Matt. 18:20 NIV). Ask the Holy Spirit to go ahead of you, to accompany every step you take, to guide and prompt you at each point in the walk. Pray for a cleansed, pure heart before God. Ask the Father to prepare the people with whom you may have opportunity to visit.

3. As you walk with your partner (or as a threesome at most), worship the Lord. Prayerwalkers are worshipers. Remember the goal of prayer and of all the Christian life: "The chief end of man is to glorify God and enjoy Him forever." Enjoy Him as you prayerwalk! Delight in Him. Adore Him. You are bringing glory to Him! There is a wonderful freedom in prayerwalking, for it calls for getting in step with the Father and His desires.

4. Ask the Holy Spirit to bring to your mind what He wants you to pray. Listen. Then pray aloud those thoughts. Every thought can be turned into meaningful prayer— some thoughts may need to be turned into a prayer for forgiveness! If thoughts do not formulate, wait. Be comfortable with silence before Him.

5. Pray the Scriptures. Claim His promises. "We do not know what we ought to pray for, but the Spirit himself intercedes for us"(Rom. 8:26 NIV).

6. Keep in mind that there is no wrong way to prayerwalk as long as you talk to the Father from your heart. Speak to Him naturally, informally, transparently, conversationally. Avoid lengthy monologues. Feel free to intersperse talking to God and talking to your partner.

7. Greet the people you encounter as you walk and pray. As the Holy Spirit leads, stop and engage them in conversation. Tell them what you are doing and ask if there is a concern for which they would like for you to pray. Pray for them on the spot. Follow through in any possible way with ministry and witness.

8. When you are a part of an organized prayerwalk, come back together at a designated time and place and share your experiences, observations, insights, and possible follow-through.

9. As you personally prayerwalk your own neighborhood, pray as specifically as possible for your neighbors and their life situations. Always lift them and their needs into the presence of Jesus and His love. Ask the Father to give you a genuine love for them, a love that will come through to them as His love. Ask the Lord to draw them to Him and sensitize them to spiritual matters, including the state of their own souls. Pray that God will do the same thing within you. Offer to follow His leadership in being willing to witness and minister to your neighbors, or to anyone toward whom He directs you. Amazing experiences follow when consistent, cumulative, genuine prayer for neighbors takes place.

This dimension of prayer lends itself delightfully to family participation—especially in terms of neighborhood prayerwalking. Create family prayerwalks, praying for your neighbors in the light of your understanding of their needs. With the freedom and naturalness of prayerwalking, children quickly pick up on it and enjoy the uniqueness.

Prayerwalking is profound, yet very simple; do not allow it to become complicated. Reading a book or participating in a workshop on prayerwalking can be helpful. However, prayerwalkers can be effective without formal training.

Prayerwalking lends itself to being a part of one's personal prayer strategy, one's family prayer strategy, and a church's prayer strategy. Prayerwalkers are needed and wanted locally and around the world—to do strategic missions praying for the fulfillment of God's heart's desire. Prayerwalking is thus hastening the day when people of all nations will gather around His throne. Prayerwalking is powerful because God is powerful.

Prayerwalking brings glory and joy to God and deep spiritual pleasure to the prayerwalker.

Questions for Reflection
Think of specific times and places you can naturally and intentionally incorporate prayerwalking into your daily life: walking for exercise, walking from your car to your office, etc.

What are some sites or locations off your beaten path that could be possibilities for prayerwalking?

Will you consider sharing this concept with a group? Your Sunday School class?

Is God leading you to initiate and organize a prayerwalk?

Is God stirring within you about the possibility of being a part of an overseas prayerwalking team?

[1]S. D. Gordon, *Quiet Talks on Prayer* (Grand Rapids: Baker Book House, 1980), 12.
[2]Steve Hawthorne and Graham Kendrick, *Prayerwalking* (Orlando, FL: Creation House, 1993).

Afterword

Lingering Reflections

"I will give you a new heart and put a new spirit in you" (Ezek. 36:26 NIV).

"For we are God's workmanship, created in Christ Jesus to do good works, which God prepared in advance for us to do" (Eph. 2:10 NIV).

"When you pray, rather let your heart be without words than your words without heart."—John Bunyan

I t is time to click on Exit. How do we conclude our thinking together about the strategic possibilities of the life that prays? Perhaps we should end by reflecting on the very basic and specific question: How does the life that prays happen?

I am convinced the life that prays happens because of that which takes place in the heart. Another way of putting it is that, as we devote ourselves daily to being close to Him (Jer. 30:21), God gifts us with a heart for prayer.

The Heart
The word *heart* is one of the most familiar words in the English language. An incredible bundle of muscles and nerves about the size of a fist, the heart pumps millions of gallons of blood through the body during one's lifetime. But the heart is much more than a pump. It is the center

of who we are, the seat of our emotions, beliefs, and decisions. The heart is the home of our character and will, the seedbed of our spiritual formation. Most amazing of all, this inner base of our thinking, loving, and choosing has the potential of Christlikeness. Thus, the physical, emotional, and spiritual dimensions of life all urge us to give priority attention to the heart.

God Is a Heart Specialist

God is in the business of radical dealings with hearts. His specialty is heart transplants! "I will give you a new heart," Ezekiel quotes God as stating. The new heart He gives in the new birth represents a radical operation designed to transform one's life at every level—a whole new way of living. This process of transformation is designed to keep on happening. Indeed, we are His workmanship, His continuing work of divine art. He wants to make a masterpiece of each one of us, to make us more and more like Jesus.

But, are we being transformed in the way that we think, live, and relate to Him and others? Are our hearts becoming more like His? Are our lives a testimony of His creative expertise to those who know us? Jesus made a sobering statement (in Mark 7:6 NIV), quoting the words from Isaiah, "These people honor me with their lips, but their hearts are far from me."

Check on the Condition of Your Heart

Almost daily, this statement comes into my consciousness: "Check on what is going on in your heart."

For a number of years, from time to time, some specific Scripture verse has lodged in my heart. You have probably had this experience. Usually, the Scripture passage has lingered with me for several months, and then, finally, another one comes into focus, shifting my attention to yet another verse or passage upon which to reflect, ponder, and apply.

220

At one point, for an unusually long time that seemed
not to end, a certain familiar verse settled into my soul,
surely placed there by the Lord. After awhile, I thought I
ought to move on to another verse, but it did not happen—the verse stayed. It had to do with my heart: "Keep
your heart with all diligence, for out of it spring the issues
of life" (Prov. 4:23 NKJV).

Finally getting it that the Father saw my need to go deeper
into the verse, and deeper into my heart, I began looking at
other Scriptures related to the heart. Out of the hundreds in
the concordance, I selected a few to keep immediately before
me. "Search me, O God, and know my heart. . . . See if there
is any offensive way in me" (Psalm 139:23–24 NIV). "The
sacrifices of God are . . . a broken and contrite heart" (Psalm
51:17). "Man looks at the outward appearance, but the Lord
looks at the heart" (1 Sam. 16:7). "You will seek me and find
me when you seek me with all your heart" (Jer. 29:13). "I
will give you a new heart" (Ezek. 36:26). "Set your hearts on
things above" (Col. 3:1). And the warning: "The heart is deceitful above all things" (Jer. 17:9).

Familiar words—all of them. Yet they were freshly probing as I placed them in my real-life context. I could not
shake them. It was not a new thought, of course, but I
pondered how possible it is to appear to be one way and in
actuality be entirely different within. Jesus said the Phari-
sees were like that—whitewashed sepulchres on the outside, and full of dead men's bones on the inside. What they
had in their hearts was more important to Him than their
outward rituals and routines. Therein lie the issues of life.
This truth looms before me today and every day.

What is going on in your heart? In light of Jesus' intention that we be transformed into the life that prays, since
He desires that every Christ follower have a heart for
prayer, is there need for one more reality check? What are
some of the characteristics of the life that prays, of the life
that has a heart for prayer?

A Personal Checkup

The life that prays knows the ultimate importance of daily "keeping the heart with all diligence," keeping the heart clean, humble, repentant, tender, gentle, obedient. In and through the life that prays, the Holy Spirit plants and produces His fruit: love, joy, peace, patience, kindness, goodness, faithfulness, gentleness, and self-control. The ultimate goal of the life that prays is to bring glory to God by becoming increasingly like Jesus; to be a loving, obedient servant like He was on earth, reaching out to a world that is lost, without hope, and without Him.

The life that prays gives close attention to the issues of life: developing an accurate understanding of God, really knowing and loving Him; making Jesus one's daily Teacher (Matt. 11:29), and thus being continually transformed "until Christ is formed in [us]" (Gal. 4:19); becoming His close, intimate partner through prayer in what He wants done in the world. Every moment and every experience give us one more opportunity to become more of what He created us to become. The life that prays demonstrates a life in which Christ is Lord—in the deepest, most intimate places of the praying heart as well as in the outer reaches of one's obedience.

Symptoms of a Clogged Heart

My own experiences reveal that there are times when our hearts get clogged, and even hardened. Subtly, we become focused on self and place at the center of our lives our own comfort, convenience, ease, expectations, ego, ambitions, hurts, and disappointments. Our view of God gets distorted; Jesus' teachings float out beyond the periphery of our awareness. We begin to ignore the disciplines of Bible study and application, solitude with the Father, service, witness, stewardship, simplicity.

Inwardly, we turn away from spiritual realities. In this state, it rarely occurs to us to seek God's face and internalize

His wisdom. We get discontented and frustrated with the people and happenings around us. We fail to invite the Holy Spirit into the midst of our daily activities. The fruit of His Spirit within withers. Words of prayer become rote, routine. One's mouth may continue to say prayer-type words, but the heart does not pray. The heart clogs.

A Capacity for Deceitfulness and Spiritual Cosmetology

Consider again the words of the prophet Jeremiah: "The heart is deceitful above all things" (17:9). Often I am overwhelmed by the profound truthfulness of this statement in my own experience. Prayerful people often do not take sin seriously enough; sometimes we do not even see the sin lodged in the crevices of our deceitful hearts. We glaze it over, ignore it, deny it, rationalize it, simply neglect to weigh it in as plain old sin. But God sees and knows and grieves, for sin is serious business. It clogs our hearts. In fact, the clogged heart may be on its way to becoming hardened. Do you recognize the symptoms?

Unclogging the heart is a work of the Holy Spirit in response to our grief and deep confession, our repentance, brokenness, and recommitment to living life honestly and authentically before God and others. Otherwise, it is possible to keep going through the motions and actions of Christ following when all the while, more and more spiritual makeup is being applied to cover up the hypocrisy. Spiritual cosmetology, a whitewashing cover-up job, provides a temporary attempt for remedy; or, perhaps even worse, going though the motions of spirituality eventually burns us out.

A Prescription for Unclogging the Heart

Every Christian has probably struggled with a clogged heart. To whatever degree the condition exists, it needs immediate, direct attention. However, there are no new and revolutionary answers. The prescription is in the Scriptures. Again and again, I have found these five simple steps dependable and productive because God is so dependable and responsive.

1. Get alone with the Father to be still and quiet. This statement sounds oversimplified, but it is difficult to do. We live in a day of incessant sounds and constant noise. Many distractions attack the Christ-following life. The soul needs quietness for intimate connection with God. Oh yes, He can and does connect with His children in the midst of noise, but we are the ones who are vulnerable to losing our focus or missing Him altogether. Our hearts desperately need quietness.

Not only are we bombarded by noise, we also live in a world of hurry and rush. Hurry clogs the heart. Yet the deeper experiences with the Father rarely, if ever, take place on the run. Yes, we can connect with the Lord as we dash around doing good things. But those times of connection are only glances, quick heart cries. Ordinarily, a period of time is required for the heart to slow down and move into deep communion with the Lord of the universe. Again and again, I rediscover that I must reorder my life to include that quiet time and space where the Holy Spirit can and will settle in with me. It is not easy, but it is essential.

2. Get into God's Word—and stay there. We need to reflect upon, absorb our Lord Christ's teachings. We must take them into our clogged hearts and embrace them all over again. We must think through them to specific ways to apply them to current attitudes, relationships, situations. We must ask the Holy Spirit to reveal clearly what confessions, restitutions, and/or other actions we need to take to cleanse and clear our hearts and reestablish the full and free flow of the sweetness and joy of the Christ-following life.

As I feed my soul some of the passages that bring back again the free flow of God's life, love, joy, and Spirit in and through my heart, these especially come to my mind: Matthew 5; 6; 7; 22:37–40; 28:19–20; John 3:14–18,30; 10:10; 14:15; Romans 8; Galatians 5:22–25; Ephesians 4: 20–27; 5:1; 6:10–18; Philippians (all 104 verses!); Colossians 1:9–14; 3:1–4,12–17; 1 Thessalonians 5:16–18; 2 Thessalonians 2:16–17; 1 Timothy 4:7*b*–8; 2 Timothy 1:7; 3:16; Hebrews 10:19–25; 12:1–3; 13:1–7; James 1:17–27; 3:13–18; 5:16; 1 Peter 1:15; 2:9–12; 5:6–9; 2 Peter 1:3–11; 1 John 3:1–3; 4:7–21; Revelation 3:19–20; Exodus 20:1–17; Psalm 25:4–5; 62:5–8; 63:3–4; 57:9–10; 96:3; 100:4–5; 119:10–16; 145:3; Proverbs 18:10; 19:17; 24:3–4; 27:19; Ecclesiastes 12:13–14; Isaiah 26:8; 40:29–31; 43:18–19; 58:11; 66:2; 32:17; Nahum 1:7; Micah 6:8; Habakkuk 3:2; etc. Keep a list like this handy for the first signs of a clogging heart.

3. Get with the people who love God with a free-flowing devotion. Authentic fellowship with authentic Christ followers can do wonders for the heart. God's people can sometimes get crossways in their fellowship and love for one another, which contributes decidedly to the clogging of the heart. How we need to be alert and serious in seeking to be faithful to His plan that we love one another, care for and minister to one another, tenderhearted, forgiving one another (Eph. 4:32 to 5:2). We know backwards and forwards the greatest commandment. Do we obey it? Do we love God supremely (and show it) and then love others (and show it)? This is how the world will recognize that we are authentic Christ followers (John 13:35). Opening ourselves to allow God's love to flow into our lives from others, and to flow through our lives to others, renews our love for God and His people, and unclogs the heart.

4. Be consistent in living a life of plain, old-fashioned service.

Many years ago the little book *Try Giving Yourself Away*
made an indelible impression upon me. I still think of it
often. Granted, I am very imperfect in my service to God
and others, but one of my favorite joys is finding some
form of giving myself away—being of service to someone.
Some of my service involvements are intentional, regular
commitments; some are spontaneous and unplanned. I
gain the most pleasure when no one else knows about the
service and I receive no credit, as the book suggests. This
concept of service is one of the dynamic messages of the
Bible, and Jesus is so clear: it is another mark of the Christ
follower. I wonder what percent of those in our worship
services on Sundays are actively involved in some form of
continuing service? How many of those who come to
church have clogged or hardened hearts? With all the biblical emphasis on service ("We are . . . created in Christ Jesus
to do good works" [Eph. 2:10]), there may be a relationship between lack of service and the clogged heart.

On the other hand, those with activist tendencies can
become vulnerable to substituting good works for solitude
time with the Lord—that lingering time with Him of
thinking through the complexities of our days, discerning
His perspective, seeking His wisdom, and opening ourselves to His resources. Rather than making it an either/or
matter, we need to aspire to a balance between solitude and
service. Each is important to the other—and to the Lord
Christ.

5. Learn to experience joy, delight, and just plain fun as an
integral part of life. Even as I live with many prayer burdens, those I choose and some I do not choose, it is essential that I include in my days some spots of time and
activity that give periodic relief to the heaviness. My husband, who revered God and His Word with all his heart,
mind, and soul, used to call this consecrated common
sense. Finding time is always a factor, but this is another

226

essential step in the abundant life Jesus came to give to all who will follow Him.

Realistically, every heart, not only the clogged ones, needs these steps regularly. Even as they are among God's remedies, they also serve as a preventative to the clogging of the heart.

Blending the Life That Prays and a Heart for Prayer
Let's come back to where we began. The life that prays happens because of what is going on in the heart. When the heart

- is sensitively, tenderly, consistently desiring to know God in Christ intimately;
- loves Him deeply and worships Him joyfully and spontaneously each day—in addition to scheduled corporate times of worship and fellowship with other believers;
- dwells in His Word and is committed to live out His teachings in attitudes, habits, perspective, and relationships;
- is clean, humble, and contrite;
- is so filled with Christ's love that His love flows into even casual encounters;
- wants to live life as Jesus taught and as He lived His own life;
- responds to the Great Commission and is actively concerned about the eternal salvation of all people, close at hand and to the ends of the earth;

then not just one's mouth prays, but one's life prays with words forming in the heart and going to the heart of the Father.

The life that prays is grounded in a personal, close, costly love relationship with Jesus. It is guided by God's Word and empowered by the Holy Spirit. It grows in Christlikeness and practices the living out of faith and love in a spiritual family (church). It is involved in getting the gospel to all the peoples of all the world.

A heart for prayer creates the life that prays. Conversely, the life that prays takes form, shape, and power because of the existence of a genuine heart for prayer.

A Most Special Benediction

Somehow it seems appropriate to conclude with a benediction. With my heart full of worship and praise of our living, reigning Lord, I feel compelled to pray a benediction I heard my husband pray hundreds of times. Huber also heard it prayed hundreds of times as he was growing up under the ministry of George W. Truett, who, so far as I know, originated the benediction. Truett was Huber's *model* (although we did not use that word back then) of a preacher/pastor/leader. He frequently quoted Truett in his conversations, his teaching, and in his preaching. I want to honor my husband's memory as I share this with you— and offer it to our Lord—from my heart to His.

Now, as we go our many scattered ways, may the blessings of God, bright like the light when the morning dawneth and gracious as the dew when the eventide cometh, be granted to us all and each; to teach us and keep us in the right way today, tomorrow, and forevermore. Amen.

A Parent's Prayer Program[1]

Bob Hostetler gives helpful suggestions for a refreshing plan for parents in praying for their children. The idea actually came from his pastor's wife who was concerned that her children develop strong Christian morals and the fruit of the Spirit. Hostetler followed her example and developed a parent's prayer program of his own.

Each day of the month, he prays for the safety of his children and for concerns related to that day. He also prays for a specific character trait, virtue, or fruit of the Spirit to be planted and nurtured in his children, quoting and paraphrasing from the Scriptures listed.

His list includes:

Day 1: Salvation (Isa. 45:8; 2 Tim. 2:10)
Day 2: Growth in grace (2 Peter 3:18)
Day 3: Love (Eph. 5:2; Gal.5:22)
Day 4: Honesty and integrity (Psalm 25:21)
Day 5: Self-control (1 Thess. 5:6)
Day 6: A love for God's Word (Psalm 9:10)
Day 7: Justice (Psalm 11:7; Mic. 6:8)
Day 8: Mercy (Luke 6:36)
Day 9: Respect—for self, others, authority (1 Peter 2:17)
Day 10: Strong, biblical self-esteem (Eph. 2:10)
Day 11: Thankfulness (1 Thess. 5:18)
Day 12: A passion for God (Psalm 63:8)
Day 13: Responsibility (Gal. 6:5)
Day 14: Kindness (1 Thess. 5:15)
Day 15: Generosity (1 Tim. 6:18–19)
Day 16: Peace, peaceability (Rom. 14:19)
Day 17: Hope (Rom. 15:13)
Day 18: Perseverance (Heb. 12:1)

228

Day 19: Humility (Titus 3:2)
Day 20: Compassion (Col. 3:12)
Day 21: Prayerfulness (Eph. 6:18)
Day 22: Contentment (Phil. 4:12–13)
Day 23: Faith (Luke 17:5–6; Heb.11)
Day 24: A servant heart (Eph. 6:7)
Day 25: Purity (Psalm 51:10)
Day 26: A willingness and ability to work hard (Col. 3:23)
Day 27: Self-discipline (Prov. 1:3)
Day 28: A heart for missions (Psalm 96:3)
Day 29: Joy (1 Thess. 1:6)
Day 30: Courage (Deut. 31:6)

[1]Bob Hostetler, "A Parent's Prayer Program," *Focus on the Family,* February 2000.

Praying for a Lost Person

• Keep in mind that the earnest prayers of a righteous person are powerful and effective (James 5:16*b*). Ask God to cleanse your life as you come to Him in intercession for someone's soul.

• Claim God's promise that it is not His will that anyone should perish, but that all should come to repentance (2 Peter 3:9). Do not become discouraged. Be consistent and faithful in your intercession (Luke 18:1).

• Pray that God will bring circumstances into the life of the person that will cause him or her to give attention to the spiritual aspect of life.

• Ask God to bring a realization of a desperate need that has gone unmet by current commitments and realities. Pray there will be an unrelenting awareness of a "hole in the soul."

• Pray that God, in His timing, will bring the right person or persons into this life to communicate the love and claims of the Savior. Consider the possibility that "thou art the one." Express your willingness to Him.

• Ask the Holy Spirit to convict of sin and ready the heart for His message of forgiveness, freedom, and life eternal, beginning now.

• Ask the Lord to give you sensitivity and agape love in discerning if you should speak a witness or relate in some other way at this time.

• Pray there will be a true grasp of Who Jesus is and what He has done in providing the means of escape from the wages of sin.

• Pray that your *life* will be an enhancement to the person's understanding of the difference Christ makes in one's life and relationships.

• Pray for other believers to intercede for the salvation of this person and represent before him or her an authentic testimony of Jesus' love and grace.

• Ask God to bring great joy to this person when the time of acceptance and commitment comes.

Praying for Your Ministerial Staff

"Therefore encourage one another and build each other up, just as in fact you are doing. Now we ask you, brothers, to respect those who work hard among you, who are over you in the Lord and who admonish you. Hold them in the highest regard in love because of their work. Live in peace with each other" (1 Thess. 5:11–13 NIV).

Praying for your ministerial staff is the best gift you can give them. Let them know how you are praying for them.

Relationship with God
•Pray for them to have a consistently intimate relationship with the Father.
•Pray that they will grow to be more and more people after God's own heart.
•Pray that they will continually hide God's word in their hearts.
•Pray that they will be filled daily with the Holy Spirit and all of the fruit of the Spirit.
•Pray that the love of Christ will dominate their lives—their attitudes, actions, relationships.

Relationship with Family
•Pray that they will have healthy, close, loving, joyful relationships with their spouses.
•Pray that they will be sensitive, considerate, fun parents to their children.
•Pray that their children will walk in the ways of the Lord.
•Pray that they will give quality time to their families.

Relationship to Church and Ministry

•Pray that they will be people of prayer devoted to the God of prayer.

•Pray that they will be devoted to studying, preaching, and living God's Word.

•Pray that they will be effective in leading your church to be the congregation God has in mind in worship, evangelism, missions, discipleship, and ministry.

•Pray that they will bear much fruit in their ministry.

•Pray that they will be balanced in their emphases and realistic in their expectations of themselves and others.

•Pray for them to have good health and vitality.

•Pray that the congregation will be considerate and realistic in their expectations of them.

•Pray that your congregation will keep your ministerial staff lifted to God in prayer.

Evidences That a Church Is a House of Prayer

•A majority of the congregation understands biblical truths related to prayer.

•A good percentage of members are serious about prayer in their lives and in the life of the church.

•The leadership of the church believes they have been called individually to a ministry of prayer.

•Prayer is at the center of the church's life. The organizational entities, councils, committees, boards, classes, choirs, and events give priority to prayer.

•The church provides a variety of opportunities, at different levels of intensity, for the congregation to participate in aspects of prayer ministry. Most members are involved in some form of prayer ministry. The church has a prayer strategy—by whatever name—that provides opportunities of prayer participation.

•Members have opportunities to lead in public prayer during worship services and other gatherings of the congregation. Public prayer is not only, or even largely, for the church's staff and congregational leadership. It is for every Christ follower to experience as God's people come together.

•The congregation prays for local, personal needs, but also has prayer burdens for the rest of the world and its lostness. A church that is a house of prayer has a missions heart.

234

Praying for Your Community and Beyond

Neighbors. Pray for the salvation of those who are lost, for the spiritual growth of those who are believers, for God's blessing and grace upon their homes and families, for specifics of which you are aware.

"Your name and renown are the desire of our hearts" (Isa. 26:8 NIV).

Schools. Pray for students, teachers, administrators, school boards, and counselors. Pray for an atmosphere that encourages ethical and moral values as well as healthy development of every student.

"Only be careful, and watch yourselves closely so that you do not forget the things your eyes have seen or let them slip from your heart as long as you live. Teach them to your children and to their children after them" (Deut. 4:9–10).

Businesses. Pray for the owners, employees, and customers. Ask God to impress each with the importance of integrity, fairness, and reliability in their dealings with one another and the community. Pray they will be rewarded with success as they relate honestly with customers.

"Now we ask you, brothers, to respect those who work hard among you" (1 Thess. 5:12).

Local officials. Pray for the mayor, city council, congressmen, police officers, firefighters, and judges. Pray they will

be open to doing their work in ways that will be good for
your community and thus pleasing to God.

"I urge, then, first of all, that requests, prayers, intercession
and thanksgiving be made for everyone—for kings and all
those in authority" (1 Tim. 2:1–2).

Medical personnel. Pray for all those who are responsible
for the physical well-being of the community. Pray they
will turn to God for His guidance in the heavy responsibilities and decisions that relate to life and death.

"He went to him and bandaged his wounds, pouring on
oil and wine. Then he put the man on his own donkey,
took him to an inn and took care of him" (Luke 10:34).

Churches of all denominations. Pray that Christian people
will become authentic followers of Christ. Ask God to
bring revival to the churches and spiritual awakening to
your community, town, or city.

"If my people, who are called by my name, will humble
themselves and pray and seek my face and turn from their
wicked ways, then will I hear from heaven and will forgive
their sin and will heal their land" (2 Chron. 7:14).

High-crime areas. Pray for the redemption of the areas of
your town or city where crime, pornography, prostitution,
and violence prevail. Pray for the salvation of those involved in these lifestyles.

"For everything in the world—the cravings of sinful man,
the lust of his eyes and the boasting of what he has and
does—comes not from the Father but from the world" (1
John 2:16–17).

Prayerwalking from A to Z

A group organized for a prayerwalk comes together to systematically cover with prayer a neighborhood or specific area of concern. Neighborhoods, schools, government buildings, church buildings (classrooms, worship center, etc.), entire towns, cities, associations, new church start areas, locations above cities, high-crime areas, university campuses, shopping malls—prayerwalking can happen anywhere.

To prepare a group for prayerwalking and lead them through an experience:

A. Explain the simple how-tos of prayerwalking. See (I) through (V) below.
B. Ask a knowledgeable person to give a brief orientation of the physical, historical, and spiritual needs of the area you will prayerwalk.
C. Divide participants into partners or groups of no more than three.
D. Allow participants to choose their own partners, if they prefer.
E. Provide assignments of the specific area to be walked, preferably "mapped out" on index cards.
F. As an important concluding part of the orientation, pray, asking God to go before the prayerwalkers, give guidance to every step, and prompt every prayer *He* wants the prayerwalkers to pray.
G. Even in this time of group prayer, pray in the prayerwalking "mode," with eyes open and head up, in order that those new to the experience will begin to be comfortable praying in this manner.

H. Set a time for the prayerwalkers to reassemble following
the prayerwalk.

I. As you prayerwalk, worship God.

J. Pray the Scriptures.

K. Claim God's promises.

L. Talk to the Lord conversationally, informally, from your
heart—as you would your best friend—because He is!

M. Avoid long monologues. Don't try to sound "spiritual."

N. Feel free to intersperse talking to God and talking to
your partner. Prayerwalking is free-flowing, natural.

O. Ask God to heighten and deepen your sensitivities.

P. Periods of silence are OK, but also pray aloud.

Q. Remember that there is no wrong way to prayerwalk, as
long as you are talking to the Father from your heart to
His.

R. Listen, observe, open yourself to the Holy Spirit and the
situation where you are walking and praying.

S. Remember that you are doing the powerful work of intercession.

T. Allow yourself to sing or hum if you desire.

U. As the Holy Spirit leads, stop and relate to someone
you encounter. Talk to them with warmth and caring.
If you feel led, tell them what you are doing and ask if
they would like for you to pray for them. If so, do it!

V. Be alert to follow-up opportunities in witness and/or
ministry.

W. At the completion of your assignment, reassemble for a
brief reporting time.

X. Share experiences, impressions, reflections, and opportunities for follow-up.

Y. Set the next time and place for prayerwalking.

Z. Conclude with praise and benediction.

Praying for an MK

Missionaries often say that the *most* helpful way to pray for them is to pray for their children. Some of their main concerns include:

Contentment. Many missionaries' kids (MKs) live away from home and attend boarding schools. Homesickness is prevalent, not just for parents but also for family members and friends in the US. Homesickness can extend to such favorite things as hamburgers and youth activities "back home." Many MKs are extremely attached to their missions field countries and have homesickness in reverse when coming to the States for college and career. This, too, is a matter of prayer concern, and a ministry we can have as we pray for specific MKs in their specific situations.

Relationships with Other Mission Families. Missions field relationships are especially important to missionary families because of the absence of extended family. Other missionaries and their children become the extended family, without the benefit of mutual backgrounds and previous understandings and sensitivities. Pray that MKs will experience healthy, joyful relationships with adult missionaries and other MKs.

Relationships with Nationals. Potential frustrations multiply in some countries, depending on the culture, the ages of the children, and the availability of friendships with the local children. In some locations, restrictions limit relationships with children in the host countries, especially among teenagers. Ask God to be very tender and loving to the MKs in difficult living conditions overseas. Pray that teens will find fulfilling ministries themselves in their years of living in other countries. Ask God to provide meaningful experiences that will compensate for situations lacking in their surroundings.

Relationship with God. More than anything else, pray for this essential matter. Sometimes MKs (like preachers' kids [PKs]) get "too much of a good thing." Often they feel as called to the missions field as their parents, but that is not always true. In many circumstances, their worship experiences are not in their heart language, making it difficult for authentic worship. Overexposure to their parents' devotion to witness and ministry can bring negative responses. Pray that MKs will have a growing, personal relationship with the Father. Ask the Lord to draw them into a close walk with Him. Pray for them in the same way you pray for your own children and grandchildren.

Perspective on Life. In some ways, MKs have a lifestyle superior to children in this country. Many of them believe that and appreciate it. Pray for those who do not have that perspective. Ask the Father to minister to their deep feelings and give them the ability to be honestly positive about the unique life they are living. Pray especially for those coming to the States for college. To some, this is a strange land and a time of crucial adjustment. If they are attending a college or university in your area, seek them out and become home and family to them. Pray with them, as well as for them.

Praying for a People Group

How do we pray for people who have no foreseeable way to hear the gospel? A people who have no Bible in their language, no missionaries, no churches, no Christian neighbors?

• Open your heart to the prompting of the Holy Spirit. Ask the Father to bring to your mind His word, His promises, and the longings of His heart for the lost.

• Intercede for the leaders of the people. Pray that they will be fair and just in their treatment of the people. Pray that the eternal God will stir the spiritual aspect of their natures. Pray that they will have a longing to know the one true God and His Son, Jesus the Christ.

• Pray that the people's eyes will be opened and they will experience a disappointment and disillusionment with their pagan gods.

• Ask God to release His power in ways that cause the people to recognize His hand and His work in their midst. Ask Him to reveal Himself in supernatural ways.

• Pray that the day will come soon when there will be a spiritual harvest among these people and that many will be saved.

• Pray that those whom God is calling to be workers among these people will hear His call and respond.

• Read *the COMMISSION* magazine, which carries monthly prayer information on unreached people groups.

• Contact missions organizations relating to people groups for prayer information. See resource section.

Daily Prayer Calendar for the Last Frontier

Day 1: Pray for special needs today that cannot be shared. Remember that God is working even where no one else knows the need.

Day 2: Pray that necessary secrecy will be maintained in working in these areas. Ask God to provide safe places for believers to meet for worship, Bible study, and training.

Day 3: Pray for encouragement and strength for imprisoned, persecuted believers; provision for needs of families of imprisoned believers; and release from imprisonment as God wills.

Day 4: Pray that the eyes of government officials, censors, and others will be blinded when necessary to protect national believers and Christian workers.

Day 5: Pray that nationals will experience dissatisfaction with false religious traditions. Ask God to take away their spiritual blindness, bringing responsiveness and a willingness to change belief systems.

Day 6: Pray for wisdom as prayer requests and information are disseminated; for protection from unwise distribution of information by well-meaning persons; and for faithful, efficient, and widespread dissemination of information that can and should be shared.

Day 7: Pray for the emotional needs of Christian workers in Last Frontier areas. Ask God to help them deal with loneliness, family separations, and the stress that comes from living in sensitive and dangerous situations.

Day 8: Pray that the attitudes of governments and opposing religious leaders will change. Ask God to open the eyes of those in opposition to the truth and bring conviction to persecutors and prosecutors. Pray for political stability in these areas and good interpersonal relationships with local officials.

Day 9: Pray that training materials and training in Bible, theology, and leadership will be available and accessible for pastors and church leaders in these areas.

Day 10: Pray for the financial needs of ministries in these areas, and pray that national churches and ministries will become self-supporting as soon as possible and advisable.

Day 11: Pray that, just as God broke down the Iron Curtain, He will break down other religious "curtains" in these areas. Pray that individuals, people groups, and entire areas will break free from the spiritual bondage in which they live and be delivered from blindness and misunderstandings.

Day 12: Pray that those who support believers in these sensitive areas will be faithful in prayer for them, even without specific details of needs and victories. Ask God to provide many more intercessors to enter the battle to take back territory from Satan for the Lord God. Pray that the Holy Spirit will direct and burden people's hearts to pray for particular persons, places, and situations in time of need.

Day 13: Pray for God to call more creative cross-cultural workers to these difficult areas and that those who are called will heed the call. Ask God to give them victory over fear, doubt, attraction of materialism, etc.

Day 14: Pray that Christians in these areas will have the wisdom to know the most effective approaches to use and revelation to see specific opportunities and methods that will be effective in pulling down the strongholds that support the core false belief systems.

Day 15: Pray that the gospel will penetrate these areas, that light will replace darkness, by radio, TV, tapes, videos, email, Internet, and every other possible means. Pray for the wise use of satellites and the newest technology.

Day 16: Pray that God will soon raise up many more national leaders, pastors, evangelists, and other workers for the most needy, though dangerous, areas. Pray for the spiritual and moral integrity of national church and ministry leaders.

Day 17: Pray that both national believers and Christian workers will have faith, boldness, and courage, tempered with wisdom and tact.

Day 18: Ask God to bring true conversions of multitudes, the raising up of great numbers of courageous believers from every sensitive area.

Day 19: Pray that constitutional guarantees for freedom of religion will be implemented. Ask God to expose those restricting religion illegally and unfairly.

Day 20: Pray that many strong local churches will be established and that national believers can overcome suspicions and distrust. Pray that Christian workers will provide wise, efficient assistance to national believers, leaders, and organizations.

Day 21: Pray for careful and strategic distribution and use of Scriptures and other Christian literature and that the fear and distrust of Christian literature will be overcome. Ask God to provide a strong, growing desire of many to know the truth, and pray that the Holy Spirit will reveal truth to them as they receive Scripture and other Christian materials.

Day 22: Pray that Scriptures can be translated very soon for those language groups without them. Ask God to protect translation teams and give them the ability to put key scriptural concepts into accurate and understandable terms, both for translators and for those evangelizing and teaching.

Day 23: Pray for harmonious relationships, spiritual unity, and good cooperation among expatriates, especially in multicultural, co-worker situations; among national believers; and between expatriates and national believers, leaders, and organizations. Pray that God will help them avoid or overcome misunderstandings.

Day 24: Pray that Christian workers learn the language and understand their host culture. Ask God to help them develop fluency in speaking and the ability to communicate well.

Day 25: Pray that Christian workers will be faithful in personal spiritual disciplines. Ask God to help them maintain quality time and a vital personal relationship with Him, resulting in biblical, spirit-directed attitudes and actions.

Day 26: Pray for protection of missionary families. Ask God to meet their children's needs for education and nurture and the special needs of single missionaries.

Day 27: Pray that Christian workers will experience victory over fear and discouragement and will recognize Satan's lies and deceptions. Ask God to give them eyes to see what He is doing and be encouraged. Ask God to give them strength and perseverance in the daily spiritual battles that come.

Day 28: Pray that anti-Christian groups, organizations, and propaganda will be ineffective and defeated. Ask God to protect national believers and Christian workers from "traitors" and informers.

Day 29: Pray for the spiritual growth of "secret" believers. Ask God to give them courage and wisdom to know what and when to speak, when not to speak, and when to make open confessions of faith.

Day 30: Pray for the physical, medical, and health-related needs of Christian workers and their families.

Day 31: Pray that Christian workers will get rest and encouragement for continuing the task while they are on stateside assignment. Ask God to give them safety in travel, at home, on the field, and in between.

Prepared by a Last Frontier missionary. Reprinted by permission.

Selected Bibliography

Billheimer, Paul E. *Destined for the Throne*, Fort Washington, PA: Christian Literature Crusade, 1975.

Blackaby, Henry T., and V. King. *Experiencing God*. Nashville: Broadman and Holman Publishers, 1994.

———. *Fresh Encounter*. Nashville: Broadman and Holman Publishers, 1996.

Bounds, E. M., *The Essentials of Prayer*. Grand Rapids, MI: Baker Book House, Direction Books, 1979.

———. *Power Through Prayer*. Springdale, PA: Whitaker House, 1983.

Bright, Bill. *The Coming Revival*. Orlando: New Life Publications, 1995.

Bright, Vonette, and Ben A. Jennings, eds. *Unleashing the Power of Prayer*. Chicago: Moody Press, 1989.

Bryant, David. *In the Gap: What It Means to Be a World Christian*. Ventura, CA: Regal Books, 1984.

———. *With Concerts of Prayer: Christians Joined for Spiritual Awakening and World Evangelization*. Ventura, CA: Regal Books, 1984.

Carver., W. O. *When Thou Prayest*. Nashville: Broadman Press, 1987.

Chambers, Oswald, *My Utmost for His Highest*. New York: Dodd, Mead and Company, Inc., 1935.

———. *Still Higher for His Highest*. Grand Rapids, MI: Zondervan Publishing House, 1970.

———. *A Holy Occupation*. Grand Rapids, MI: Discovery House Publishers, 1992.

Cho, Paul Y. *Prayer: Key to Revival*. Waco, TX: Word Books, 1984.

Christenson, Evelyn, and Viola Blake. *What Happens When Women Pray*. Wheaton, IL: Victor Books, 1976.

———. *A Time to Pray God's Way* and *A Study Guide for Evangelism Praying*. Eugene, OR: Harvest House Publishers, 1996.

Crawford, Dan R. *The Prayer-Shaped Disciple*. Peabody, MA: Hendrickson Publisher, Inc., 1999.

248

Cymbala, Jim. *Fresh Wind, Fresh Fire*. Grand Rapids, MI: Zondervan Publishing House, 1997.

Davis, Walter Bruce. *William Carey: Father of Modern Missions*. Chicago: Moody Press, 1963.

Deweese, Charles W. *Prayer in Baptist Life*. Nashville: Broadman Press, 1986.

Dake, Cindy Lewis, comp. *The Best of Prayer Patterns*. Birmingham, AL: Woman's Missionary Union, 1999.

Drummond, Lewis A. *The Awakening That Must Happen*. Nashville: Broadman Press, 1978.

Drumwright, Huber L. *Prayer Rediscovered*. Nashville: Broadman Press, 1978.

Duewel, Wesley L. *Touch the World Through Prayer*. Grand Rapids, MI: Zondervan Publishing House, 1986.

Dunn, Ronald. *Don't Just Stand There—Pray Something*. San Bernardino, CA: Here's Life Publishers, Inc., 1991.

Eastman, Dick. *Love on Its Knees*. Old Tappan, NJ: Fleming H. Revell Company, 1989.

————. *The Hour That Changes the World*. Grand Rapids, MI: Baker Book House, Direction Books, 1980.

Foster, Richard J. *Celebration of Discipline: Paths to Spiritual Growth*. New York: Harper and Row, 1979.

————. *Prayer: Finding the Heart's True Home*. New York: HarperCollins Publishers, Inc., 1992.

————. *Streams of Living Water*. New York: HarperCollins Publishers, Inc., 1998.

Gordon, S. D. *Quiet Talks on Prayer*. Grand Rapids, MI: Baker Books, 1980.

Grubb, Norman. *Rees Howell, Intercessor*. Fort Washington, PA: Christian Literature Crusade, 1952.

Hawthorne, Steve, and Graham Kendrick. *Prayerwalking*. Orlando: Creation House, 1993.

Huegel, F. J. *Prayer's Deeper Secrets*. Grand Rapids, MI: Zondervan Publishing House, 1959.

Hallesby, O. *Prayer*. Minneapolis: Augsburg Publishing House, 1931.

Hunt, T. W. *The Doctrine of Prayer*. Nashville: Convention Press, 1986.

Hunt, T. W., and Catherine Walker. *PrayerLife: Walking in Fellowship with God*. Nashville: Convention Press, 1988.

————. *The Mind of Christ*. Nashville: Broadman and Holman Publishers, 1995.

Hunter, W. Bingham. *The God Who Hears*. Downers Grove, IL: InterVarsity Press, 1986.

Hurnard, Hannah. *God's Transmitters*. Wheaton: Tyndale House Publishers, Inc., 1988.

Johnstone, Patrick. *Operation World*. Grand Rapids, MI: Zondervan Publishing House, 1993.

————. *The Church Is Bigger Than You Think*. Great Britain: Christian Focus Publications, 1998.

Kane, J. Herbert. *Wanted: World Christians*. Grand Rapids, MI: Baker Book House, 1986.

Kelly, Thomas R. *A Testament of Devotion*. New York: Harper and Row, 1941.

Kempis, Thomas à. *The Imitation of Christ*. Grand Rapids, MI: Baker Book House, 1982.

Laubach, Frank C. *Prayer, the Mightiest Force in the World*. Old Tappan, NJ: Fleming H. Revell Co., 1946.

Law, William. *A Devout and Holy Life*. Springdale, PA: Whitaker House, 1996.

Lawrence, Brother. *The Practice of the Presence of God*. Ashland City, TN: Brightside, 1996.

Lindsell, Harold. *When You Pray*. Grand Rapids, MI: Baker Book House, 1975.

Lord, Peter. *Hearing God*. Grand Rapids, MI: Baker Book House, 1988.

MacDonald, Gordon. *Restoring Your Spiritual Passion*. Nashville: Thomas Nelson Publishers, 1986.

Martin, Glen, and Dian Ginter. *Powerhouse: A Step-by-Step Guide to Building a Church That Prays*. Nashville: Broadman and Holman Publishers, 1994.

Marshall, Catherine. *A Closer Walk*. New York: Avon Books, 1987.

————. *Meeting God at Every Turn*. Toronto: Bantam, 1985.

Murray, Andrew. *The Ministry of Intercession*. Westwood, NJ: Fleming H. Revell Co., 1952.

————. *With Christ in the School of Prayer*. Old Tappan, NJ: Fleming H. Revell Co, 1953.

————. *The Inner Life*. Springdale, PA: Whitaker House, 1984.

Myers, Warren. *Pray. How to Be Effective in Prayer*. Colorado Springs: Nav-Press, 1983.

Nee, Watchman. *The Normal Christian Life*. Fort Washington, PA: Christian Literature Crusade, 1961.

Nouwen, Henri. *With Open Hands*. New York: Ballantine Books, 1972.

Packer, J. I. *Rediscovering Holiness*. Ann Arbor, MI: Servant Publications, 1992.

Parker, William, and Elaine St. Johns. *Prayer Can Change Your Life*. Carmel, NY: Guideposts, 1957.

Parks, Helen Jean. *Holding the Ropes*. Nashville: Broadman Press, 1983.

Piper, John. *Desiring God*. Portland, OR: Multnomah Press, 1986.

————. *Let the Nations Be Glad! The Supremacy of God in Missions*. Grand Rapids, MI: Baker Books, 1993.

Ravenhill, Leonard. *Revival Praying*. Minneapolis: Bethany Fellowship, Inc., 1962.

Rinker, Rosalind. *Prayer: Conversing with God*. Grand Rapids, MI: Zondervan Publishing House, 1959.

Sanders, J. Oswald. *Prayer Power Unlimited*. Minneapolis: World Wide Publications, 1977.

Schaeffer, Francis. *True Spirituality*. Wheaton, IL: Tyndale House Publishers, 1971.

Sjogren, Bob. *Unveiled at Last*. Seattle: YWAM Publishing, 1992.

Tippit, Sammy. *Fire in Your Heart*. Chicago: Moody Press, 1987.

Thomas, Gary. *Seeking the Face of God*. Nashville: Thomas Nelson Publishers, 1994.

—. The *Glorious Pursuit*. Colorado Springs: NavPress, 1998.

Thompson, Larry L. *Watchman Intercessory Prayer Ministry*. Nashville: Life-Way Christian Resources, 1992.

Torrey, R. A. *How to Pray*. Chicago: Moody Press, 1900.

Tournier, Paul. *The Whole Person in a Broken World*. New York: Harper and Row, 1964.

Trueblood, Elton. *The Validity of the Christian Mission*. New York: Harper and Row, 1972.

Whiston, Charles. *Pray: A Study of Distinctively Christian Praying*. Grand Rapids, MI: William B. Eerdmans Publishing Company, 1972.

Willard, Dallas. *The Divine Conspiracy*. San Francisco: HarperCollins Publishers, Inc., 1998.

Winter, Ralph. *Penetrating the Last Frontiers*. Pasadena, CA.: William Carey Library Publications, 1978.

Willis, Avery, Jr. *The Biblical Basis of Missions*. Nashville: Convention Press, 1979.

—. *MasterLife*. Nashville: LifeWay Christian Resources, 1996.

Prayer Resources, Movements, Organizations, Networks, and Initiatives

This section seeks to give an overview of some of the current, available prayer resources and opportunities for life-changing, world-changing prayer involvement. The following listing is not comprehensive, but representative of many other organizations, movements, and networks that are also working and praying effectively. You will find that some of the resources relate to personal praying while many others relate specifically to kingdom (Great Commission) praying.

International Mission Board, SBC
P. O. Box 6767
Richmond, VA 23230
1-800-866-3621
www.imb.org

For information about international missions, a catalog listing describing printed and audiovisual resources is available by calling 1-800-866-3621 or by emailing a request to resource.center@imb.org. Also available on the Internet at www.imb.org.

"On Mission with God . . . Through Prayer" is a brochure describing various ways intercessors can receive prayer needs and participate meaningfully in praying for the nations of the world. To order, call 1-800-866-3621 or email resource.center@imb.org.

PrayerLine gives up-to-the-minute missions needs from around the world. Call toll free 1-800-395-PRAY 24 hours a day. These messages are also available by email. Contact prayeroffice@imb.org.

CompassionNet is Southern Baptists' worldwide computer-based prayer network. It contains prayer folders for countries where Southern Baptists have work, as well as for megacities, unreached people groups, and population segments. It is updated daily, Monday–Friday. To subscribe, visit the International Mission Board's Web site at www.imb.org or call 1-888-462-7729.

Global PrayerGram provides a monthly printed list of prayer requests and prayer answers from missions fields around the world. To subscribe, call 1-800-866-3621 or email resource.center@imb.org.

PRAYERplus features a church's participation in a prayer relationship with a specific unreached people group plus the added dimension of members of the congregation following God's leadership into personal, on-site overseas involvement. Efforts by the church and the IMB personnel are coordinated in seeking to evangelize the people group. For more information, call toll-free 1-888-462-7729 or email prayerplus@imb.org. Visit www.imb.org.

"Prayer Guides for Unreached Peoples" provides a quarterly profile of a specific unreached people group to congregations committed to pray for those living in areas where access to the gospel is restricted by resistant governments or religions. Each new prayer guide gives detailed information about the group receiving the current prayer focus. The guide may be duplicated and distributed throughout the congregation. For information on how your church may participate, call 1-888-462-7729 or email resource.center@imb.org. or prayeroffice@imb.org.

"Missionaries Need 'Real-Life' Prayer" was written by Marina Menzies, missionary to Honduras, and published in *the COMMISSION*. This article has been widely circulated, for it gives realistic help in praying insightfully for missionaries living and working in an overseas assignment. Call 1-800-866-3621 or email resource.center@imb.org.

National Prayer Partnerships is an emphasis on prayer partnerships between associations or conventions and "open" nations around the world. Ministry and evangelism involvements often grow out of these prayer partnerships. For information, call toll free 1-888-462-7729. Visit www.imb.org.

"Pray for Missionaries from A to Z" guides the pray-er through the alphabet suggesting prayer needs in the missionary's daily life. Place orders by calling 1-888-462-7729 or email resource.center@imb.org.

Prayer Mobilizer Kit is provided by the International Prayer Strategy Office. The materials will assist in training leaders to enlist and mobilize intercessors for meaningful and powerful prayer for overseas missions. Email prayeroffice@imb.org.

Ministers' World Missions E-Link provides concise, urgent, ready-to-use prayer items prepared for church bulletins as missions moments for congregational prayer. For free subscription, ministers may call toll-free 1-888-462-7729.

the COMMISSION magazine, published monthly, offers

extensive, invaluable missions information and inspiration about missionaries and the peoples of the world. Included are profiles of people groups. To receive this publication, call 1-800-866-3621 or email resource.center@imb.org.

On Mission with God is a monthly videotape ($3.95 per month) that brings overseas missions to life. To order this resource, call 1-800-866-3621.

Become a Global Priority Church by giving missions a major focus throughout the life of your congregation. The leadership of the pastor and staff are essential. Aspects of the experience are permeating prayer, missions education, giving, short-term missions projects, the adoption of an unreached people group and/or IMB personnel. Call toll-free 1-877-462-4721 or email globalpriority@imb.org.

Ramadan: Fasting and Seeking God takes the intercessor through the days of the Muslims' holy month of prayer and fasting, giving information and guidance for focusing prayer on Muslims. Prayer guides are also available for praying for Jews: "Days of Awe"; for Hindus: "Divali: Festival of Light"; and for Buddhists: "Days of Enlightenment." To order or to receive information, call 1-800-866-3621 or email resource.center@imb.org.

Adopt a Missionary gives your church opportunity to have a personal relationship with international personnel and be a part of their lives and ministries through your praying and caring. Call 1-800-362-1322 or email adoptamissionary@imb.org.

"Prayerwalking" is a brochure for introducing this simple but profound dimension of prayer. To order, call toll-free 1-888-462-7729 or email resource.center@imb.org.

Prayer Journeys to possible overseas destinations can be researched by visiting www.imb.org/pray or calling 1-888-462-7729.

North American Mission Board, SBC
4200 North Point Parkway
Alpharetta, GA 30022
(770) 410-6000
www.namb.net

On Mission Prayer Map—A comprehensive map including many helps in praying for North America, such as (1) seven keys to an effective missions-centered prayer life; (2) how to pray for believers; (3) how to pray for unbelievers; (4) how to pray for states, provinces, and countries; (5) how to pray for evangelism and missions efforts, etc. To order, call 1-800-448-8032 or email customerservice@lifeway.com. (Item 0-8400-8506-0)

The map guides the intercessor over a 31-day period to pray for all the states/provinces in the United States and Canada as well as one's specific concerns. Every 7th day, believers pray for national political leaders listed on the map as well as local church and community leadership. Included is a helpful map key to explain the different elements of the daily and weekly prayer list concerns.

Prayer Partners—A complete NAMB missions personnel birthday prayer calendar. Included are features with information and pictures of personnel and their ministries. Order by calling 1-800-448-8032.

North American Missions Prayer-Gram—Prayer needs published monthly. To request, call 1-800-448-8032.

258

North American Missions PrayerLine—Daily prayer needs
for the United States and Canada. Call 1-800-554-PRAY
or visit www.namb.net/prayer.

Spiritual Awakening Video Series—Twelve messages on
preparation for revival. To order, call 1-800-448-8032.

Regional Conferences and Seminars—Focusing on preparation for revival. To order, call 1-800-448-8032.

Prayer Journeys in North America—For information, visit
www.namb.net/vols/prayerjourneys.

Taking Prayer to the Streets: Prayer Journey Resource Kit—
Instructions and training for Lighthouse of Prayer participants. (Item 0-8400-9632-1**)

Prayer for Revival and Spiritual Awakening—Gives suggestions for praying for revival and spiritual awakening. (Item
0-8400-8843-4**)

Lighthouse of Prayer Starter Kit—Equips individuals and
families to pray, care, and share Christ with their neighbors. Item 0-8400-9634-8**

"Praying Your Friends to Christ"—A helpful brochure in
giving help in praying for the lost. Comes in pack of 100.
(Item 0-8400-6728-3**)

Praying Your Friends to Christ Instruction Manual—A tool
for teaching how to pray for the lost. (Item 0-8400-8837-
x**)

**To order these items, call 1-800-448-8032 or email
customerservice@lifeway.com. Order online at www.lifeway.com.
For further information, call (770) 410-6333.

WMU
P. O Box 830010
Birmingham, AL 35283-0010
1-800-968-7301
www.wmu.com

To order materials, email customer_service@wmu.org
or call 1-800-968-7301.

WMU's vision is to challenge Christian believers to understand and be radically involved in the mission of God.
Many resources are available to encourage churches,
WMU members, families, children, and youth to be faithful in prayer and to grow in their spiritual lives. Magazines
for all ages feature many aspects of one's relationship with
God through worship, confession, petitions, and intercessions for missionaries and the people to whom they witness, disciple, and minister. For full information on the
resources, visit www.wmu.com.

Prayer Patterns—Offered in *Missions Mosaic,* magazine for
Women on Mission, published by WMU. Included are devotional thoughts, a prayer focus, and a Scripture verse to
pray. Very importantly, a missionary birthday calendar lists
missionaries according to their birthdays, including their
missions assignment and country of service. Prayer Patterns gives opportunity for intercessors to pray around the
world day by day. For subscription information, call
1-800-968-7301, fax (205) 414-8657, or email
customer_service@wmu.org.

Transdenominational Organizations, Movements, Resources

America's National Prayer Committee
This group, comprised of 400 of the nation's prayer leaders, seeks to give servant leadership to the strengthening of the growing prayer movement in the United States. America's National Prayer Committee sponsors and/or relates to numerous prayer events, conferences, and organizations, including the National Day of Prayer, the nationally broadcast Concert of Prayer, and the Denominational Prayer Leaders Network. David Bryant, founder of Concerts of Prayer International, is chairman. Address: P. O. Box 770, New Providence, NJ 07974. Call (908) 771-0146. For information, call (877) NOW HOPE. Email: Natlpray@aol.com. Visit www.nationalprayer.org.

Campus Crusade for Christ International
Campus Crusade is fulfilling a major role in multiple prayer initiatives around the world. PrayWorld! 2001, The Macedonian Project, Fasting and Prayer Gatherings, and the *Jesus* Film represent some of the comprehensive endeavors in CCCI's global outreach. For information, visit www.ccci.org or call (407) 826-2000.

PrayWorld! 2001
A most comprehensive new prayer movement is PrayWorld! 2001 (with the year in the title advancing every 12 months). This annual global call is for 40 days of united, simultaneous prayer and fasting of believers around the world during Lent. The goal is to unite churches in every

nation of the world in praying for the same concerns at the same time.

With the arrival of the millennium, Praying Through the Window was phased into yet another dimension with plans to expand its reach into all the nations of the world through PrayWorld! 2001. In concert with many agencies and organizations, Vonette Bright and Ben Jennings of Campus Crusade have been asked to assume the servant leadership of this newly unfolding prayer movement. An International Prayer Council is directing the development of PrayWorld! 2001 plans. Among the goals is to assist in the formation of a national prayer committee in every nation of the world. These national prayer committees will in turn lead the believers of their nations in 40 days of intense prayer for the lost people of their country.

A 40-day calendar of daily topics and Bible verses is available in English, Chinese, Korean, Spanish, French, and Hindu. For a single-sheet, reproducible prayer calendar (one copy—no charge), send a business-size, self-addressed, stamped envelope to Campus Crusade at 100 Lake Hart Drive, Orlando, FL 32832. The calendar is also available on the Web site of the National Prayer Committee: www.nationalprayer.org. For information and prayer calendars, call 1-800-569-4825. Other resources are available. Visit www.usprayertrack.org.

The Macedonian Project
The Macedonian Project calls forth the mobilization of intercessors to go as prayer journey teams to the unreached peoples, often where missionaries have not yet been assigned. In addition to the emphasis on prayer, each team is encouraged to make local connections, such as a teacher with a local school, to present a gift of the *Jesus* film, or a businessman making contact with a similar business in the

locale. Teams are also encouraged to motivate followup "back home," even to the point of arranging other teams to return to the same area. The goal of the Macedonian Project is to establish an indigenous ministry. Training for participation is available. For information, call (877) 622-7765. Email: macprojectus@ccci.org. Visit www.macproject.com.

Fasting and Prayer Gatherings

These large events taking place across America are inspired by Bill Bright, founder and president of Campus Crusade, and author of *The Coming Revival: America's Call to Fast, Pray, and Seek God's Face*. Satellite locations are an important part of the movement. For information, call 1-800-888-FAST. Visit www.fastingprayer.com.

The Jesus Film

Now available in more than 550 languages, this film is the most effective evangelistic tool around the world. A ministry of Campus Crusade, copies may be ordered from 1-800-432-1997. It is also available in video. To order by mail, write: The *Jesus* Film Project, P. O. Box 72007, San Clemente, CA 92674-9207. (Video: $19.95 plus $4.50 shipping/handling). Email: jfp@ccci.org. Visit www.jesusfilm.org.

The original classic *Jesus* film has been adapted for children and is available in a 62-minute color video. Visit the *Jesus* Film Project Web site at www.jesusforchildren.org. Call 1-800-432-1997 or fax (949) 492-0381 ($14.95 plus $4.50 shipping/handling). Email: jfp@ccci.org.

Center for Ministry to Muslims

Sponsored by the Assemblies of God, this center informs Christians about the needs of the world's 1.2 billion Muslims. The center's Jumaa Prayer Fellowship encourages

Christians to omit lunch every Friday and pray for Muslims. Training seminars for working with Muslims are conducted in 50 countries where 20,000 workers have been trained. The center also publishes *Hoor Ul Haq* (Light of Truth) magazine, which presents the gospel from a Muslim perspective in 84 countries. Email: owner-fia-news@xc.org.

Christian Women United
Led by Evelyn Christenson and Kathryn Grant, with an emphasis on evangelism praying, Christian Women United began as a part of the AD 2000 North America Women's Tract. Now related to Mission America, Christian Women United has added the Lighthouse Movement emphasis to the organization's purposes. Resources available are *Study Guide for Evangelism Praying* and *Love Your Neighbor as Yourself*. Order from Christian Women United, P. O. Box 472247, Charlotte, NC 28247-2247. For information, call or fax (612) 566-5390.

Evelyn Christenson Ministries, Inc. reaches out to women throughout the world teaching prayer evangelism, recommending the triplet method. Address: 4265 Brigadoon Drive; St. Paul, MN. Call or fax (612) 566-5390.

Concerts of Prayer International
David Bryant is the founder of this movement that has grown to dynamic proportions in America and many nations of the world. Concerts of Prayer International promotes, equips, and mobilizes movements of united prayer that seek God for revival, spiritual awakening, and worldwide evangelization. COPI also provides many resources for equipping city prayer movements and local churches in prayer and revival. This movement has been transformed into a ministry of America's National Prayer Committee, a coalition of 400 leaders committed to strengthening the national prayer movement. Address: P. O. Box 770, New

Providence, NJ 07974. For information, call (877) NOW
HOPE or (908) 771-0146. Fax: (908) 665-4199. Email:
copi@aol.com. Visit www.nationalprayer.org.

Every Home for Christ

Led by Dick Eastman, this network's goal is to place a simple gospel presentation in every home in the world, supported by a massive prayer focus on world evangelization
and the 10/40 Window. Almost 2 billion gospel messages
have been distributed globally, each with a decision card.
Over 19 million of these decision cards have been returned
to 1 of 80 offices. Each response is followed up with a
four-part correspondence course with the vision of getting
each responder into a group of worshiping believers. Eastman, through this ministry, features the Change the World
School of Prayer. Address: 7899 Lexington Drive, Colorado Springs, CO 80920. For information, call 1-800-423-
5054. Email info@ehc.org. Visit www.ehc.org.

Global Mapping International

Maps of Affinity Blocs of peoples (grouped by affinities of
language, history, culture, etc.), Light the Window maps,
wall maps, as well as many other resources are provided by
Global Mapping International, 7899 Lexington Drive,
Suite 200A, Colorado Springs,CO 80920. Email
info@gmi.org. Visit www.gmi.org. Call (719) 531-3599.

Great Commission Round Table

Three international organizations—Lausanne Movement
for World Evangelization, World Evangelical Fellowship,
and the A.D. 2000 and Beyond Movement—have combined forces to lead in the formation of a network designed to create Christian cooperation on a global scale.
Many other networks sharing the same values and goals are
being added to the Round Table. One of the ten agreed-
upon values is "unleashing the entire Church into global

intercession, giving special focus in prayer and ministry to those who have never heard the gospel or received Christian ministry—the 3,000 peoples with less than 5 percent Christian (2.24 billion people)."

For information, email John Robb, international coordinator of the Great Commission Global Round Table: John_Robb@wvi.org. Call (626) 301-7713 or fax (626) 301-7789.

Intercessors for America
This organization calls for the first Friday of each month to be a day of united prayer and fasting for national leaders with an emphasis on prayer revival and spiritual awakening. A monthly newsletter is offered to give prayer news and motivation and to support the First Friday prayer focus. For information, write P. O. Box 4477, Leesburg, VA 20177; call 1-800-USA-PRAY or (703) 589-1032; or fax (703) 777-2324. To subscribe to the newsletter, email usapray@aol.com. Visit www.ifa-usapray.org.

International Prayer Ministries, Inc.
International Prayer Ministries mobilizes prayer for personal revival, spiritual awakening, and world evangelization through prayer revivals and conferences. Led by Glenn Sheppard, 3322 Irwin Bridge Road, Conyers, GA 30012. Call (770) 388-7616; fax (770) 483-8606; email: gshep10143@cs.com. Visit www.internationalprayerministries.org.

Light the Nations
Light the Nations relates to First Nations Forum, a ministry network of Mission America, comprised of Native American ministry leaders throughout North America. Light the Nations sponsors Forty Days of Prayer and Fasting during the November time frame. Christians across

America are invited to join the Native American believers in praying for every Native American home on every reservation and in every community. For information, call Mark Custalow at (615) 896-0036 or email mcustalow@namb.net. For a "Light the Nations: Five Blessings" brochure, write HOPE, P. O. Box 141312, Grand Rapids, MI 49514; call 1-800-217-5200; fax (616) 235-6650; or email info@hopeministries.org. Visit www.hopeministries.org.

Lydia Prayer Fellowship International
With a national network of women members committed to intercession, this ministry calls for fasting one day each month to pray for church, community, country, and the nations of the world. A number of free resources are provided, including book-size prayer cards listing names of our President, cabinet members, Supreme Court members, and other officials. Cards come in packs of 100 or 1,000. To order, email tryna@bahl.com. Write: P. O. Box 4509, 2140 Garden Terrace, Mountain View, CA 94040. Email lydia@lydiafellowship.org. Visit www.lydiafellowship.org.

March for Jesus
With a focus on the worship of God and praying for the world, March for Jesus draws participants in cities worldwide into mass prayer and praise on the streets. More than 100 nations participate. Headquarters are in the UK, where this movement originated. For information, call (404)-627-3267; email mfjusa@compuserve.com. Visit www.mfj.org or www.Jesusday.org.

Mission America
Mission America is an interdenominational coalition of more than 500 national Christian leaders representing 81 denominations, 300 parachurch ministries, 57 ministry networks, and 200,000 churches. The coalition, including

Celebrate Jesus 2000, the North American Mission Board, the Mapping Center for Evangelism, Houses of Prayer Everywhere, and many other organizations, is co-sponsoring the Lighthouses of Prayer Movement (see below). Visit www.missionamerica.org. and www.lighthousemovement. com.

Lighthouses of Prayer

The goal of Lighthouses of Prayer is to enlist Christian homes to pray for, care for, and share the gospel with every man, woman, young person, and child in America. In this unique endeavor, Mission America is bringing together the evangelical community of our nation in a prayer and evangelism campaign. For information, write Mission America, 5666 Lincoln Drive, Edina, MN 55436; call 1-800-995-8573; or email missionamerica@compuserve.com. To order materials, call (888) 323-1210. Brochures are also available from LifeWay Christian Resources 1-800-448-8032. Visit www.missionamerica.org and www.lighthouse-movement.com.

Houses of Prayer Everywhere

HOPE is also a component of the Lighthouse Movement. A Church Lighthouse Kit is available by writing P. O. Box 141312, Grand Rapids, MI 49514. For information and additional resources, call 1-800-217-5200. Email info@hopeministries.org. Visit www.hopeministries.org.

Moms in Touch International

A worldwide network, this transdenominational movement mobilizes mothers to come together weekly to pray for their children and the schools they attend. Their goal is to raise up moms to intercede for every school across the US and around the world. For information, contact Fern Nichols, P. O. Box 1120, Poway, CA 92074. Call 1-800-949-MOMS or (858) 486-4965, or fax (858) 486-5132.

Email MITIHQTRS@compuserve.com. Visit www.mom-sintouch.org.

National Day of Prayer Task Force

First observed in our country over two centuries ago, the National Day of Prayer was established, as an act of Congress in 1952, to be observed on the first Thursday of May every year. More than 2 million Americans gather in an estimated 20,000 locations for personal repentance and prayer, and for corporate prayer for our nation and its leaders. Americans of all faiths are urged to find a place where an observance of the day is taking place and join with others in praying earnestly for revival and spiritual awakening. The national observance is sponsored by the National Prayer Committee. Shirley Dobson is chairman of the task force responsible for the event and the related observances in Washington, D.C., and throughout America. Write P. O. Box 15616, Colorado Springs, CO 80934-5616 (mail only) or P. O. Box 15440, Colorado Springs, CO 80935-5440 (mail orders only). For ideas and details, call (719) 531-3379; fax (719) 548-4520. To place an order for resources related to the National Day of Prayer, call 1-800-444-8828; email ndptf@aol.com. For more information, visit www.nationaldayofprayer.org.

In conjunction with the National Day of Prayer, a three-hour nationally broadcast concert of prayer is led by Christian leaders from across America. This event is called the world's largest prayer meeting. For more information, visit www.concertofprayer.org.

National Pastors Prayer Network

The NPPN seeks to identify and encourage pastors' prayer groups in cities and communities across America. The network provides information on its Web site and through email contact. Phil Megliorattis is the facilitator. Email

praychgo@flash.net. Visit www.homestead.com/nppn. To
subscribe to the newsletter, email subscribe@nppn.org.

Operation Torch
Operation Torch is enlisting volunteers to pray earnestly
for the people groups of North Africa. Hundreds are
needed to participate in prayer journeys to the region.
Each team links up with a strategy leader advocate for one
of the people groups in the region.

Those interested in praying for North Africa and going on
a prayer journey to North Africa through Operation Torch
may contact Gerry Volkart at the International Mission
Board by email: gerry.volkart@imb.org or call toll-free
1-800-999-3113, ext. 1328 or ext. 1704. The Operation
Torch Web site is www.optorch.com.

Prayer for the Persecuted Church
The International Day of Prayer for the Persecuted Church
is a global day of compassionate intercession for persecuted
Christians worldwide. Millions of believers throughout the
world join in prayer for brothers and sisters in Christ who
suffer because of their faith. World Evangelical Fellowship
(WEF) coordinates the emphasis overseas and the International Day of Prayer for the Persecuted Church promotes
the efforts in the United States. For information, call (888)
538-7772. Visit www.persecutedchurch.org.

Renovare
Led by author Richard Foster, this ministry seeks to motivate individuals and churches toward spiritual renewal
with special emphasis on the disciplines of the spiritual
life. Regional conferences take place nationwide. Address:
8 Inverness Drive East, Suite 102, Englewood, CO 80112-
5609. For information, call (303) 792-0152 or fax (303)
792-0146. Email 103165.327@compuserve.com.

See You at the Pole
On the third Wednesday of September each year, this movement mobilizes youth nationwide to gather around their schools' flagpoles for united prayer. For information, contact Billy Beacham, P. O. Box 60134, Fort Worth, TX 76115. For information year round, call (858) 592-9200. For promotional materials for each September's observance of SYATP, call in the summer (817) HIS PLAN (447-7526) Visit www.syatp.com. For other information, call (858) 451-1111. Email: pray@syatp.com.

The Caleb Project
This project challenges churches, missions agencies, and other ministries to complete the task of world evangelization by taking the gospel to the least-evangelized people groups. Resources include prayer guides, prayer cards, partnerships, unreached peoples videos, missions drama scripts, and many more helps for ministry. Advocacy training is also at the heart of the ministry. For information, email training@cproject.com. The Caleb Project provides a manual: *Prayer Journeys: A Leader's How-to Manual.* Address: 10 W. Dry Creek Circle, Littleton, CO 80120. Phone: (303) 730-4170, ext. 343. Fax: (303) 730-4177. Email: info@cproject.com. Visit www.calebproject.org.

The Esther Network International
This unique children's prayer movement came out of Global Consultation on World Evangelism (GCOWE) with the original name of Children's Global Prayer Movement. Children are enlisted and trained as intercessors for the lost of the world. More than 1 million young prayer warriors participate.

The Joshua Project
The Joshua Project was launched in 1990 for the purpose
of compiling strategic information on the unreached peoples of the world. The data is a combination of research
from SIL/Wycliffe, International Mission Board, Operation World, and A.D. 2000. The original list of 1,750
major unreached peoples has been reduced to 1,600, and
church planting efforts are underway in more than half of
these. Less than 200 remain untargeted by any missions
agency. Joshua Project profiles can be found at
www.bethany-wpc.org. Click Links to bring up profiles.

The Harvest Information System (HIS) Database
Building on the foundation of the Joshua Project, an even
more extensive missions information system is being
formed as additional organizations (such as the Billy Graham Center, Global Mapping, A.D. 2000 staff) and many
individuals are becoming a part of the new Harvest Information System (HIS) Database. Also, thousands of database partners on the field will provide real-time up-to-date
information which will be available to the whole body of
Christ. Included is the listing of untargeted people—those
peoples that do not have a reported church planting team
on-site and no missions organization committed to evangelization or church planting among them. For information, email hisquery@egroups.com or dan@ad2000.org.
Visit www.hiservices.org (as of this writing, soon to be operational). People group profiles can be found at www.
bethany-wpc.org. Click Links to bring up profiles.

The Mapping Center for Evangelism
Colaboring with Mission America and in cooperation with
the North American Mission Board and Campus Cru-sade
for Christ, The Mapping Center for Evangelism is making
available neighborhood maps, demographic information, a
custom compact disc, neighborhood lists for prayer and

personal evangelism, and many other resources. A training video is also available. For information, call (913) 438-7301 or email support@map4jesus.org. Visit www.map4jesus.org.

US Center for World Mission

The US Center for World Mission is a hub for many aspects of global evangelization. Almost 50 agencies have offices in the 35-acre complex located in Pasadena, California. The center has 19 regional centers in different parts of the US and a number of affiliated centers in other parts of the world. In addition to study and degree programs, *Mission Frontiers* and the *Global Prayer Digest* are published. The Adopt-A-People Campaign is at the heart of the center's ministries. Many resources are available. Also located in the complex is the William Carey Library. For information, visit www.uscwm.org.

World Prayer Center

The World Prayer Center is a transdenominational communications center serving Christians throughout the world by linking strategic prayer requests and practical needs with intercessors. Located in Colorado Springs, Colorado, the center uses the latest in technology to receive, compile, and disseminate prayer needs and requests from every continent. Local churches and individual intercessors are invited to receive the weekly email and bimonthly newsletter filled with needs from around the world. Send name, organization, address, city, and state to info@wpccs.org. Visit www.wpccs.org.

YWAM

YWAM is an international movement of believers responding to the Great Commission. The movement sponsors a vast array of ministries with 700 "bases" in 130 countries around the world. In cooperation with WorldChristian

News, YWAM sponsors a monthlong prayer initiative, 30 Days Muslim Prayer Focus. Any 30-day period may be chosen for the emphasis. Also available are the *Hindu Prayer Focus* guides and the *Intercessor's Prayer Guide to the Jewish World.*

For information and to place orders, call (888) 926-6397. Email wcn@xc.org. Visit www.ywam.org for many more resources.

YWAM Strategic Frontiers International has released a video series to generate prayer for some of the 127 key unreached people groups in the 10/40 Window. There are 13 videos in the series ($99.95 for the series, or $15.00 each) To order, call 1-800-FOR-YWAM or (719) 226-3006, or email WaitingWorld@sfcos.org.

Additional Resources

A House of Prayer: Prayer Ministries in Your Church, compiled by John Franklin, gives guidance for establishing or strengthening the church's prayer ministry. LifeWay Christian Resources, 127 Ninth Avenue, North, Nashville, TN 37234-0151. Call 1-800-458-2772, email customerservice@lifeway.com, or order online at www.lifeway.com. Also available through LifeWay Christian Stores.

A Walk with the Master: Praying Men, by Don Miller is available in tape form from NAMB. Call 1-800-233-1123 or fax (615) 251-5983. Or write Don Miller, P. O. Box 8911, Fort Worth, TX 76124; (817) 429-6917.

"Brigada" is a weekly email newsletter providing a gateway to missions networking. It is compiled by Doug Lucas who calls it the missionary helper newsletter. With a major

274

focus on unreached people groups, the weekly communication is filled with information—and quite a bit about prayer. To subscribe, email Brigada-today-subscribe@egroups.com. Visit www.brigada.org.

Church Prayer Ministry Manual, by T. W. Hunt. Hunt is considered the most respected teacher and leader in the field of establishing and maintaining church prayer ministries. The manual includes a section on the Watchman Prayer Ministry. Call 1-800-458-2772 or email customerservice@lifeway.com.

Doorknob hangers can be used by neighborhood prayer-walkers. Message may read, "We have prayed a blessing upon your home. We welcome you to attend our church," or whatever words you choose. One location for orders: (619) 420-6007. Address: 303 W. 35th Street, Suite E, National City, CA 91950. Email durraink@aol.com.

Echo is published three times a year and distributed to 100,000 students and young adults. It presents worship, discipleship, and missions involvement as the biblical model for Great Commission Christians. Phone: 1-800-352-7225. Email: echo@echomagazine.com. Visit www.echomagazine.com.

Global Prayer Digest is a monthly prayer devotional guide with news of what God is doing around the world. Included is a daily unreached people profile, a daily missions-related Scripture verse, and commentary. Available in English, Spanish, Portuguese, and Korean. To order in email form, email hub@xc.org with the following message: *Subscribe brigada-pubs-globalprayerdigest.*

How to Build a Praying Church, by Tom Lovorn, is a notebook of extensive helps plus four tapes by Tom Lovorn.

Order from Church Growth Institute, P. O. Box 4404, Lynchburg, VA 24502. Call 1-800-553-4769.

If My People . . . Pray, by Elaine Helms, is the work of the experienced, effective prayer ministry coordinator of the Noonday Baptist Association and the Johnson Ferry Baptist Church. She can be contacted by calling (772) 993-8915.

Lausanne NewsLetter is published quarterly with prayer requests from around the world. To subscribe, email Lausanne@xc.org. Visit www.lausanne.org.

Mission Frontiers is the bulletin of the US Center for World Mission. To subscribe, email mission.frontiers@uscwm.org or call (626) 797-1111. Fax: (626) 398-2263. Write: 1605 Elizabeth, Pasadena, CA 91104. Subscriptions are by suggested donation of $15.00. Visit www.mission-frontiers.org. Also available by email from Brigada.

Native American Prayer Alerts (NAPA) are newsletter/prayer guides provided by Intercessors for America to those desiring awareness of Native America Indian happenings and want to be included as partners in prayer. To be added to the list, email usapray@aol.com. Visit www.ifa-usapray.org. A one-sheet listing of the names and addresses of 225 Native American Indian tribes is available by sending a stamped, self-addressed business-size envelope to P. O. Box 4477, Leesburg, VA 20177.

A brochure, "Healing for the Past . . . Hope for the Future . . .," may be ordered from the Native American Resource Network, P. O. Box 1417, Castle Rock, CO 80104. Email: ircoal@aol.com. Phone: (303) 660-9258. Fax: (303) 660-0621.

276

Powerhouse: A Step-by-Step Guide to Building a Church That Prays, by Dian Ginter and Glen Martin. Published by Broadman and Holman. The authors give valuable assistance to churches that take seriously Jesus' instruction, "My house shall be called a house of prayer."

Pray! is a magazine published bimonthly by the Navigators in cooperation with America's National Prayer Committee, Mission America, the Denominational Prayer Leaders Network, and the National Association of Evangelicals. The goal is to encourage "a passion for prayer." To subscribe (16.97 per year), call (760) 781-5219, fax (760) 738-4805, or email navpress@pcspublink.com. Visit www.praymag. com.

PrayerLife: Walking in Fellowship with God, by T. W. Hunt and Catherine Walker, is a 13-week "Life" course available in written form and in tape form. Call 1-800-458-2772 or email customerservice@lifeway.com.

Praying the Heart of God, by Ted Elmore, is available in both English and Spanish. This resource teaches how to pray the heart of God in three areas: the lost, the church, and our families. The material can be used for seminars, small groups, and personal study. Each participant will learn not only the intent and purpose of God in these areas but also how to focus prayer from a scriptural basis. Available from the Baptist General Convention of Texas Evangelism Division, 333 North Washington, Dallas, TX 75246-1798; or call (214) 828-5115. For information, email elmore@bgct.org or tedelmore@aol.com.

The Praying Church Sourcebook, a Complete Guide to Developing Your Prayer Ministry, by Alvin J. Vander Griend, with Edith Bajema, features many ideas for enhancing your church's life of prayer. CSC Publications. Call 1-800-333-8300.

The Role of Prayer in Spiritual Awakening is a 26-minute video of a powerful message by J. Edwin Orr, foremost teacher on revival and prayer. To order, call Keynote at 1-800-352-8273 ($19.98 plus $5.25 shipping/handling).

William Carey Library, located at 1705 North Sierra Bonita, Pasadena, CA 91104, as a part of the US Center for World Mission, has the most comprehensive list of missions titles available. Categories include World Christian Books, Prayer Resources, Missionary Biographies, Assistance to Local Churches, etc. Books are sold at discount prices. For prices and ordering information, call 1-800-647-7466, fax (626) 794-0477, visit www.uscwm.org, or email orders@wclbooks.com.

Minette Drumwright, a native Texan, grew up in San Antonio and graduated from Baylor University. Her late husband, Huber Drumwright Jr., served Southwestern Baptist Theological Seminary as professor of New Testament and later as dean of the School of Theology. Mother of two daughters and grandmother of three, Drumwright has been involved in Baptist life at many levels. After her husband's death, she served on the staff of the Foreign Mission Board, SBC (now International Mission Board, SBC), directing the work of the Office of International Prayer Strategy. In retirement, she teaches and speaks in churches and leads retreats and seminars both in the United States and overseas.